The Revival of Civic Learning

A Rationale for Citizenship Education in American Schools

by

R. Freeman Butts

**William F. Russell Professor Emeritus
in the Foundations of Education
Teachers College, Columbia University**

A Publication of the Phi Delta Kappa Educational Foundation

Cover design by Victoria Voelker

©1980 R. Freeman Butts
Library of Congress Catalog Card Number 80-81870
ISBN 0-87367-423-5
Printed in the United States of America

Table of Contents

Publication of this monograph has been financed in part through a generous contribution from Miss Bessie Gabbard, a member of the Ohio State University Chapter of Phi Delta Kappa and a member of the Phi Delta Kappa Educational Foundation Board of Governors.

A Personal Note

This little book is frankly a very personal statement of my views concerning the civic role of American schools. It does not represent the views of any organization or association. In it I have tried to bring together ideas that I have expressed in one form or another over a period of years. I have tried to make it as coherent as I can in view of the fairly long period of time and the variety of experiences I have had with what I prefer to call *civic education*.

In fact, as I think about it, I believe the concern began in mature and critical form in my first weeks as a freshman in the Experimental College at the University of Wisconsin where the required reading for all students was Plato's *Republic*, and the required subject of discussion was to grapple with Socrates and Thrasymachus over the meaning of justice. And I soon began to learn about freedom from Alexander Meiklejohn, who was later to instruct the U.S. Supreme Court on that subject in relation to the First Amendment. And perhaps I had imbibed something about equality from earlier schooling in the shadow of Abraham Lincoln in Springfield, Illinois. But this is not to be an autobiography.

Yet, I believe the reader is entitled to know something about, in the present idiom, "where I am coming from." For 40 years at Teachers College, Columbia University, the problem of education in a democratic society was a continuing subject of study, teaching, and writing during which I learned a great deal from working with and teaching with George Counts, John Childs, Bruce Raup, Harold Rugg, Lyman Bryson, and a number of other colleagues in the Department of Social and Philosophical Foundations. I was a little surprised to remind myself by looking at their books again recently that they—and I—talked unashamedly about citizenship and citizenship education.

I learned about diversity by teaching courses and workshops on intercultural education (one particularly memorable workshop with Margaret Mead in New Rochelle, N.Y.) at Teachers College and at the University of Wisconsin in the 1940s. During the 1950s I learned more about freedom and especially about due process and the difference between authority and authoritarianism while I fought the cold war against McCarthyism in the ranks of the Academic Freedom Committee of the American Civil Liberties Union. As a member of the executive committee of the Academic Freedom Project at Columbia University, I helped in the planning and critique of the major studies by Robert M. MacIver and the histories by Richard Hofstadter and Walter Metzger.

In the 1960s I learned a great deal about international human rights and "cultural imperialism" while I was directing the far-flung international programs of Teachers College in Asia, Africa, and Latin America. In the 1970s I again learned a great deal about due process and "participation" as I experienced them in both the raucus "participatory democracy" of the campus crises at Columbia and in the quieter realms of designing broadened faculty and student roles for the governance of Teachers College.

If the reader should have the patience or interest to get to Chapter 5, I hope my references here to justice, freedom, equality, diversity, due process, authority, participation, and human rights will take on more meaning.

Finally, a word about my credentials in writing about civic education, more specifically conceived as programs of teaching and learning in the schools. These, too, go back further than it is probably politic to mention. However, one of my early memories about my schooling in the 1920s has to do with the day I went shyly as an eighth-grader down to the big auditorium at Springfield High School to receive the history medal for winning a citywide essay contest sponsored by—yes—the Daughters of the American Revolution. Mercifully, I don't believe that essay is extant, but surely it had to do with good citizenship and could not possibly have overlooked Washington, Jefferson, and Lincoln. But to come, hurriedly, closer to the present.

In connection with the large and handsomely financed Citizenship Education Project in the 1950s at Teachers College, I was a continuing consultant and drew up historical outlines for the "Premises of American Liberty." In the 1960s I was on the executive board of the Center for Research and Education in American Liberties sponsored jointly by Columbia and Teachers College under the leadership of Alan Westin.

Following my retirement from Teachers College in 1975, I was enabled to continue my studies with the aid of a Rockefeller Foundation Humanities Fellowship and by appointment as Distinguished Professor of Education at San Jose State University. I am especially grateful for these opportunities.

At last, in the 1970s I was fortunate to be deeply involved in a number of special civic education projects, some of which I mention in this book. Especially useful in my learning has been my membership on the Advisory Commission of the Special Committee on Youth Education for Citizenship of the American Bar Association and membership on the executive committee of the Law in a Free Society Project. And I owe special thanks to the Danforth Foundation, which, with the Kettering Foundation, sponsored the National Task Force on Citizenship Education. I served on the advisory committee of that task force and I was invited by the Danforth Foundation to act as consultant on civic education in 1977-78, during which time I learned far more from the projects the foundation was helping to support than I could possibly contribute.

I make no apology for focusing this book on the schools. They, of course, cannot do the whole job of civic education; a great many persons and agencies are attending to the education of citizens by all sorts of organizations and media. I believe that more explicit and concerted attention should be given by the public and by the profession to what the schools can and should be doing. This book is my personal effort to increase and inform that attention.

R. Freeman Butts
Palo Alto, California
June 1980

Chapter 1

The Challenge of the 1980s:
Privatism in Politics and Pluralism in Education*

T he decade of the 1980s brings us to the 200th anniversary of the
decade American historians have commonly called "The Critical
Period." In the 1770s the American colonies had declared their
independence of the British Crown and Parliament, the several states
had formed their constitutions, and the Articles of Confederation had
proved sufficient (but only barely so) to enable the colonies to cooperate
in winning the war and signing the peace in 1783. Many outward signs
were favorable to national expansion—finances were becoming
stabilized, commerce was increasing, and the economy and the
population were on the rise. But by all accounts, the sense of unease,
malaise, and crisis became ever more prevalent in the 1780s, leading
more and more voices to declare that the Revolution, in the face of
accelerating self-interest, was failing for want of a sense of the public
good. A major historian of the period, Gordon S. Wood of Brown
University, sums up a prevailing view of the 1780s as follows:

> Not only were the new popular state legislatures creating a new
> unexpected kind of tyranny with their confusing and unjust laws, but
> the American people were showing by their intense interest in making
> money that they were not the stuff republicans were made of. Classic
> public spirit was being eclipsed by private interests, individualism, and
> selfishness. Such behavior foreshadowed the fate that had befallen the
> ancient republics, Great Britain, and other corrupt nations....By the
> middle '80s many reformers were thinking of shifting the arena of
> constitutional change from the states to the nation and were looking
> to some sort of modification of the structure of the central government
> as the best and perhaps the only answer to America's political and
> social problems.[1]

My point here is not so much to draw a parallel between the 1780s and
the 1980s as it is to underline a remarkable difference. The critical
period of the 1780s saw a great national debate concerning what to do
about the relatively weak state and national governments in face of a
growing privatism. The eventual result was a strengthening of the
national government through the constitutional convention of 1787, the

---

*Portions of this chapter are based upon and drawn from Chapter 12 of my *Public
Education in the United States* (New York: Holt, Rinehart and Winston, 1978).

1

adoption of the U.S. Constitution and its installation in 1789, and the final acceptance of the Bill of Rights in 1791. This was, in effect, the establishment of a sense of legitimacy for the new federal government that finally replaced the Articles of Confederation. And much of the discussion about education in the 1780s and 1790s had to do with its new role in helping to prepare youth for their role in the new political community that was being created. The idea of a common public education was born with the idea of a common political community.

Privatism in Politics

The thing that strikes me regarding the 1980s is the fact that today a marked trend toward private interests is taking place during *this* "critical period" after a decade or more of alienation directed against the very federal government that was set up 200 years ago. The sense of legitimacy attached to government at all levels has increasingly been eroded, and the private interest is increasingly being praised as a necessary brake on the role of government in American society. The cry to limit government has been heard ever more insistently, and the efforts to reduce its role and its support have been more and more successful. Whereas the 1770s and 1780s witnessed an extraordinary process of constitution making, it is ironic that the Constitution's bicentennial in the 1980s may become a critical period of constitution *unmaking* if forces partial to private rather than public enterprise have their way.

The most obvious symbol of the constitution unmaking process was, of course, Proposition 13 in California which, by initiative vote in June 1978, amended the state constitution, reducing local property taxes to 1% of the assessed valuation as of 1975-76, prohibiting their increase, and requiring a two-thirds vote of the legislature to increase state taxes. As Robert Lekachman, economist at the City University of New York, said, "The public mood is sour, cynical, and self-regarding." His prediction about the movement toward the new conservatism, heralded by Proposition 13, was as follows:

> The process under way is the return of many functions of government to private markets and entrepreneurs. The shrinking resources devoted to public schools and public universities must lower their quality and encourage parents and students to prefer private substitutes. Acceleration of the existing movement away from public education will shrink its remaining constituency and increase the political support for such proposals as Senator Moynihan's tuition tax credit.[2]

The Moynihan-Packwood proposals to grant income-tax credits to parents whose children attend private elementary and secondary schools was defeated in the Senate in October 1978, but Senator Moynihan of New York promised he would be back with the proposal again. Meanwhile, over half the states began some movement toward

2

limiting taxes or government spending. California Governor Edmund G. Brown and economist Milton Friedman led the parade to hold a constitutional convention to amend the U.S. Constitution to this same end; and more than 30 states soon took some sort of action. As more and more states acted quickly—and some rather thoughtlessly—the specter of a constitutional convention in the midst of a rising tide of conservative privatism could pose an even more serious threat to the very idea of a common public national purpose. The social welfare and reform gains of half of century could be threatened along with the very idea of a common public education.

Proposition 13 did not spring full grown from the two heads of California politicans Howard Jarvis and Paul Gann. The public mood has been taking shape for much of the past decade-and-a-half, during which many of the exhilarating hopes of John F. Kennedy's New Frontier and Lyndon Johnson's Great Society were frustrated and complicated by a variety of forces that Sydney E. Ahlstrom, Yale historian, has called "The Traumatic Years" when "the nation's sense of purpose fell to its lowest ebb," and many elements of a national consensus were shattered. Ahlstrom lists five issues that gained massive public attention and served to replace the relatively placid and bland decade of the 1950s and the vital reforms of the early 1960s with years that were "tumultuous, troubled, and traumatic":

> They can be briefly listed: 1) race and racism; 2) war and imperialism; 3) sex and sexism; 4) exploitation and environmentalism; and 5) government and the misuse of power. Underlying all of these was the fundamental question of Justice, which is the first virtue of any society. Because young people took such an unprecedented role among those who were active in these interconnected moral campaigns, the nature and function of educational institutions also became prime objects of concern—and sometimes of overt assault.... If these several protest and reform movements are seen as a whole they constitute a full-scale critique of the American way of life: both the social injustices of the system itself and the ideological, philosophical, and theological assumptions that have justified and legitimated the existing social order.[3]

As Ahlstrom says, the *Brown* decision by the U.S. Supreme Court in 1954 was the decisive event in race relations, but it was not until the mid- and late-1960s that the moral commitment to racial justice peaked under the leadership of Martin Luther King, Jr. At the same time, the riots in the ghettos, the burning of the cities, and ultimately the massive political divisiveness over busing produced enormous trauma in community after community. The other most visible and emotionally disturbing issue was the anti-Vietnam War movement that swept from the campuses to the cities in the wake of Kent State and Jackson State killings. The intensity of the animosity and frustration that convinced thousands of students that their colleges and universities should be shut

3

down because of their complicity in the war was unique in American history.

The feminist movement and the sexual revolution affected the personal, family, and interpersonal relations of men and women in the quiet, private precincts of the household but also in the streets and legislative halls. Pro-abortion and anti-abortion drives, Equal Rights Amendment (ERA) and anti-ERA debates, birth control and sterilization, divorce and non-marital cohabitation, open homosexuality, pornography, abuse of women and children, women in the work force, children in one-parent families—all these issues spilled over, creating deep consternation in those who held traditional values of family integrity and sexual morality.

Probably the ecological issues and the erosion of a sense of legitimacy in government raised the most troublesome and fundamental conflicts over the role of the private and the public in American life. From Rachel Carson's *The Silent Spring* in 1962 to Barry Commoner's "Reflections on Solar Energy" in *The New Yorker* in 1979, the underlying issues were exploitation or preservation, growth or no growth, public control or private control. Eventually, the recurrent gasoline shortages and the frightening insecurities of nuclear power plants began to compete with a desire for lower taxes and higher profits or wages in the consciousness of ordinary persons as well as national leaders. Barry Commoner posed the issues and argued that the solution to each energy issue depends on the single larger issue of "social governance":

> The resolution of the energy crisis—the solar transition—is an opportunity...to embark on a historic new passage. But to find our way we will need to be guided by social rather than private interests. There are many known ways—and many yet to be invented—of introducing social governance into production: national planning; local or regional planning; public utilities; cooperatives; and, if need be, public ownership on a national or local level. These measures will, of course, clash with the notion that every productive decision must be privately governed, for private profit, in order to insure economic efficiency. But we know from the energy crisis that these inefficiencies are outside the realm of private governance, and are accessible only to social decisions.
>
> It will be difficult—some say impossible—to learn how to merge economic justice with economic progress, and personal freedom with social governance. If we allow the fear of failing in this effort to forestall the effort to make it, then failure is certain. But if we firmly embrace economic democracy as a national goal, as a new standard for political policy, or even only as a vision of the nation's future, it can guide us through the passage that is mandated by the energy crisis and restore to the nation the vitality inherent in the richness of its resources and the wisdom of its people.[4]

I believe that Commoner correctly argues that the outcome of the energy crisis depends a great deal upon whether it is governed by the values of the private interest or the public interest. In this most vital of economic issues the role of government will be central, as indeed it is in the social issues of race and racism and the survival issues of war and peace. It is thus excruciatingly troublesome to realize that the traumatic era has bequeathed to us, along with all the other traumas, a loss of confidence in the very means of last resort upon which people must rely to restore a sense of national purpose: the constitutional government.

I need not restate the succession of opinion polls and scholarly judgments that have verified the growing cynicism and skepticism about government, the alienation from politicians and public institutions, including autocratic school administrators, insensitive bureaucracies, and militant, bargaining, striking school teachers. Ahlstrom describes the long crisis of confidence in government as the ultimate trauma of the traumatic years:

> The era was marked throughout by a steady deterioration of national trust of a dozen different kinds dependent on as many grounds of dissatisfaction. Inequities in the military conscription system, racial discrimination, the impersonality of big government, the venality of small government, corruption in high places, desolated cities, the harshness of the police, and official dishonesty about the war—all of these played their part.... Because deep suspicions remain, reformist zeal and political concern is replaced by self-seeking and privatization, even though the need for reform and political activism is greater than ever.[5]

Not only did the historians and the polls find an erosion in the public's sense of legitimacy toward government and a rise in the sense of privatism, but political leaders, scholars, and public interest groups were finding disunity, inefficiency, and weakened authority within the government itself. A good example of this was a series of analytical articles by John Herbers in *The New York Times* following the congressional elections of 1978. The recurrent theme was the escalation of special interest politics and the decline of concern for the public good. Herbers quotes John Gardner as saying the nation is being whipsawed by a multiplicity of special interest groups, resulting in a paralysis in national policy making; and Stuart Eizenstat, President Carter's chief advisor on domestic policy, as saying that we are an increasingly fragmented and Balkanized society. Herbers summarized as follows:

> What is different now from anything the nation has seen in the past, according to a wide range of authorities, is the convergence of a number of forces, some new and some old, that have been building for several years and that came into focus in the recent election campaigns.
>
> Those forces include the organization of political movements around single issues rather than parties, a quantum jump in lobbying and campaign contributions on the parts of the public and special

interests, a decline in the moral authority of the Presidency and of government at all levels, enormous growth in centralization of the Federal Government, and decentralization of Congress.

There is disagreement as to which of those is most important. But there is a consensus that no coalition of interests is strong enough to set priorities for the overall public good, to effect reforms that have wide public support, to root out inefficiency and corruption in government programs, and to inspire confidence in political leadership.[6]

The traumatic era produced a curious anomaly. Public opinion polls showed a drastic decline of confidence in the executive branch of government (from 41% in 1966 to 23% in 1976) and in Congress (from 42% in 1966 to 17% in 1976); and a general rise in distrust of political authority (from 20% in 1958 to over 50% in 1976). Yet, the evidence cited by Herbers shows that an increasing number of Americans were turning to government to lobby for funds or practices or policies that would benefit their particular group. Not only is it business and labor, but hundreds of special groups rally around single issues: anti-abortion, anti-gun control, anti-busing, anti-taxes, anti-nuclear energy, pro-oil, pro-gas, pro-trucking, pro-railroads, pro-environment protection. And now that Congress has some 385 subcommittees, its decentralized decision-making process makes the policy makers more accessible to the hundreds of special interest groups but makes it more difficult for the congressional leadership to define and implement broad policy goals. A 1980 report by Common Cause called *The Government Subsidy Squeeze* gives details on how the "Special Interest State" fuels inflation.

While adults were professing political alienation and staying away from the polls, yet besieging Washington and the state capitals for their special interests, what of youth? The evidence seems to be that privatization has become the mode for both college and noncollege youth following the extreme activism of the late 1960s and early 1970s. A Yankelovich survey of the changing values of youth published in 1974 found the years from 1967 to 1973 to be a period of startling shifts in values and beliefs that marked the end of one era and the beginning of a new one. What was labeled the "new values" of a minority of college students in 1967 had spread to the entire youth generation by 1973. The survey referred to three categories of new values:

1. *Moral norms:* More liberal sexual mores; a lessening of automatic obedience to and respect for the established authority of the law, police, government; a lessening of the church and organized religion as a source of guidance for moral behavior; and a decline in traditional concepts of patriotism and automatic allegiance to the idea of "my country right or wrong."

2. *Social values:* Changing attitudes toward the work ethic,

marriage, family, and the role of money in defining success.

3. *Self-fulfillment:* A "greater preoccupation with self at the expense of sacrificing one's self for family, employer, and community."[7]

The pollsters called attention especially to the trend of "deauthorization," i.e., the marked rise since 1969 in the values assigned to privatism and a corresponding decline in values assigned to constituted authority, obligation to others, and patriotism—and this applies to noncollege as well as to college students. In 1969 only one college student in three called patriotism a very important value; in 1973 this had dropped to one in five. In 1969 three in five noncollege students called patriotism a very important value; in 1973 this had dropped to two in five. So the vast majority of *all* American youth had little use for patriotism as they understood it. More generally, the majority of both college students and noncollege students were labeled "political skeptics." More than 60% believed that American society is democratic in name only, that "special interests" run the political machinery of the nation with little true participation by the mass of American citizens, and that the political parties need fundamental reform. A whole generation does not believe what the society preaches or what the schools teach.

Especially discouraging was the evidence from surveys that high school and college students felt they had little obligation to take part in the political system. Alexander Astin's survey reported in the *Chronicle of Higher Education* for 13 January 1975 revealed an apparent "political withdrawal." Only one-fourth to one-third of college freshmen in 1974 believed that "participating in community action programs" or "keeping up with political affairs" or "influencing social values" were essential or very important objectives for them as individuals. And only 12% to 15% thought that "influencing the political structure" was essential or very important. These were students who started college a month after the House voted for impeachment and Richard Nixon resigned and who were graduated from college in 1978 or 1979. And what of prospective teachers? The Study Commission at the University of Nebraska reported in October 1974 that of all teacher candidates in all subjects only 2.6% felt that it was essential for them to influence the political structure and only 10.8% that it was very important to do so.[8] Prospective teachers were only a few percentage points below all undergraduates, and potential secondary school teachers were only slightly higher.

Looking beyond our national boundaries, the most appalling feature of all is the massive public ignorance and indifference concerning the relation of the American community to the emerging but inchoate world community. The issue of world interdependence is plain enough to the academic profession as well as to the public, if we but think a moment of the facts of energy, population, food, trade, oil, war, finance

7

and space. But few, even in academia, translated the facts, the dangers, and the possibilities of interdependence into a primary educational purpose. The decline in financial support from government and foundations for international education was one of the dreariest statistics of the 1960s. The International Education Act of 1966 was still waiting for its first funding in 1979.

One more major effort was being made in the late 1970s to reverse the trend. The reports of the President's Commission on Foreign Languages and International Studies, headed by James A. Perkins, were issued in November 1979, just before the crises in Iran and Afghanistan enveloped America's foreign policy. It remained to be seen whether international education funds or budget cutting would win out. Meanwhile, Stephen Bailey reminded us that only 3% of all undergraduate students were enrolled in any courses that dealt with international events or discussed in any way foreign peoples and cultures.[9] This amounts to less than 1% of the total college-aged youth in the U.S. And in 1973 only about 5% of all teachers in training had any exposure to international content or perspectives in their coursework for teacher certification.

The reports from the campus since 1975 are mixed, but the general view is that a heightened competition for grades and academic success has been stimulated by the competition for jobs in the more remunerative professions. This turn from liberal arts studies to professional training in college is deplored by those in the humanities. Meanwhile, fraternities, sororities, and football have been rediscovered. Philip Altbach, a perceptive analyst of student movements around the world, finds the underlying privatism to be a major element in student life of the 1970s:

> The religious revival, and especially interest in personalistic Eastern religions, is part of a widespread concern evident on campus, as well as in the middle class generally, for psychological self-improvement. The popularity of books like *I'm OK, You're OK*, the EST movement, transcendental meditation, and similar currents are all indicative of this significant strain in campus life. In a sense, the idealism that was focused on political and social concerns in the 60s has been directed toward the "inner life" in the 70s. Even the most popular campus social cause of the 70s, the environmental issue, is very much related to this current.[10]

The anomaly of cultivating the "inner life" alongside competing for grades and jobs caused the Carnegie Council to worry about the rise of unethical practices among students scrambling for places in prestigious institutions and among faculty and administrators of colleges and universities facing lower enrollments in a declining higher education market:

> We see certain signs of deterioration of important aspects of academic life, and in particular:

8

- A significant and apparently increasing amount of cheating by students in academic assignments,
- A substantial misuse by students of public financial aid,
- Theft and destruction by students of valuable property, most specifically library books and journals,
- Inflation of grades by faculty members,
- Competitive awarding of academic credits by some departments and some institutions for insufficient and inadequate academic work,
- Inflated and misleading advertising by some institutions, in the search for students.[11]

Pluralism in Education

I mention these several examples of the rise in privatism in political and educational practice in order to illustrate one major aspect of the "critical period" that must be faced by civic education in the 1980s. A second major element, and one that will make privatism in politics even harder to cope with, is a growing stress upon the values of pluralism in educational thought and practice that germinated in the 1960s and blossomed during the 1970s. This attraction to pluralism resulted no doubt from the loss of credibility in governmental authority and from an emerging attitude that glorified "doing one's own thing." But as seen by serious scholars and analysts of the contemporary social and educational scene, the phenomenon was much more than that. It is nothing less than a new search for a legitimate authority upon which to base educational goals and practices. From a variety of sources, arguments have been propounded that the authority for education should rest primarily with the diverse pluralistic communities in American society rather than primarily in the common political or civic community. I have found it convenient to contrast these two views in the oversimplified terms "pluralism" and "civism."

Pluralists seek moral authority and legitimacy for education in the many different communities that serve to bind individuals and groups together on the basis of religious, racial, ethnic, linguistic, or cultural unity. They see such positive values in the diversity and variety of pluralistic associations that they consider them to be the essence of community around which education and schooling should cluster. Most pluralists are exceedingly critical of public education for being so conformist in outlook and practice. Their remedies cover a wide range of reform. Some recommend that public schools should emphasize ethnic studies, multicultural studies, bilingual studies, and in general should reflect the enormous diversity of their respective cultural communities. Other pluralists see no special authority in public education, viewing it as no more legitimate or authoritative than private schools or any number of other educative agencies, such as families, churches, and voluntary associations of all kinds. Still others view

9

public education as positively *illegitimate*, because of its historic connection with an exploitative, capitalist, corporate state.

By contrast, "civicists" seek the principal authority and legitimacy for public education in the common civic or political community.* They argue that public education has a special responsibility for being a positive force in promoting the values, the knowledge, and the skills of participation required for maintaining and improving the democratic political community and for strengthening the values of freedom, equality, justice, and popular consent as set forth in the Declaration of Independence, the Constitution, and the Bill of Rights. For these values to provide protection for the diversity of groups in a pluralistic nation, they must be held in common or else privatism, contention, and conflict may threaten the welfare of all but the most powerful groups in the society.

Pluralism has had a rapid rise in popularity among an increasing number of critics of public education during the past decade or so. It has been picked up enthusiastically by many professional education groups, especially under the heading of "cultural pluralism," a term usually associated with Horace M. Kallen, who was for many years a professor of philosophy at the New School for Social Research in New York City and a vigorous advocate of liberal and progressive views in education.

The popular rebirth of cultural pluralism in the 1960s has come from several sources, only a few examples of which I will mention here: 1) the new ethnicity; 2) the rise of a neo-conservative view in political and economic philosophy; 3) certain advocates in philosophy of education; and 4) prominent policy advisors who work both within and without the educational establishment.

While blacks achieved some success in the civil rights movement of

---

*Though not often found in current usage, I derive the word "civicist" from civics (the study of government) as physicist is derived from physics. In fact, however, the words "civism" and "civicism" are perfectly good, but seldom used, English words, included in both *Webster's Unabridged Dictionary* (Second Edition) and the *Oxford English Dictionary*. Civism is taken from the French *civisme* (taken in turn from the Latin *civis* meaning citizen), which the French coined to refer to the devotion or disposition toward the new nation they established in their Revolution of 1789. In English the word civism refers generally to the "citizen principle" as envisioned in the ancient Greek and Roman republics, especially the tradition of self-sacrifice for the public good. It came then, by extension, to mean the principles of good citizenship. Civism is a useful single shorthand term for the longer phrase "principles of good citizenship in a republic." It connotes the need for building a sense of cohesion that will bind citizens together into a viable political community. Civicism is defined in *Webster's New International Dictionary of the English Language* as "principles of civil government" or "devotion, adherence, or conformity, to civic principles or to the duties and rights belonging to civic government." See the use of the term by George Armstrong Kelly, "Who Needs a Theory of Citizenship?" *Daedalus* (Fall 1979), p. 27. This whole volume of *Daedalus* is devoted to "The State." See especially Harry Eckstein, "On the 'Science' of the State," and James Fishkin, "Moral Principles and Public Policy."

10

the 1960s, other forms of discrimination continued to frustrate the descendants of white immigrants from Europe. As a result, a new and sometimes fierce pride in ethnic traditions has appeared both in professional and popular literature and has reappeared as a lively political force in the elections of the 1960s and 1970s. Books and articles by Michael Novak, formerly on the staff of the Rockefeller Foundation; Nathan Glazer of Harvard; Daniel Patrick Moynihan, formerly of Harvard and now U.S. Senator from New York; and Rev. Andrew Greeley, director of the Center for the Study of Pluralism at the University of Chicago, are among the best known.[12]

The new ethnicity is defined by Novak as:

> ...a movement of self-knowledge on the part of members of the third and fourth generations of southern and eastern European immigrants in the U.S. In a broader sense, the new ethnicity includes a renewed self-consciousness on the part of other generations and other ethnic groups: the Irish, the Norwegians and Swedes, the Germans, the Chinese and Japanese, and others....[13]

Novak argues for the introduction of ethnic studies into the public school curriculum as follows:

> With even modest adjustments in courses in history, literature, and the social sciences, material can be introduced that illuminates the inherited patterns of family life, values, and preferences. The purpose of introducing multicultural materials is neither chauvinistic nor propagandistic but realistic. Education ought to illuminate what is happening in the self of each child.[14]

From views and sentiments like those of Novak has arisen the demand for ethnic heritage studies and multicultural studies in the public schools. But another approach arising from the new ethnicity argues that *ethnic schools* would be better than common public schools. Andrew Greeley implies this when he argues that an "ethnic miracle" has been achieved by some of the immigrant groups in rising out of poverty and combating hatred and discrimination by their own efforts and in spite of the public schools. In fact, their own parochial schools aided Irish Catholics, Italians, and Poles to achieve financial success and middle-class status in a matter of a few decades after their arrival in the U.S. The public high school did not assist in this process because the immigrants' financial success came *before* they began to flock to high schools. It was rather their family life, their hard work, their ambition, their courage, their work ethic, and their sacrifice. They were given no favors and no help, but they *were* given personal freedom and the chance to turn their hard work into economic progress.

The message for social policy in all this is that public funds should go to aid ethnic schools that have been so important in the "ethnic miracle" of the past. In Greeley's view:

> ...one might take it as a tentative hypothesis that the school is a rather poor institution for facilitating the upward mobility of minority

groups—until they first acquire some kind of rough income parity.
The naive American faith that equality of education produces equality
of income seems to have been stood on its head in the case of the
ethnics. For them, better income meant more effective education.

Nor did the public schools play the critical "Americanization" role
that such educators as Dr. James B. Conant expected them to play in
the 1940s and 1950s. Even taking into account parents' education and
income, the most successful of the ethnics—educationally,
occupationally, and economically—went to parochial schools, and
they did so at a time when the schools were even more crowded than
they are today, staffed by even less adequately trained teachers, and
administered by an even smaller educational bureaucracy than the
very small one that somehow manages to keep the parochial schools
going today. Again: a social policy hint: Maybe what matters about
schools for a minority group is, as my colleague Professor William
McCready has remarked, that they are "our" schools (whoever "we"
may be).[15]

A second fountainhead for the new pluralism springs from a variety
of neo-conservative analyses in the fields of moral, political, and
economic philosophy in which fundamental questions are being raised
concerning the future of the institution of public education itself and,
more broadly, the whole range of institutions that make up liberal
democratic government in America.

It seems clear that during the early 1970s there has been a growing
conservative reaction against the educational and social reform efforts
of the 1960s. One could cite Robert Nisbet of Columbia in historical
sociology, Robert Nozick of Harvard in political philosophy, Milton
Friedman of Chicago and the Hoover Institution at Stanford in
economics, and Harvard's Nathan Glazer in education and social
structure.

Theirs is a call for the reassertion of the values of private freedoms,
individual rights, the free market mechanism, the minimal state, the free
play of voluntary groups, mutual aid associations, and the
reinforcement of pluralistic racial and social groupings of all kinds.
Along with the positive values associated with freedom for the "100
flowers to bloom" comes an attack upon the overweening welfare state,
the inquisitional and repressive measures of bureaucracy, the leviathan
mentality, and in general a disenchantment with the liberal welfare state
and its policies.

Let me give just one example of the new conservatism. Robert Nisbet
of Columbia begins his book *The Twilight of Authority* by saying:

> I believe the single most remarkable fact at the present time in the
> West is neither technological nor economic, but *political*: the waning of
> the historic political community, the widening sense of the
> obsolescence of politics as a civilized pursuit, even as a habit of mind.
> By political community I mean more than the legal state. I have in
> mind the whole fabric of rights, liberties, participations, and

12

protections that has been even above industrialism, I think, the dominant element of modernity in the West....

We are witnessing...a gathering revolt...against the whole structure of wealth, privilege, and power that the contemporary democratic state has come to represent.[16]

Nisbet's prescriptions for the restoration of authority are to recover the central values of social and cultural pluralism rather than political cohesion and to revive the prestige of the private as contrasted with the public. In briefest terms, Nisbet defines four central values of pluralism. Correctly understood, 1) it preserves functional autonomy of the major social institutions (avoiding intrusion of the state into the spheres of school, university, family, and religion); 2) it decentralizes power into as many hands as possible; 3) it recognizes that hierarchy and stratification of function and role are unavoidable and honorable and to be preserved from intrusion by the arbitrary power of regulatory agencies in the "name of a vain and vapid equality"; and 4) it relies as much as possible upon informal custom, folkway, spontaneous tradition—sanctioned habits of mind—rather than formal law, ordinance, or administrative regulation.

Thus, Nisbet argues for the renascence in education of pluralism, privatism, kinship, localism, and voluntary association. For example, regarding kinship, it was a great mistake of democratic dogma to think that political institutions like the public school could do better than the family in the realm of education. Regarding localism, the opposition to busing springs from pride of attachment to neighborhood rather than from racism. Regarding voluntary association, the prime agents of human accomplishment are the intimate, free, relevant, and spontaneous associations of self-help and mutual aid, the best illustration of such laissez-faire phenomena being Milton Friedman's proposal for educational vouchers. In other words, private schools under the auspices of churches, labor unions, cooperatives, neighborhoods, and families have been notably less expensive and more efficient than public schools:

From what labyrinths of bureaucracy we would be saved in the grim worlds of social workers and educational administrators had there been instituted in the beginning a system of education whereby a natural, already existing social group—the household—would be the means of distributing public funds for welfare and for education.[17]

In the concluding paragraphs of his book, Nisbet argues that it all comes down to the way we conceive of the nature of citizenship:

If there is to be a citizenship in the useful sense of that word, it must have its footings in the groups, associations, and localities in which we actually spend our lives—not in the abstract and now bankrupt idea of *patrie*, as conceived by the Jacobins and their descendants.[18]

Now, if the signposts of the future are the new thrusts of ethnicity, localism, regionalism, religion, and kinship, this is exactly what we had

200 years ago when the founders of the American commonwealth sought to overcome these very pluralistic elements by establishing a political community and a constitutional order whose motto became *E Pluribus Unum*. And Nisbet's notions of private education based upon these same elements of traditional pluralism were exactly the characteristics of the schools and colleges of the colonial period that the founders and their successors sought to replace by their proposals for a public education that would be universal, free, common, and eventually secular and compulsory.

A third source of demand for pluralism has arisen from philosophy of education. One line of reasoning, identified with the so-called "romantic critics," has led to the conclusion that the public school system cannot be reclaimed and should be replaced by voluntary efforts of many kinds. Another line of argument has led to proposals for all sorts of "alternatives" to loosen up and introduce flexibility into the public school system itself. These two refrains became dominant themes of professional education discussions of the 1960s and 1970s.

Henry Perkinson, educational historian at New York University, accurately sums up the essence of the romantic critics:

> One after another the romantic critics have uncovered layers of authoritarianism in our educational arrangements. To a man they reject imposition and advocate a child-centered or learner-centered education. The smorgasbord curriculum of John Holt, the inquiry method of Postman and Weingartner, the open classroom of Herbert Kohl, the free school of George Dennison, the learning web of Ivan Illich—all point to an educational process where people learn what, how, and when they like.[19]

The embracing of pluralism in education can scarcely go further. The concern specifically for political community is scarcely in evidence, except for a minor refrain of somehow removing the evils of a capitalist system. The overall impact of the romantic critics is probably much more important, though less direct, than often admitted by the educational establishment. Another kind of pedagogical pluralism, that which emanates from within the establishment and focuses upon reforms of the public schools in the direction of greater alternatives, reflects much of the orientation if not the fire and outrage of the romantics. Philosophers of education, educational policy advisors, national commissions, federal programs, and national association projects begin to echo if not incorporate the pluralistic criticisms that have reverberated through the press and other mass media for over a decade.

Philosophy of education, which had been socially oriented to the ideals of democracy and individual development in the spirit of John Dewey's pragmatism and experimentalism through most of the period from the late 1920s to the early 1950s, began to be absorbed by linguistic analysis of philosophical problems in the 1950s and early 1960s. Then

14

philosophy of education began to rediscover the individualistic and pluralistic side of Dewey's philosophy and especially that of Horace Kallen.[20] The essence of that philosophy is the idea that primary human associations are the most basic communities, consisting of natural affinities and sentiments. The individual can most readily develop his personality and self-fulfillment in and through such associations. A genuine pluralistic society will thus honor and encourage the diversity of the natural primary groups based upon kinship, language, religion, culture, and locality. Education should therefore recognize and encourage such diverse loyalties, both as the essence of democracy and of personal development. Obviously, this revival of the philosophy of cultural pluralism fits nicely with the rise of the new ethnicity and a non-authoritarian political philosophy, whether stemming from conservative, liberal, or radical sources.

Some philosophers and practitioners of education, imbued with the pluralistic emphasis upon individual and primary group attachment, argue that the public schools should stress the pluralistic character of American society through multicultural studies. Others find no place or a greatly reduced place for public education as it has been historically developed. One of the most forthright statements of this philosophy of education is that of Seymour Itzkoff of Smith College, whose recent book is interestingly titled *A New Public Education*. He finds a large place for private voluntary effort and little for a public governmental role in education. His conception of the "new public education" is so new that it really means private education supported by public funds.

Calling as witnesses Horace Kallen, John Dewey, and Thomas Green, Itzkoff argues that the local autonomous cultural community is the natural context and authority for education. He argues that the educational system can be reformed by a gradual shift to voluntarism and eventually a full voucher system. In this way the stagnant, bureaucratized, politicized public system can be given over to those who will be the ultimate beneficiaries; parents and children will have maximum opportunity to realize their value commitments in a wholly voluntary system of community-based schooling.

Itzkoff concludes that the legitimacy of the public school and the moral authority it once had have been irretrievably lost, confounded at least in part by the new stress on an aggressive equality by government fiat, forced integration, affirmative action, and proliferation of quotas enforced by the intercession of government:

> The traumas that the schools have recently undergone have arisen precisely because of our waning confidence in the school. The moral consensus that undergirded the public school for so many decades has dissolved. And in its absence the state schools have fallen prey to a host of political locusts. Drained of its integrity, public education has become an automatic target for every new political grab. This has

15

caused many thoughtful people to abandon hope for the public school as a functioning national institution in its traditional moral as well as skill-training role.[21]

In place of the *common* public school should arise a pluralism of voluntary schools around which individuals with similar values, social concerns, and cultural ideals could cluster. Itzkoff opts for unregulated vouchers so that the greatest kind of differentiation (except racial) could lead to schools based on special interests, special talents, special cultural and ethnic orientations, and specialized admission policies:

> Free choice is the key, the right to be taught by whom one chooses, and the right to teach only those one feels will benefit from one's skills.[22]

Now it is still too early to record the disappearance of the public school as Itzkoff proposes, but prominent voices on the policy scene are giving notice that its role and importance should be viewed as greatly diminished in comparison with nonschool agencies of education. Only one or two examples can be cited.

In the policy pronouncements summarized in his book, also interestingly titled *Public Education*, my former colleague Lawrence A. Cremin, now president of Teachers College, Columbia University, notes that one of the failings of the progressive theory of education was that it focused too exclusively on the public schools as agencies of social reform and thus ignored the possibilities of other educative institutions. In his chapter on "Public Education and the Education of the Public" Cremin puts his policy observations this way:

> The fact is that the public is educated by many institutions, some of them private and some of them public, and that public schools are only one among several important public institutions that educate the public. There are, after all, public libraries, public museums, public television, and public work projects (the most extensive of which are the military services)....[23]

Now, Cremin does not flagellate the public schools as many other pluralists do, but his thesis that they are only one among many educative agencies apparently means that they have no special primacy of place in a democratic society, and I find him giving them no distinctive purpose that other educative agencies cannot fulfill:

> In sum, then, to think comprehensively about education we must consider policies with respect to a wide variety of institutions that educate, not only schools and colleges, but libraries, museums, day-care centers, radio and television stations, offices, factories, and farms. To be concerned solely with schools, given the educational world we live in today, is to have a kind of fortress mentality in contending with a very fluid and dynamic situation.[24]

Though public schools are not specifically denigrated in Cremin's views, they come off diminished in importance in comparison with all the other educative agencies he mentions. I would ask which of these

16

have as their *primary* purpose the formation of good citizens? Cremin does not propose priorities in this fashion. He seems simply to be asking for public debate about the alternatives. His view thus lends itself in *other* hands to a reification of "alternatives" as the be-all and end-all of educational policy.

One such policy position was taken recently by Theodore R. Sizer, former dean of the Harvard Graduate School of Education, who argued for a pluralism of educational institutions as the best solution for the future. He acknowledged that he had been particularly influenced by Cremin's *Public Education*, Tyack's *One Best System*, Glazer's *Affirmative Discrimination*, and Glazer and Moynihan's *Ethnicity*. Sizer's policy proposals are threefold. First, we must not simply reassert that the public schools are the one best system:

> ...the sooner those responsible for public education recognize that nonpublic schools, the so-called deschooling movement, the alternative education movement, and the advocates of neighborhood community schools all in their several ways represent a new reality in American educational politics, so much the better for the children. It is no surprise that efforts at a national unified teachers union have lost momentum and the political interest for increased federal involvement in the "improvement" of education has slowed. Disaggregation is a policy with new adherents. One need only look at the growing edge of the curricula of teacher training institutions to see the interest in alternatives and in the special educational needs of special groups, increasingly ethnic as well as racial groups. The *common* school, the single institution built around a common American creed, never was and clearly never will be.[25]

A second pluralistic injunction from Sizer rests on Cremin's argument that the part that schools can play in the education of children is limited. In fact, he goes so far as to acknowledge that Cremin's message on configurations of education will serve to bury the public school:

> Cremin would include, along with the school, the church, the family, and the ethnic group. *The times are ready for a new kind of pluralism in schooling*, a pluralism which relates the schools with other institutions in carefully contrived and thoughtfully constructed ways. Cremin's "Public Education" drives the final nail into the coffin of the late-Nineteenth Century nativist creation of a "one best system." The sooner that the educational establishment at large recognizes this, the better (again) for the children.[26]

Sizer is not worried about the segregative aspects of alternative schools. He believes that the "thread of nationhood" and social cohesion will be adequately served by the much more powerful mass media. He is apparently willing to leave the "common thread of nationhood" to Walter Cronkite, Harry Reasoner, and Ann Landers. So, he comes to his third proposal that youngsters could well divide their time between different kinds of schools: ethnic schools, community schools, regional schools, yes, even "national schools." So his final message is that there should be multiple opportunities for all children and parents to choose complementary institutions: a smorgasbord of schools.

All in all, then, whether it comes from outside or from inside the education establishment, the call for "alternatives" has become one of the most popular terms in the educational lexicon of the 1970s. It has been applied to all manner of undertakings, from well-thought-out programs to almost any kind of improvisation that will take bored, restless, or disruptive youth off the backs of embattled and harrassed public school administrators and teachers. Several national commissions have tried to tackle the problem, and in its own way the federal government has responded to the political interests of particular target groups: the Teacher Corps for the disadvantaged, the Bilingual Act for those with limited English, and the Ethnic Heritage Act for special ethnic groups. And above all, the major professional groups have taken up the call for multicultural studies with enthusiasm, if not always with deep understanding of the implications of cultural pluralism.

An example of the enthusiastic embracing of multicultural education and cultural pluralism is the American Association of Colleges for Teacher Education (AACTE), which appointed its Multicultural Education Commission in February 1971 and officially adopted its statement titled "No One Model American" at its Board of Directors meeting in November 1972. The statement quoted here indicates its strong attachment to the philosophy of cultural pluralism:

> Multicultural education is education which values cultural pluralism. Multicultural education rejects the view that schools should seek to melt away cultural differences or the view that schools should merely tolerate cultural pluralism. Instead, multicultural education affirms that schools should be oriented toward the cultural enrichment of all children and youth through programs rooted to the preservation and extension of cultural diversity as a fact of life in American society, and it affirms that this cultural diversity is a valuable resource that should be preserved and extended. It affirms that major education institutions should strive to preserve and enhance cultural pluralism.[27]

A careful reading of the full AACTE statement will reveal not only the obvious concern for the pluralistic communities, but also virtually no reference to the common elements that bind the different groups together. In this respect it appears to me that the National Education Association, the Association for Supervision and Curriculum Development, the National Council for the Social Studies, and many other enthusiastic proponents of multicultural education have forgotten or little noticed a major tenet that Horace Kallen, the father of cultural pluralism, always insisted upon; namely, that the fundamental principles of *political* democracy must underlie the diversities of *cultural* pluralism. Horace Kallen always gave primacy to the public schools. It was only upon this foundation that

> ...the outlines of a possibly great and truly democratic commonwealth become discernible. Its form would be that of the federal republic; its substance a democracy of nationalities, cooperating voluntarily and autonomously through common institutions in the enterprise of self-realization through the perfection of men according to their kind. The common language of the commonwealth, the language of its great tradition, would be English, but each nationality would have for its emotional and involuntary life its own peculiar dialect or speech, its own individual and inevitable esthetic and intellectual forms. The political and economic life of the commonwealth is a single unit and serves as the foundation and background for the realization of the distinctive individuality of each *nation* that composes it and of the pooling of these in a harmony above them all. Thus, "American civilization" may come to mean the perfection of the cooperative harmonies of "European civilization"— the waste, the squalor and the distress of Europe being eliminated—a multiplicity in a unity, an orchestration of mankind.[28]

And when Kallen came to identify the "common institutions" fundamental to the political commonwealth, he always gave primacy to the public schools. He was opposed to separate schools for separate cultural groups except as supplementary and voluntary additions to the common public schools that he urged all to attend. He opposed the injection of pluralistic religion into the public schools, and he opposed public support for private or ethnic schools. When he came in 1956 to define the elements of the "American Bible," which summed up for him the common creed of all Americans, he included not only the Declaration of Independence; the Constitution; the great credos of Washington, Jefferson, Madison, Lincoln, Wilson, Holmes, Brandeis, F.D. Roosevelt, and Truman on civil rights; and the U.S. Supreme Court rulings on separation of church and state, but also Horace Mann's *Twelfth Report to the Massachusetts Board of Education*[29] on education.

As the 1970s ended and the 1980s opened, a particularly formidable alliance between privatism in politics and pluralism in schooling began to be forged around the voucher idea. Not surprisingly, the movement gained headway in California on the heels of Proposition 13 and the gathering momentum to cut taxes, reduce governmental expenditures, and limit the role of governmental services.

The ideological framework was supplied by a book titled *Education by Choice; The Case for Family Control* by John E. Coons and Stephen D. Sugarman, professors of law at the University of California, Berkeley.[30] The basic assumption is that parents and families should be the primary authorities in guiding the education of children. These "private sovereigns" are more likely to know best and care most for the welfare of their children and to provide effective care for the children's interests. Therefore, the family or family-like clusters should have priority in educational decisions over the "public sovereigns" of children, i.e., teachers, social workers, juvenile courts, and other professionals. The power of educational choice should thus be kept as close as possible to the individuals whose interests are at stake. In order to enlarge parental control over the education of children, *all* children should be eligible to receive scholarships provided by public funds to enable them to attend any certified school of their parents' choice, whether public, private, parochial, or profit-making.

The family-choice initiative thus would redefine by constitutional amendment the meaning of common schools in California:

> There shall be three classes of common schools for grades kindergarten through twelve, namely, public schools, public scholarship schools, and private scholarship schools. Public schools are those publicly owned, funded, and administered and not certified to redeem scholarships. Public scholarship schools are those organized by the authority of public school districts or public institutions of higher learning and which are certified hereunder to redeem scholarships. [These must be non-profit corporations.] Private scholarship schools are those privately organized and certified hereunder to redeem scholarships. [These may be non-profit or profit-making corporations.][31]

Although the purposes of the proposition for vouchers stress the values of freedom of religion and elimination of racial segregation in schooling, I find no mention or special concern for the civic purposes of education or the preparation of citizens for participation in a common, democratic political community. The whole emphasis is upon fulfilling the private wants and desires of parents with regard to the education of their own children. This proposal, I believe, seeks to reverse the 200-year effort to surmount the potential divisiveness of the many segments in America through common public schools. This proposal seeks to solidify the differences and the diversities of a pluralistic society by embedding public support for differences in the state constitution. It does not recognize the validity or legitimacy of the state's concern to promote the values and ideals of a democratic political community through the agencies of common public schooling.

We must readily admit that the goals of common schooling have not always been achieved in public schools, but now I believe the effort of the family-choice initiative to redefine the meaning of common schools would entail giving up even the *ideal*. The choice in such a proposition is whether or not the ideal of a common school system devoted primarily to the task of building a civic community among the vast majority of

20

citizens shall be given up in favor of promoting with public funds the extension of private choice.

Despite wide and favorable publicity in the nation's mass media and despite numerous changes in the proposed proposition (profit-making schools were not to be eligible), the Coons-Sugarman initiative did not obtain enough signatures to qualify for the June 1980 ballot in California. Nearly all observers agreed, however, that the proposal would reappear in some form.

I believe this proposal is in essence an effort to do away with the public schools as a proper governmental function achieved over the past 200 years and to return educational control to the private markets and entrepreneurs who dominated the educational field in the eighteenth century.[32] This would increase public malaise about the public schools; encourage the rising fever that already beckons parents in an affluent society to desert the public schools for secular day schools, fundamentalist Christian academies, and all sorts of alternative schools. In none of these movements do I find a well-formulated conception of the common public good or of the obligation of schooling to try to promote a sense of civic community. Today, even the *rhetoric* of "good citizenship" as the prime purpose of education is all but missing from the educators' and the public's lexicon. We need to remind ourselves of the historic meaning of the idea of citizenship and the historical efforts of public schools to make it a reality.

Chapter 1 Notes

1. Bernard Bailyn et al., *The Great Republic, A History of the American People* (Boston: Little, Brown, 1977), pp. 322, 324.

2. Robert Lekachman, "Proposition 13 and the New Conservatism," *Change* (September 1978): 28.

3. Sydney E. Ahlstrom, "National Trauma and Changing Religious Values," *Daedalus* (Winter 1978): 20.

4. Barry Commoner, "Reflections: The Solar Transition," Part II, *The New Yorker* (30 April 1979): 93.

5. Ahlstrom, "National Trauma," p. 22.

6. John Herbers, "Governing America," *The New York Times* (12 November 1978).

7. Daniel Yankelovich, *The New Morality: A Profile of American Youth in the Seventies* (New York: McGraw-Hill, 1974), pp. 5-6.

8. Nebraska Curriculum Development Center, Study Commission on Undergraduate Education and the Education of Teachers (Lincoln, Nebraska: University of Nebraska, October 1974).

9. Stephen K. Bailey, *College Board Review*, No. 97 (Fall 1975): 3.

10. Philip G. Altbach, "Whatever Happened to Student Activists?," *The Chronical of Higher Education* (26 March 1979): 56.

11. Carnegie Council on Policy Studies in Higher Education, *Fair Practices in Higher Education; Rights and Responsibilities of Students and Their Colleges in a Period of Intensified Competition for Enrollments* (San Francisco: Jossey-Bass, 1979), p.3.

12. See, e.g., Michael Novak, *The Rise of the Unmeltable Ethnics* (New York: Macmillan, 1972); Nathan Glazer and Daniel Patrick Moynihan, *Beyond the Melting Pot* (Cambridge, Mass.: M.I.T. Press, 1963); Lawrence H. Fuchs, ed., *American Ethnic Politics* (New York: Harper and Row, 1968); Edgar Litt, *Ethnic Politics in America* (Glenview, Ill.: Scott Foresman, 1970); Andrew M. Greeley, *Why Can't They Be Like Us?* (New York: American Jewish Committee, 1968); and Peter Schrag, *The Decline of the WASP* (New York: Simon and Schuster, 1971).

13. Michael Novak, "The New Ethnicity," *The Center Magazine* (July/Aug. 1974): 18.

14. Ibid., p. 25.

15. Andrew M. Greeley, "The Ethnic Miracle," *The Public Interest*, No. 45, (Fall 1977), p. 29. See also, Greeley, *The American Catholic; A Social Portrait* (New York: Basic Books, 1977).

16. Robert Nisbet, *Twilight of Authority* (New York: Oxford University Press, 1975), pp. 3-5.

17. Ibid., p. 278.

18. Ibid., p. 286.

19. Henry S. Perkinson, *Two Hundred Years of American Educational Thought* (New York: McKay, 1976), pp. 307-308. For an excellent brief bibliography of the major writings of the romantic critics, see pp. 310-312.

20. See, e.g., Horace M. Kallen, *Culture and Democracy in the United States* (New York: Boni & Liveright, 1924); William Greenbaum, "America in Search of a New Idea: An Essay on the Rise of Pluralism," *Harvard Educational Review* 44 (August 1974); several articles in *Philosophy of Education 1976: Proceedings of the Thirty-Second Annual Meeting of the Philosophy of Education Society* (Urbana, Ill.: Educational Theory, 1976); Charles A. Tesconi, Jr., *Schooling in America; A Social Philosophical Perspective*, Part IV (Boston: Houghton-Mifflin, 1975); and Thomas F. Green, *Education and Pluralism: Ideal and Reality* (Syracuse, N.Y.: Syracuse University, 1966).

21. Seymour Itzkoff, *A New Public Education* (New York: David McKay, 1976), pp. 333-334.

22. Ibid., p. 356.

23. Lawrence A. Cremin, *Public Education* (New York: Basic Books, 1976), p. 58.

24. Ibid., p. 59.

25. Theodore Ryland Sizer, "Education and Assimilation: A Fresh Plea for Pluralism," *Phi Delta Kappan* (September 1976): 34.

26. Ibid.

27. William A. Hunter, ed., *Multicultural Education Through Competency-Based Teacher Education* (Washington, D.C.: American Association of Colleges for Teacher Education, 1974), p. 21. See also, e.g., "Alternative Approaches to Teacher Education," *Journal of Teacher Education* (Jan./Feb. 1977); and National Council for the Social Studies, *Curriculum Guidelines for Multiethnic Education* (Arlington, Va.: N.C.S.S., 1976).

28. Horace M. Kallen, *Culture and Democracy in the United States* (New York: Boni and Liveright, 1924), p. 124.

29. Horace M. Kallen, *Cultural Pluralism and the American Idea; An Essay in Social Philosophy* (Philadelphia: University of Pennsylvania Press, 1956), p. 87.

30. John E. Coons and Stephen D. Sugarman, *Education By Choice; The Case for Family Control* (Berkeley: University of California Press, 1978).

31. John E. Coons, "An Initiative for Family Choice in Education," a proposed amendment of the Constitution of California, draft of 5 March 1979.

32. See my debate with Coons in "Educational Vouchers: The Private Pursuit of the Public Purse" versus Coons, "Of Family Choice and 'Public' Education," *Phi Delta Kappan* (September 1979): 7-13.

Chapter 2

The Idea of Citizenship

T hose of us born and brought up in modern nation-states are likely to think that citizenship in such political organizations is "natural" and something to be taken for granted. But those who have been born in one country and have immigrated to another to become "naturalized" citizens are not nearly so likely to take citizenship for granted. And those who are "stateless" know only too well the handicaps, if not the terrors, of having no citizenship at all in a world made up of nation-states. I begin, then, with a reminder about the origin of the idea of citizenship that long antedated the modern nation-state but which is now tightly bound up with it.

The idea of citizenship was forged in two major formative periods. The first formulation occurred during the rise and fall of the Greek city-states from roughly the seventh to the fourth centuries B.C. and was carried over with modifications to the Roman Republic and Empire. The second took place in connection with the growth of the modern nation-states in the revolutionary era of Western Europe and America from the seventeenth to the nineteenth centuries. We in the U.S. are inheritors of both periods. The founders of the American Republic not only drew heavily upon both the Greco-Roman and Western European traditions of citizenship, but they made significant contributions of their own to the idea of democratic citizenship. As the twentieth century draws to a close it is clear that we are in a third formative period when the idea of citizenship will again need to be reformulated to take account of the drastically changed world situation, which the men of the eighteenth century could not foresee.

The Origin of Citizenship in Greco-Roman Republics

It can be argued that the idea of citizenship can be traced further back than the Greeks. In fact, I have so argued on the basis of scholarly accounts of the rise of the Sumerian city-states in the period from 3000 to 2500 B.C. But the history is so fragmentary and the influence upon the Western tradition so tenuous that I start where the historical record is more than ample and the significance for us is direct and telling. Even so, the history is long and complicated, so I can touch only the high spots and must be very selective.[1]

Two main points about the origin of the idea of citizenship are: 1) citizenship was based upon membership in a political community regulated by man-made laws rather than upon membership in a family, clan, or tribe based upon kinship, religion, ethnic background, or inherited status; and 2) the predominant view of citizenship in fifth-century Athens was that citizenship meant that the laws were made, administered, and judged by free citizens who were both rulers and ruled, not merely subjects of a king or priest who made or revealed the laws. In the first case citizenship entailed rights and responsibilities conferred by law (achieved status) in contrast to roles and obligations conferred by inherited class, kinship, or sex (ascribed status). In the second case the free citizens were members of a democratic or republican political community in which the citizen class participated actively in the affairs of the state.

The significant fact about the rise of the Greek city-states from the seventh to the fifth centuries B.C. was that authority for governing, for maintaining social order, and for administering justice was transferred from household patriarchs, tribal chiefs, military nobles, literate priesthoods, or hereditary kings to the political community centering upon the city-state or polis. While some of the outward forms and terminology of tribe and clan were often kept for the sake of ethnic pride, the Greek city-states dropped the essentially ascriptive characteristics of kinship ties typical of traditional folk societies and established citizenship in the polity as the overarching tie of unity that bound the community together. The bonds of sentiment and loyalty to the territorial state became the primary forms of social cohesion, superior to family or kin, class or caste, or any kind of voluntary association. The key personality in this fundamental change was the powerful Athenian statesman, Cleisthenes, whose political reforms apparently were effected in the last decade of the sixth century B.C.

This transfer of legitimate authority from kinship lineage to polity is nicely described by Robert Nisbet, Schweitzer Professor of the Humanities at Columbia:

> What we see, therefore, taking place with revolutionary suddenness and sweep is a total transformation of a social system. Instead of the traditional, kinship-based pluralism of Athenian authority, there is now a monolithic unit that arises from a governmental system reaching directly down to the individual citizen. Instead of a system of law based upon immemorial tradition, its interpretation subject to the elders of kinship society and always slow and uncertain, we have now a system of Athenian law that is prescriptive, that is made, rather than merely interpreted out of tradition, and that is deemed binding upon all Athenians irrespective of kinship lineage. We see, too, a growing commonality of all Athenians, one that did not and could not exist so long as the sense of community rose primarily from the fact of

25

generation, through tribe or clan. And finally, there is in the new Athens a manifest individualism, sprung from the fact that henceforth the individual, not the kinship group, was the irreducible and unalterable unit of the Athenian military-political system.[2]

While Nisbet is pleased to refer to the new polity as a "monolithic unity," the rise and decline of the Greek polis from 800 to 300 B.C. would scarcely justify universal application of such a description, especially for Athens. In the seventh century B.C. independent farmers were drawn into the rolls of citizens to fill the ranks of infantrymen alongside the mounted cavalrymen of nobles. And under Cleisthenes propertyless artisans and sailors in the mercantile and military navy also gained citizenship. These trends provided a broader base of citizenship in Athens than in many other Greek polities, leading to its boast of becoming a democracy. And the florescence of drama, art, architecture, literature, and philosophy that was the glory of fifth-century Athens both sprang from and centered upon the polis as the symbol and culmination of a citizen's fulfillment. A classic statement of the ideal of Athenian citizenship was expressed by Pericles in his funeral oration in the first year of the Peloponnesian War in 431 B.C. While it was indeed an idealized version, nevertheless it had some of the same claim upon the loyalties and commitments of Athenians that Lincoln's address on the battlefield at Gettysburg came to have for Americans:

> Our constitution...favours the many instead of the few; this is why it is called a democracy. If we look to the laws, they afford equal justice to all in their private differences; if to social standing, advancement in public life falls to reputation for capacity, class considerations not being allowed to interfere with merit; nor again does poverty bar the way, if a man is able to serve the state, he is not hindered by the obscurity of his condition. The freedom which we enjoy in our government extends also to our ordinary life. There, far from exercising a jealous surveillance over each other, we do not feel called upon to be angry with our neighbor for doing what he likes.... But all this ease in our private relations does not make us lawless as citizens....
>
> We throw open our city to the world, and never by alien acts exclude foreigners from any opportunity of learning or observing, although the eyes of an enemy may occasionally profit by our liberality....
>
> Our public men have, besides politics, their private affairs to attend to, and our ordinary citizens, though occupied with the pursuits of industry, are still fair judges of public matters; for, unlike any other nation, regarding him who takes no part in these duties not as unambitious but as useless, we Athenians are able to judge at all events if we cannot originate, and instead of looking on discussion as a stumbling block in the way of action, we think it an indispensable preliminary to any action at all.[3]

This Periclean view of the ideal fifth-century Athenian citizen as described by the historian Thucydides was destined, however, to be eclipsed in much of subsequent history by other conceptions of Greek citizenship formulated by Plato and Aristotle, both of whom wrote their influential treatises during the decline and crises besetting the Greek polis in the fourth century B.C. After a long and exhausting war with Sparta, the Athenian polity was weakened and eventually overcome by the Macedonian kings, Philip and Alexander. Plato attributed this decline and fall to a rampant individualism, a resurgence of traditional kinship and religious beliefs, a preoccupation with personal and private wealth, and the prejudices and ignorance of the common people (*demos*) whose passions as citizens led to successive injustices and tyranny over the best and the brightest.

It was in this setting that Plato drew up his ideal political community in the *Republic*. Impressed by the discipline and military superiority of the authoritarian Spartan state in contrast to the factional rivalries of democratic Athens, Plato visualized a state that would be ruled by a wise, just, and well-educated class of guardians who could subordinate their passions for the good of the state. In contrast to the Periclean ideal that each citizen would alternately work, fight, and rule, Plato argued that justice required all persons to do only that for which they were best fitted: workers to work, warriors to fight, and guardians to rule. In a loose sense, good citizenship consisted of each class doing what it was best fitted for; in a strict sense, the only genuine citizens were the aristocratic class of guardians, selected and trained by a rigorous system of state-controlled education to perform their roles as philosopher-kings. They were the only ones who could surmount the passions of the body, the confining ties of family, kinship, wealth, and religion, and grasp the genuine truth, beauty, and goodness of the real world of ideas by means of a higher education achieved through the intellectual discipline of mathematics, metaphysics, and dialectics.

Plato's vision of the aristocratic and essentially closed political community does indeed illustrate Nisbet's term "monolithic unity." Thus, it has perennial appeal to those who have wished to overcome the excessive individualism and freedom and passions of the mob in the interests of "higher" intellectual and moral virtues as these are defined by the well-educated upper classes who have been privileged to contemplate and grasp the true ideas of reality that lie beyond the ebb and flow of practical experience.

But the other powerful voice that defined a Greek view of citizenship was that of Aristotle whose *Politics* and *Ethics* were enormously influential despite their prosaic and pedantic quality in comparison with Plato's poetic, even mystic, vision of utopia. Aristotle's views were much more pluralistic. He found some good in all three of the major forms of government, a classification of his that proved to be a starting point for political philosophers for some 2,000 years. The government, which is the supreme authority of the state, may be in the hands of one, few, or many. In each case there is a true form that may become a perversion or corruption. The test of the difference is that in a true form the ruler is ruling on behalf of the common interest of all, and in the perversion the ruler is ruling on behalf of the private interest of the ruler. So the paradigm becomes:

	True Form Serves the Public Good	Corrupted Form Serves the Private Interest of	
One	Monarchy	Tyranny	The king
Few	Aristocracy	Oligarchy	Wealthy property owners
Many	Republic or Commonwealth (Constitutionalism)	Democracy	Needy poor

Aristotle thus does not come out unequivocally for a single true form of government, but his biases are generally on the side of aristocracy or constitutionalism. His aristocratic leanings show when he would confine citizenship to the "free man," thereby ruling out women, children, slaves, mechanics, traders, and farmers who had to work for a living and who did not, therefore, have the native ability or the education or the leisure to engage fully in the task of ruling. But when he spoke about the citizen class itself, Aristotle sounded very much like a constitutionalist or a republican. The citizens are all equal in their political rights and responsibilities, for a citizen is ruled only by other citizens, all of whom take part and take turns in governing.

All citizens hold the "office of citizen." There are two kinds of office. One has a fixed term and is determinate in length. These are held by the government officials who are elected or appointed to a specific office for specific functions. The other "office of citizen" is of indeterminate or continuous duration and applies to the duties and responsibilities that *all* citizens have in their capacities as rulers, deciders, and judgers in the legislative assemblies and courts of the commonwealth. Aristotle thus clearly distinguishes free and equal citizens, who share in ruling the state, from the subjects who have no voice in their government and have no legal rights of redress or protection, as in the case of slaves who are entirely subjected to the absolute rule of the master, or children who are subjected to the benevolent rule of their parents. In contrast, citizens engage in self-government, taking turns in ruling and being ruled by their equals:

> [The citizen's] special characteristic is that he shares in the administration of justice, and in offices. Now of offices some are discontinuous, and the same persons are not allowed to hold them twice, or can only hold them after a fixed interval; others have no limit of time—for example, the office of [juryman] or [assemblyman*]. Let

*All Athenian citizens were members of the popular assembly throughout their adult life. The assembly had judicial as well as legislative functions.

28

us, for the sake of distinction, call it "indefinite office," and we will assume that those who share in such offices are citizens. This is the most comprehensive definition of citizen....He who has the power to take part in the deliberative or judicial administration of any state is said by us to be a citizen of that state; and, speaking generally, a state is a body of citizens sufficing for the purposes of life.[4]

Despite their differences as to the essential qualities of the truly just state (Plato's more absolutistic and Aristotle's more pluralistic), they agreed on two major characteristics that I would like to stress. One was that the *political* community was seen as the most valuable means for human fulfillment and justice; the other was that education should be a public function of the polity rather than a private function of family, kinship, or religion. On the first point, Aristotle put it this way:

Every state is a community of some kind, and every community is established with a view to some good....But if all communities aim at some good, the state or political community, which is the highest of all, and which embraces all the rest, aims at good in a higher degree than any other, and at the highest good.[5]

Since the ultimate object of the state is the good life, then the citizens must be led to virtue by the inculcation of virtuous habits and rational principles:

A city [state] can be virtuous only when the citizens who have a share in the government are virtuous, and in our state all the citizens share in the government.[6]

And how is this to be achieved? By a common public education conducted for all citizens by the state. Aristotle's ideas concerning citizenship contained in the preceding quotations and in the following quotation were expressed over and over by the framers of the American Republic in the late eighteenth century:

No one will doubt that the legislator should direct his attention above all to the education of youth; for the neglect of education does harm to the constitution. The citizen should be molded to suit the form of government under which he lives. For each government has a peculiar character which originally formed and which continues to preserve it. The character of democracy creates democracy and the character of oligarchy creates oligarchy; and always the better the character, the better the government.

...since the whole city [state] has one end [virtue], it is manifest that education should be one and the same for all, and that it should be public, and not private—not as at present, when everyone looks after his own children separately, and gives them separate instruction of the sort which he thinks best; the training in things which are of common interest should be the same for all. Neither must we suppose that any one of the citizens belongs to himself, for they all belong to the state, and are each of them a part of the state, and the care of each part is inseparable from the care of the whole.[7]

That education should be regulated by law and should be an affair

29

of the state is not to be denied, but what should be the character of this public education, and how the young should be educated, are questions which remain to be considered.[8]

Unfortunately, Aristotle does not get around in his *Politics* to telling us what the proper political education for citizens should be, beyond mentioning the usual elementary subjects taught in most city-state schools: reading and writing, gymnastics, music, and possibly drawing. It would have been interesting to see what differences he would have prescribed for the education of citizens in each of his types of government: monarchy, aristocracy, and constitutional republic. We do, however, get some insight into Aristotle's views of higher education in his *Ethics* where he outlines the proper subjects of study for a free man, that is, a liberal education.

When it came to a liberal education, Aristotle the philosopher and scientist won out over Aristotle the political theorist and realist. In his *Ethics* Aristotle argued that the highest form of virtue was pure speculation. Man as knower and thinker was higher in the scale of human values than man as doer and citizen. Man's rational nature has a higher aspect and a lower. The higher is made up of the intellectual virtues and the lower of the moral virtues. These moral virtues, which are the outcome of habit formation, constitute the character of persons and are molded in the earlier years of life and schooling.

The higher intellectual virtues, which are the outcomes of teaching, are also of a higher and lower type. The more noble is *theoretical reasoning* that aims at knowledge for its own sake, formulates the first principles that describe the unchanging reality lying behind the natures of man, nature, and the universe, and determines the truth or falsity of propositions that define the unchanging aspects of existence. The liberal studies that best aid the intellectual faculties to discover these first principles are from higher to lower: theology, metaphysics, ontology, cosmology, physics, astronomy, psychology, biology, mathematics, and logic.

The less noble of the intellectual faculties is *practical reasoning* which aims at knowledge having to do with action or conduct (prudence) or the making and producing of things (art). The practical reasoning thus deals with the changeable and the variable in events as an aid to guiding human conduct and formulating rules for action. Here the citizen is guided through his study of politics, ethics, economics, rhetoric, and the arts.

In this preference for the theoretical studies over the practical studies, Aristotle lent the weight of his influence to that of Plato in forming a Western intellectual and academic tradition that has long viewed theory to be valued more than practice in a liberal education, truth-seeking to be a higher goal than the goals of morality and justice, and acquisition of organized knowledge to be preferred to the development of normative judgments about right and wrong.

This is one of the great ironies of the Greek tradition of philosophy as represented by Plato and Aristotle. Although both of them found the highest form of human collective life to reside in the political community rather than in traditional family, ethnic, kinship, religious, or warrior/military communities, and although both agreed that education was a prime function of the political community, neither of them developed a curriculum that focused upon an education that would directly promote a democratic state. Plato despaired of democracy and directed his guardians to contemplate the pure reality that lies behind the rough and tumble of practical affairs. Aristotle found more of value in republican government, but he too viewed scientific knowledge and theoretical speculation as more noble than moral and practical conduct.

Perhaps this is to be expected of philosophers and scientists whose views of the just and authoritative political community have little place for freedom and none for equality, except within very circumscribed conditions applying to a small minority of citizens dependent on large populations of workers, aliens, and slaves. The mainstream of the Western intellectual tradition found the Greek tradition to be quite congenial until the democratic revolutions of the seventeenth and eighteenth centuries.

There was, however, a major exception to this Platonic-Aristotelian philosophic tradition, and it had a considerable influence upon educators of the Roman Republic period but it apparently could not compete during the Roman Empire period and the Middle Ages. This was the rhetorical tradition exemplified by the great Athenian teacher of rhetoric, Isocrates, a contemporary of both Plato and Aristotle. Isocrates carried on a running battle with the philosophers and the philosophical schools of his day. He had little good to say about the abstract and irrelevant "academic" studies of Plato's Academy and Aristotle's Lyceum.

Isocrates argued instead that the fateful problems facing the Athenian polis following the Peloponnesian War could only be remedied by an education that faced head-on the problems posed by factionalism, excessive individualism, poverty, overpopulation, corruption, and despair. Isocrates argued that the highest human good was to be realized in and through the political community and that the chief forms of human excellence rested in service to the polity. The chief means to this end resided in man's reason, which gave him the ability to conduct discourse that could lead to sound practical judgments. Man may be "a political animal" as Arisotle said, but his genius is that he can be "a persuading animal," communicating with others to establish a polity under the rule of law.

The ideal citizen is thus the *rhetor*, or orator, not the philosopher or scientist. He heaped scorn on the idea that the good citizen can be formed by long years of immersion in purely abstract academic studies like mathematics, science, or metaphysics. In contrast, the orator is a man who is devoted to public affairs, accepts the duties and obligations of citizenship, and informs himself thoroughly by a broad range of studies, including not only rhetoric, but logic, literature, history, political science, and ethics. With this kind of "practical" education, the orator is ready to develop a sense of good judgment about the problems facing the polis and to enter into reasoned discussions in the public forums with other citizens in order to arrive at just decisions of public policy.

One matter of special note was that Isocrates was an ardent advocate of a Pan-Hellenic union among the warring city-states as the only solution to the competition, rivalry, and warfare pandemic among the many, small, individualistic city-states. But Isocrates lost his campaign for *e pluribus unum* among the several city-states. The Greeks left it to Macedonian conquerers and later to the Roman conquerers to impose a kind of external order upon the political pluralism that they themselves could not overcome.

Isocrates' proposals were apparently too slow and too democratic for his times. He argued for the process of public discussion and discourse as the means of arriving at accurate and valid judgments, based upon persistent study of relevant factors and rational influence free from emotional bias. He admitted that man cannot achieve irrefutable, certain knowledge in human affairs.

But in the recurring crises of the fourth century B.C. that plagued the several city-states of Greece, people wanted social, moral, and political certainties. Some people found these, they thought, in philosophy, in mysticism, and in religion rather than in the political community. Others found or tried to find greater certainty in a new kind of political community that stressed the centralized authority of large-scale empire, first under the Macedonian Empire that extended from Greece to India and Egypt and then under the Roman Empire that extended from the Middle East and Egypt to Britain.

The one point I wish to make here is that the early Roman experience paralleled somewhat the Greek shift from kinship to polis. For example, during the Roman Republic (from the fifth to the end of the first century B.C.) the authority of the Roman state was overlaid on an extremely powerful network of authority that rested very largely in the hands of the father of a family (*pater familias*) or household that often consisted of relatives, clients, servants, and slaves as well as wife and children. This authoritarian structure of authority and protection centered in the power of the father (*patria potestas*) who was responsible for the safety, security, and welfare of the kinship group. The family rather than the individual was the basis of legal, religious, and social unity.

The family, not the individual, was the irreducible unit of tradition and law in the Roman Republic down until the time of the Augustan reforms....Until very late in the history of the republic, the family was made to bear responsibility for most individual offenses, and it was the prime agency of retribution for injuries suffered by one of its members. Something akin to a highly stabilized, fully accepted blood feud existed under the *patria potestas*....Offenses such as murder, assault, arson, trespass, and injury were held by the Romans to be private offenses, to be privately negotiated, and not, as we today regard them, crimes against the state itself.[9]

Thus the family had great autonomy and collective power in law, in religion, and in property and wealth. Individuals could not own property except with the express authority of the *pater familias*. This autonomy also prevailed in education. By custom the sons of upper-class patrician families were educated in and through the family, whereas the children of plebeian classes seldom had very much schooling of a literate sort. But the power and autonomy of the kinship groups under the Republic began to give way during the third and second centuries B.C. as a result first of incessant foreign wars and then of the civil wars of the first century B.C. Finally, in 27 B.C. the Empire officially succeeded the Republic when the general Octavian became the emperor Augustus.

As Nisbet points out, the military necessity of soldiers to obey their commanders rather than their fathers was a key element in this transition of authority from kinship group to the state, a transition somewhat akin to that performed by Cleisthenes in Athens some 500 years earlier. Legitimate authority was transferred from the family to the state, now in the person of the emperor rather than in the Senate or the Assembly, and the power of law was directly enforced on individuals rather than mediated through families as in the Republic. The efforts of a Cicero at the end of the Republic or a Quintilian at the height of the Empire to espouse the educational ideas of Isocrates could not withstand the autocratic and authoritarian pressures of the Imperium. When rhetoric had little influence in public policy making, it became an embellishment for an ever more refined oratorical style cultivated for its own sake rather than for the art of political persuasion among free citizens. The law replaced philosophy and rhetoric in the idea of citizenship.

In the course of the next six or seven centuries, the Roman law of the Empire was interpreted and developed in ways that made it enormously influential when the nation-states of the modern period began to be formed. Nisbet applies the term "political intellectuals" to those lawyers, teachers, textbook writers, and advisors to the emperor who contributed to the basic ideas of the Roman law. The culmination of this work was the *Corpus Juris Civilis*, a masterly codification undertaken by a commission of jurists headed by Tribonian, an advisor to the Emperor Justinian. Between 529 and 565 A.D. several volumes were published, consisting of constitutions promulgated by the emperors since Hadrian in the second century A.D., the collected opinions of jurists, and a general textbook of the law.

Generally known as the Justinian code, these volumes, handed down throughout the Middle Ages, became part of the revival of classical learning that stimulated the growth of cathedral schools and universities in the twelfth and thirteenth centuries. One of the great ironies, however, was the fact that the Roman civil law gave great comfort and justification to those rulers of the fifteenth and sixteenth centuries who were seeking to establish the political legitimacy of national states, supreme in their own right and free from subservience to the overall authority of a universal Roman church or a revived Holy Roman Empire modeled upon Justinian's own vision of a Universal Christian Roman Empire.

Nisbet defines four central political principles of the Roman law that are useful for our purposes.[10] 1) The political order has sovereignty over all the other groups and interests in society; sovereignty involves the state's monopoly of legitimate force and a high degree of centralization of authority. 2) No other form of association lawfully exists in society unless it is conceded the right to exist by the political sovereign. 3) The interpersonal relations of citizens are considered legal only if based upon willing consent; hence, hereditary, ascriptive, traditional customs have no status in law unless they can be converted into contractual relations. This applies to the original "contract" by which human beings were presumed to have founded collectively the state itself. 4) The only politically recognized units in the society are individual citizens upon whom the rights and responsibilities of citizenship rest.

I began this quick review of the idea of citizenship by making two points about its origins in the Greco-Roman period. The first was that citizenship arose with the rise of political communities based upon man-made laws that took precedence over the customs and conventions of kinship, religion, or inherited status. This idea prevailed when the Greek polis replaced tribal groups and when the Roman Empire replaced the Roman Republic, which had largely recognized the kinship authority of *pater potestas*. But kinship relations and tribal authorities were reestablished in the geographic domain of the Roman Empire when it succumbed to the Germanic invasions of the fourth to the eighth centuries A.D. For some 1,000 years during the Middle Ages, citizenship in a political community was eclipsed by the pluralistic memberships that characterized medieval society:

> Kinship had almost as much sway [in medieval society] as it had had in earliest Rome, during the period of the republic, and in earliest Athens, prior to the Cleisthenean reforms. Medieval society was a vast

34

web of groups, communities, and associations, each claiming jurisdiction over the functions and activities of its members. The church was powerful; but, so, after the twelfth century, were guild, profession, monastery, and manor. It would be hard, finally, to think of two more unlike structures than feudalism, decentralized and localized in essence, and the kind of imperial Roman society that had given rise to the system of law we are here concerned with.[11]

So, after some 1,200 years of varying fortunes (roughly from the sixth century B.C. to the sixth century A.D.), the idea of political citizenship went into decline during nearly 1,000 years of the Middle Ages. It was revived, refurbished, and began to dominate the major Western societies as they formed a series of modern nation-states. In contrast to the long career of the general idea of political citizenship in the Greco-Roman period, the second point I would make is that *democratic* citizenship had only a fairly short career of a century or two, pre-eminently in Athens. It was an idea whose time had definitely not come. It could not withstand the attacks upon it from the side of pluralistic, traditional kinship and religious ties nor from the side of monistic, absolutistic, authoritarian controls exercised by military, political, or religious sovereigns who claimed to rule by higher authority than the consent of the people. It was this *vox populi* that was revived, refurbished, and reconstituted by the "political intellectuals" of the eighteenth-century democratic revolution.

The Modern Idea of Democratic Citizenship

The revival of the idea of citizenship arose in connection with the origins of the modern European nation-states in the sixteenth and seventeenth centuries, and the idea of democratic citizenship received its modern formulation in connection with the democratic revolution that swept much of Western Europe and British America in the eighteenth century. I find very illuminating the interpretation of Robert R. Palmer, Yale historian, that the democratic revolution was a single revolutionary movement that broke out in many different parts of Western civilization, especially in the decades from 1760 to 1800.[12] The first manifestation was the American Revolution; the French Revolution was the most extreme and most violent; reform movements appeared in England and Ireland; and short-lived republics were set up in Holland, Belgium, Switzerland, Italy, Hungary, and Poland in the 1780s and 1790s.

Palmer makes the point that these revolutions did not spread from America or from France to the other countries. Rather, each country had its own agitations, its own protests, and its own assaults on the established orders, which from the mid-seventeenth to the mid-eighteenth centuries had become more aristocratic, more closed, more elite, more self-perpetuating and hereditary, and more privileged. Even

35

the parliaments, assemblies, councils, and diets that were based upon some sort of representative principle had become less responsive to the welfare of the common people.

Each country had its own revolutionary upheavals aimed at more participation in government by a greater share of the populace, more equality in such participation, and greater protection for the civil liberties and civil rights of an enlarged body of citizens. But the conservative resistance in most countries was such that by 1800 the established orders had regained their powers and the republics had reverted to aristocracies or monarchies, with two exceptions. The French Revolution maintained its republican facade until the counter-revolution under Napoleon established the empire formally in 1804. The American revolution was the only one to succeed without a major reaction.

It is worth reminding ourselves what the democratic revolutionaries in the eighteenth century were revolting *against*. Palmer argues persuasively that the 40-year movement was essentially "democratic" in the sense that there was a growing desire for an equality that would do away with the inherited forms of social stratification:

> Politically, the Eighteenth Century movement was against the possession of government, or any public power, by any established, privileged, closed, or self-recruiting bodies of men. It denied that any person could exercise coercive authority simply by his own right, or by right of his status, or by right of "history," either in the old-fashioned sense of custom and inheritance, or in any newer dialectical sense, unknown to the eighteenth century, in which "history" might be supposed to give some special elite or revolutionary vanguard a right to rule. The "democratic revolution" emphasized the delegation of authority and the removability of officials, precisely because...neither delegation nor removability were much recognized in actual institutions.[13]

Now it is important to remind ourselves that the revolutionary movements of the eighteenth century have been viewed quite differently during the past 200 years. Much depends on how one views the medieval configurations of social and political order. The contrast here between Palmer, the liberal historian, and Nisbet, the conservative sociologist, is instructive. Palmer speaks of the social stratification and growing aristocracy of the "constituted orders" of the medieval and early modern period. Nisbet speaks of the "federalism" of the medieval pluralist community. He finds great value in the autonomy, decentralization, and variety of the countless customs, traditions, and networks of groups. At the base of the social structure was the strong family system of kin, household, and clan. There were towns, guilds, all kinds of occupational and fraternal associations, monasteries, parishes, universities, and courts:

> In kinship, religion, social class, local community, region, guild,

monastery, university, and various other types of community lay, then, the medieval system of federalism, one that can be truly described as a *communitas communitatum*.[14]

Describing the medieval social systems as federalist and pluralist enables Nisbet to view their values favorably in contrast to the oppressive, centralized, bureaucratized, absolutistic, collectivist, modern nation-states that attacked and replaced the medieval synthesis. It is a similar valuing of the older order and revulsion against the excesses of the later French revolutionary period that led conservatives in Britain and elsewhere to praise the freedom of the privileged social and political groups of the old regimes. Those groups performed different functions and had different interests and thus should legitimately have different rights and obligations from those of the common people.

Palmer, on the other hand, describes what these differences in rights and obligations had come to mean for the "constituted bodies" of the Western European countries by the middle of the eighteenth century:

> Persons did have rights as members of groups, not abstractly as "citizens," and all persons had some legal rights, which, however, reached the vanishing point for serfs in Eastern Europe and slaves in America...but the most noticeable similarities in the constituted bodies are to be found in two other features. First, the concept of "order"...frequently meant that there were some orders of men whose function was to fill positions of governance, in state or church, as distinguished from other orders whose functions were different. Secondly, there was a strong tendency, about a century old in the 1760s, toward inheritance of position in this governing elite, either by law or in fact, a tendency for influence to accumulate in a few families, or, in more abstract terms, for *the institution of the family to diffuse itself through the institutions of government* [italics added], not to mention those of religion....
>
> In short, the world had become more aristocratic.[15]

Palmer then describes the constituted bodies of the middle of the eighteenth century. Some examples will illustrate the two tendencies mentioned above. In Sweden in the "Age of Freedom" (1719-1772) the diet consisted of four houses: nobles, clergy, burghers, and peasants. The burghers elected only burghers, and the peasants only peasants, so that each "order" or class was separated from the other. In Poland, Hungary, and Bohemia the diets were monopolized by noble landowners. In Prussia the civil service became virtually a self-selecting estate of the realm. In the Republic of Venice the "citizens" who were qualified for office were all nobles, and nobility was hereditary. Relatively few families dominated the citizenship in some of the Swiss cantons, which meant that citizenship was virtually hereditary.

In the model republic of Geneva there were five orders of persons: citizens who were eligible to hold office; burghers who had the right to vote but not hold office; *habitants* who had the right to do business but no political rights; natives who were born in the city but not of citizen or burgher families; and subjects who lived in the country but were ruled by the city. Altogether, including the free cities of Germany and the French and English parliaments, the trend was toward more family rule, more closed corporative membership, and a tendency to self-perpetuation in office.

It was this growing dominance of preferred status favoring the rights and privileges of family, kinship, wealth, property, and social class that the revolutionary movements objected to. The doctrines of natural rights, of social contract, of equality, and of political liberty were in large part directed at doing away with the preferred status that had been made into permanent legal relationships, fixing the rights and obligations of special groups into a hierarchical political order. In this feudal context the idea of citizenship, where it was mentioned at all, had become identified with a narrowly defined and small group in society. The democratic revolution essentially aimed to broaden the meaning of citizenship to include a much wider range of male adults, if not all of them, and to redefine the role of citizens in such a way that they not only became active participants as individuals in the day-to-day political process but became, collectively as "the people," the very founders of the political compact itself.

The political thought of the seventeenth and eighteenth centuries and the course of the democratic revolution are far too complicated and controversial to be summarized here. I can only select a few points for emphasis that seem to me to highlight the formulation of a new meaning for citizenship in the U.S. as it grew out of the American Revolution and was incorporated in the new American Republic. Here I draw upon the recent scholarship of major American historians who have dealt especially with this formative period in American history.[16]

The essential point here is that, above all, the American Revolution was *political* in its intent and in its results. It was not aimed at a total overturning and reconstruction of society, as the Jacobin phase of the French Revolution turned out to be. The British-American colonies had already achieved a good deal of the social equality and had never been plagued with the hereditary aristocracy that so infuriated the French revolutionists. In America there was great faith in the virtues of independent property owners; there was little effort to achieve a radical redistribution of the economic sources of wealth or production, except for the expropriation of the lands and property of loyalists who fled to Canada.

What did influence the American patriots was the oppressive power of the British Parliament and of the royal officials who sought to compel obedience of the colonists from afar, treating them like "subjects" rather than like "citizens." Repressive compulsion by taxes, by standing armies, and by arrogant and aristocratic officials came more and more easily to be identified as tyranny and as a violation of the citizens' rights to liberty and equality.

To justify the citizens' rights, revolutionary thought in eighteenth-century America drew upon a stock of five historical ideas that Bernard Bailyn identifies as: 1) the classical literature on politics from Plato and Aristotle to Cicero, Sallust, and Tacitus who wrote on the corruption and decline of virtue that was undermining the Roman Republic; 2) the Enlightenment literature on the social contract and political reform ranging from Montesquieu and Locke to Voltaire and Rousseau; 3) the English tradition of common law stressing equity, justice, and civil rights; 4) the Puritan covenant theology that envisioned a special destiny in America for God's contract with man; and 5) especially in Bailyn's view, the radical politics of the seventeenth-century revolution in England, the Civil War, and the Commonwealth period as illustrated by John Milton, James Harrington, and Algernon Sidney. Their outlook on civil liberties helped to shape the republican ideas of Whigs in the eighteenth century in opposition to the view of Tories, who defended royal sovereignty.

The American solution was to turn away from the traditional constituted bodies and turn to "the people" as the sovereign constituent power for establishing governments that would rest upon the natural rights of liberty and equality and that would function by popular consent, political representation, independence from foreign rule, and separation of political powers.

One of the most influential statements of this redefinition of "the people" as the constituent power of the legitimate political community is, of course, the Declaration of Independence, which funneled a century of democratic revolutionary thought into the prose of Thomas Jefferson through the drafting committee consisting of Benjamin Franklin, John Adams, Roger Sherman, Robert R. Livingston, and Jefferson himself:

> We hold these Truths to be self-evident, that all Men are created equal, that they are endowed by their Creator with certain unalienable Rights, that among these are Life, Liberty, and the Pursuit of Happiness—That to secure these Rights, Governments are instituted among Men, deriving their just Powers from the Consent of the Governed, that whenever any Form of Government becomes destructive of these Ends, it is the Right of the People to alter or to abolish it, and to institute new Government, laying its Foundation on such Principles, and organizing its Powers in such Form, as to them shall seem most likely to affect their Safety and Happiness....

> We, therefore, the Representatives of the United States of America...do, in the Name, and by Authority of the good People of these Colonies, solemnly Publish and Declare, That these United Colonies are, and of Right ought to be, Free and Independent States....

Four of the 13 states, thus declared to be independent and to rest upon the sovereignty of their citizens, had already drawn up and adopted constitutions before 4 July 1776. One of the most influential in stating the basic ideas of liberty and equality was the Declaration of Rights drafted by George Mason and adopted by the Virginia Assembly on 12 June 1776 as a bill of rights to its new constitution. Its several clauses spell out for a particular state in greater detail what Jefferson's eloquent words implied that the several states held in common:

That all men are by nature equally free and independent, and have certain inherent rights, of which, when they enter into a state of society, they cannot by any compact, deprive or divest their posterity; namely, the enjoyment of life and liberty, with the means of acquiring and possessing property, and pursuing and obtaining happiness and safety.

That all power is vested in, and consequently derived from, the people; that magistrates are their trustees and servants, and at all times amenable to them.

That government is, or ought to be, instituted for the common benefit, protection and security of the people, nation or community...

...when a government shall be found inadequate or contrary to these purposes, a majority of the community hath an indubitable, unalienable and indefensible right to reform, alter or abolish it.

That no man, or set of men, are entitled to exclusive or separate emoluments or privileges from the community but in consideration of public services, which not being descendible, neither ought the offices of magistrate, legislator or judge to be hereditary.

That the legislative, executive and judicial powers should be separate and distinct.

That...all men having sufficient evidence of permanent common interest with, and attachment to the community have the right to suffrage, and cannot be taxed, or deprived of their property for public use, without their own consent, or that of their representatives....[17]

Thereupon the Declaration lists specific items of due process and civil liberties that made up a "bill of rights": the right of individuals to a speedy trial by jury with due process; prohibition of excessive bail, of inhuman punishments, and of general warrants for search and seizure; protection of freedom of the press; subordination of the military to civil power; and free exercise of religion.

The bills of rights of other states in various ways extended this list to cover a wider range of citizens' rights: freedom of speech, assembly, and petition; right to bear arms and *habeas corpus*; equal protection of the laws; inviolability of household; and prohibition against *ex post facto* laws and expropriation of property without due process of law.

The enumeration of these rights and liberties in the state constitutions, many of which were later incorporated in the U.S. Constitution and Bill of Rights, was the way the colonists sought to devise a political community in which the citizens as a body exercised the ultimate legitimate authority. This authority deserved obedience for the sake of order, but at the same time it protected the individual's rights from the coercive absolutism of a totalitarian state. The statement of rights and liberties represented the citizens' effort to solve the persistent dilemma of order based upon the sovereignty of "the people" versus liberty for the individual citizen.

It is all too evident to us today that the patriots really meant *white men* when they came to spell out the rights of the people, and they meant white men of property when it came to voting. But at least these eighteenth-century patriots opened up the closed constituted bodies of 1,000 years' standing in such a way that their successors could eventually wipe out the property qualification and the sexual, racial, and age restrictions in the definitions of full democratic citizenship.

The dilemma of securing order while protecting individual freedoms was especially acute during this process of releasing people from the coercion imposed by the aristocracy and of substituting a voluntary acceptance of authority based upon the decisions of the body of citizens—and at the same time leaving room for dissent, difference of view, and freedom of thought. In his widely influential *Social Contract*, Rousseau put it this way: "...the strength of the State can alone secure the liberty of its members."[18] Some interpreters see in this the attempt of the state to require persons to be "forced to be free." Nisbet, for example, considers Rousseau to be the epitome of the advocates of the absolutist, monolithic state in view of his almost mystical analysis of the "general will" as the egalitarian expression of the public interest as formulated by the people as a whole.[19]

Perhaps Rousseau *was* an extremist advocate of the *political* community as superior to and as embracing all other communities, as Nisbet says, but the American founders of state and federal republics accepted only selected parts of Rousseau's attacks upon the old regimes. They certainly did not adopt his view of an absolutist though egalitarian state; they were too much concerned with freedom. But some of them did borrow from him the concept of a citizen acting collectively with other free and equal citizens to form and run a legitimate political community. They also adopted his view that the individual citizen should not only voluntarily obey the laws but should be free to act, think, and believe as an individual under the freedoms secured by those laws and bills of rights.

I believe that Palmer makes the points about Rousseau that are most significant for the new conceptions of citizenship that the American revolutionaries were formulating in the 1770s and 1780s:

Jf one were to name the one book in which the revolutionary aspirations of the period from 1760 to 1800 were most compactly embodied, it would be the *Social Contract*....

The *Social Contract* remains the great book of the political revolution.... What is certain is that the greatest vogue of the book came after the fact of revolution. The book did not so much make the revolution as it was made by it....

The best way to understand the book is not to compare its propositions to later democratic practice...nor yet to view it as an anticipation of totalitarianism...but to contrast it with the attitudes prevailing at the time it was written [1762], of which one of the most fundamental was that some men must in the nature of things take care of others, that some had the right to govern and others the duty to obey....

The *Social Contract* was therefore a quest for rightful authority, for a form of state in which obedience would turn into duty, while all the while an ethical philosophy stressing individual liberty was preserved. Rousseau could find no place to locate this final authority except in the community itself. Those who obey must in the last analysis command. The subject must, in the end, be the sovereign....[20]

Palmer sums up what the *Social Contract* meant to the men of the 1760s who were in a mood of rebellion:

First of all, the theory of the political community, of the people, or nation, was revolutionary in implication: it posited a community based on the will of the living, and the active sense of membership and voluntary participation, rather than on history, or kinship, or race, or past conquest, or common inheritance, or the chance of birth into an already existent political system. It denied sovereign powers to kings, to oligarchs, and to all governments. It said that any form of government could be changed. It held all public officers to be removable. It held that law could draw its force and its legality only from the community itself....[21]

Although Rousseau may not have been the greatest influence upon the Americans who put their revolution into terms of political philosophy, there is an interesting parallel in his concept of "citizen." In the *Social Contract* Rousseau defines "citizen" this way when he is defining the social compact:

...this act of association creates a moral and collective body... receiving from this act its unity, its common identity, its life, and its will.

This public person, so formed by the union of all other persons, formerly took the name of *city*, and now takes that of *Republic* or *body politic*; it is called by its members *State* when passive, *Sovereign* when active, and *Power* when compared with others like itself. Those who are associated in it take collectively the name of *people*, and severally are called *citizens*, as sharing in the sovereign power, and *subjects*, as being under the laws of the State.[22]

Now compare this with the preamble to the Massachusetts constitution of 1780, written by John Adams, who was certainly no flaming egalitarian radical:

The body politic is formed by a voluntary association of individuals. It is a social compact, by which the whole people

42

convenants with each citizen, and each citizen with the whole people, that all shall be governed by certain laws for the common good.[23]

Palmer points out that the word "covenant" could go back to the *Mayflower Compact* but that "social" and "citizen" could very well have come from Rousseau's *Social Contract*, which Adams had read as early as 1765. Be that as it may, Palmer makes the significant point that the word "citizen" in its modern usage was brought into the English language from the French by the Americans at the time of the American Revolution. The English used the word only to refer to full inhabitants of cities. And he further points out that the phrase "We the people ordain and establish" (to express the theory that the people were the constituent power) was first used in the Massachusetts constitution of 1780 and found its way from there to the U.S. Constitution of 1787 and to many of the other state constitutions.

Running through all shades of American opinion by the mid-1780s was an uneasy feeling that something had to be done about the political process at both the state and the national levels. Alarms were being sounded throughout the land in press and pulpit and coffee house. Protests against high prices, corruption in high places, bribery and payoffs to public officials, excessive affluence among the wealthy and excessive poverty among the disadvantaged, hucksterism among land speculators, arbitrary confiscation of property, reckless issuance of paper money by capricious legislatures, the decline of religion and public virtue—all these fed the long-held suspicion of political power and tempted many to believe that unrestrained state legislatures or majority rule at home were little better than an unrestrained Crown or Parliament abroad.

The earlier republican faith that "the people" were basically virtuous or could be made so if they were given liberty to rule themselves began to weaken in the face of the mountainous problems that were piling up after a decade of experience among 13 independent states. So, more and more thoughtful people of a "federalist" persuasion began to argue that liberty alone, or religion alone, or education alone could not assure a sound political community. Constitutional reform itself and the strengthening of political institutions themselves were required in order to remedy the licentiousness and viciousness of unrestrained liberty and equality. Paramount among such reforms were a strengthening of the executive and judicial branches of government to balance the legislative and the strengthening of a senate to balance the popularly elected assembly. The Massachusetts constitution of 1780 presaged this feeling, but by the mid-1780s the feeling also grew that reforms in the state governments alone were not enough, that reform had also to extend upward to the central government. As Gordon S. Wood puts it: "State governments, however well structured, no longer seemed capable of creating virtuous laws and citizens."[24] The calling of the Constitutional Convention was thus the culmination of a decade of trial and error in the process of constitution-making.

Historians are, of course, divided as to the essential meaning of the Constitution of 1787-89 with regard to the original Revolution of the mid-1770s. In general, Gordon Wood argues that it was an aristocratic repudiation of the democratic ideology of the Revolution. Bernard Bailyn, however, argues that the Constitution was not as much a repudiation as it was "a second generation expression of the original ideological impulses of the Revolution applied to the everyday, practical problems of the 1780s."[25] And Jack P. Greene in favorably reviewing Wood's book as "one of the half dozen most important books ever written about the American Revolution," nevertheless, says:

> This faith in the efficacy of legal and constitutional arrangements may thus have made the process of constitution-making in the states the very essence of the Revolution in 1776, and the Constitution may, therefore, have been less of a repudiation and more of a fulfillment of the principles of '76 than Wood suggests. Because it did so much to reshape the political ideas and aspirations of men in America and elsewhere in the world, the innovative system of politics incorporated by the Federalists in the Constitution, far more than the genuine but transitory and limited millenialism of 1776, may have been not only the most lasting contribution but also the most radical feature of the Revolution.[26]

Within the Philadelphia convention and the subsequent debates, the prime issues centered upon reconciling and compromising the confrontation of interests represented by "federalists" and "anti-federalists."[27] Until these were worked out, the role of education would remain uncertain even in theory.

The course of events between 1787 and 1789 was, in effect, an agreement to try Madison's middle ground between a strongly centralized and consolidated nation and a loose collection of individual, independent, sovereign states. As a result it was going to be difficult to define what the role of education ought to be in view of a compromise "federal" governmental political system whose allocation of powers and function were still largely to be worked out. If Hamilton's or Jay's strongly centralized national government had clearly won out, it might have been fairly easy to design a centralized national system of education. Or, if the New Jersey plan to tinker a bit with the Articles of Confederation but leave the states fundamentally alone as Patrick Henry, Sam Adams, Richard Henry Lee, George Mason, or Elbridge Gerry wished, the authority for education would clearly have remained in state or in private hands.

But these alternatives did not win. Out of the clash of federalist and anti-federalist views came a new constitutional order that created a new federal government but did not automatically or immediately create a new or unified political community. The problem, therefore, that was bequeathed to education was how to help develop the social cohesion and the sense of community required of a republican *nation* while the educational systems remained in state, private, or religious hands. The convention debates were so engrossed in the federalist/anti-federalist opposition and in the political process of winning an argument or reconciling differences that education was either ignored or postponed until the more basic question of union or disunion was settled.

Gordon Wood argues that the differences of outlook toward the proposed constitution are not easily defined. The proponents and opponents were not easily classified according to economic or sectional groupings. He concludes that the fundamental quarrel was between aristocratic federalists and democratic anti-federalists. Federalists feared too much social mobility and social disruption and believed in the superiority of an elite of talent and learning as a natural aristocracy. Those best qualified to rule could be detected by their property, education, and cultivated refinement. They came to the conclusion that social differences were probably inevitable and that the fundamental threat to republicanism came from oppression, not of government officials or aristocratic gentlemen but of an arbitrary or capricious or uneducated majority. So both individuals and property must be protected by government through a bicameral system in which the unruly majority of the house could be checked by the greater wisdom and stability of the propertied and educated senate. *Both* should be looked upon equally as representatives of the sovereign people, as indeed also were the President and the judiciary. Sovereignty lies with the total people of the political community and *all* their representatives, not solely with the representatives in the state legislatures or the U.S. House of Representatives. Thus, the federalists argued, since all the agencies of government, both federal and state, represented the sovereign people, and since the powers of the federal government were strictly limited, and the courts were especially alert to protect individual liberties, there was no need for a particular bill of rights in the constitution.

This conclusion about not needing a bill of rights was probably the weakest argument of the federalists. It enabled the anti-federalists to picture the federalists as protectors of wealth, privilege, and power, who in effect had succeeded to the social hierarchy of the British empire and who would reinstitute monarchy if they could. The anti-federalists tried to marshal resentment against the cultivated classical education of urban or country gentlemen. They were likely to believe that hard-working ordinary people of virtue and good common sense were just as fit to rule, nay even more so, as the fine-feathered gentlemen politicians with their supercilious academic learning. They held to the earlier republican beliefs that moral regeneration was more important in the preservation of republicanism than in the legalistic machinery of

45

constitution-making. They feared the new constitution would neglect local interests, state problems, and the needs of the lowly people—this was what the Revolution of 1776 was all about. They saw a strong president and an "upper" house as negating the historic republican Whig belief in the elected legislature as the real depository of the people's liberties. How could this representative sovereignty be divided with a second house that would inevitably represent the rich and the privileged?

But the anti-federalists lost much of the argument of 1787-1789. They were poorly organized and uncoordinated in their opposition, and in essence they were looking backward to the simpler times of the seventeenth and eighteenth centuries. They were more traditional and less sophisticated in their vision of what was required of a political system needed to cope with the exigencies of large-scale organization, international affairs, trade and commerce, incipient industrialization, and scientific technology. To cope with these problems, modern political systems have developed not only differentiated governmental structures to perform specialized executive, legislative, and judicial functions, but also more differentiated political infrastructures to carry on the complicated political process through political parties, organized interest groups, well-developed mass media, and mass systems of universal education.

These characteristics of a modern political system, especially the differentiated separation of powers, were seen by the federalists as much more crucial than they had been in 1776. They argued that failure to distinguish the executive, legislative, and judicial functions was not only a fault of the Articles of Confederation but also a characteristic of traditional tyranny itself. Furthermore, the "upper" house would be not so much a repository of wisdom and privilege but a protection of small states against the tyranny of the large states, a new kind of check upon unrestrained power.

So in the end, the Madison compromise won the day, especially when he came to agree with Jefferson that a specific bill of rights was desirable and he promised that one of the first acts of the new Congress would be to draw up a bill of rights, a promise he promptly and personally carried out in the summer of 1789. A new conception of liberty was being formulated, the consequences of which could not be foreseen. Liberty was no longer to be confined simply to the older Whig meaning, i.e., the right of the people to participate in the legislative process through elected representatives. Liberty was now being extended to mean the protection of the individual and minority groups against encroachments by the government itself and especially by the legislature. It also projected the idea that a liberal government would be an active protector of individuals from whatever source the threat of tyranny is greatest, if need be from the majority itself.

Madison spelled out this view of the role of the federal government as a protector of liberty in his remarkable speech in the House of Representatives on 8 June 1789, when he presented and justified his proposals for amendments to the Constitution to incorporate suggestions made by the state conventions at the time of their ratifications. First of all, he proposed that the Constitution spell out the principle of the sovereignty of the people, i.e., he wanted to define more explicitly what we have come to call the political community that lies behind or above the constitutional order itself:

> First, that there be prefixed to the constitution, a declaration, that all power is originally vested in, and consequently derived from, the people.
>
> That government is instituted and ought to be exercised for the benefit of the people; which consists in the enjoyment of life and liberty, with the right of acquiring and using property, and generally of pursuing and obtaining happiness and safety.
>
> That the people have an indubitable, unalienable, and indefeasible right to reform or change their government, whenever it be found adverse or inadequate to the purposes of its institution.[28]

These sentences breathe the spirit and even some words of the Virginia Declaration of Rights and the Declaration of Independence. The *people* are the ultimate source of authority for government. This reflects the natural rights philosophy of the eighteenth century—civil government is to be a secular government. The rightful establishment of government is derived from the authority of the people alone, and the people alone have the right to reform or change their government. Madison's wording was not adopted, presumably because the present Preamble beginning "We, the people" was deemed sufficient to cover Madison's point here.

Thus, by the time the Constitution was debated and drawn up at the Constitutional Convention in 1787, the Preamble no longer said that the representatives were speaking "in the name of and by the authority of the people" as the Declaration of Independence did. The Preamble simply says quite directly "We the people of the United States...do ordain and establish this Constitution for the United States of America." And it might be well to recall here once again the reasons for such establishment. It was in order to:

- form a more perfect Union
- establish Justice
- insure domestic Tranquility
- provide for the common defense
- promote the general Welfare
- and secure the Blessings of Liberty to ourselves and our Posterity

As I said earlier, historians have long argued whether the framing and adoption of the federal constitution was a logical and political fulfillment of the revolutionary movement of the 1770s and 1780s or whether it was a sign of a conservative reaction against the more radical goals of the earlier revolutionary struggles within the states as well as against British rule. I cannot, of course, add much to such discussions, but it is quite clear that the reaction in the new United States was in no way comparable to that in France or Germany or Britain of the nineteenth century. The aristocratic forces in America were less extreme, less rigid, and less caste-conscious than in Europe and, conversely, there was greater willingness to admit to the possibility of social mobility and a more flexible class structure.

What seems to me to be the most important point for the idea of citizenship is that the Americans came up with the twofold proposition: Not only did the source of legitimate power reside in the people rather than in the constituted bodies of tradition, but "the people" were at one and the same time the source of legitimate authority for *both* the states *and* the federal government. The trouble with the Articles of Confederation was that the federal government drew its authority from the several states, not from the people as a whole. Now, under the new constitution both sets of governments were to be legitimized by the same source. This meant that the individual citizen was at once a citizen of a particular state *and* a citizen of the whole United States:

> The citizen... was simultaneously a citizen both of the United States and of his own state. He was the sovereign, not they. He chose to live under two constitutions, two sets of laws, two sets of courts and officials; theoretically, he had created them all, reserving to himself, under each set, certain liberties specified in declarations of rights.[29]

Although Americans arrived at a creative conception of a broadened idea of citizenship, it posed serious problems for the process of defining what the role of education should be in the new republic and in the new states. There were differences of opinion, of course, but also much ambiguity and much uncertainty. Many federalists who might have been expected to argue for a centralized national education system were also aristocratic and not particularly enthusiastic about making education universally and equally available to the lowly as well as to the well-placed. So they did not argue for federally controlled public education. Most anti-federalists were likely to be in favor of universal common education as a means of inculcating the republican virtues, but they surely did not want such an education to be centrally directed by the national government. So, proposals for a federally promoted system of education were relatively few, although they did come along within the decade following the adoption of the Constitution.

Whatever the views regarding the control or organization of education, most proposals agreed that somehow a new public education should be developed that would instill among all citizens the republican values of liberty, equality, and the public good. On these matters there was an increasing consensus among federalists and anti-federalists before the Constitution was adopted, and among Federalists and Republicans after it was adopted, but just how to implement the ideals of a new civic role for education continued to be a matter for intense public debate.

Chapter 2 Notes

1. R. Freeman Butts, *The Education of the West; A Formative Chapter in the History of Civilization* (New York: McGraw-Hill, 1973). For Sumerian city-states, see pages 41-47; for various Greek ideas of citizenship, see Chapter 3; for Rome, see Chapter 4.

2. Robert Nisbet, *The Social Philosophers: Community and Conflict in Western Thought* (New York: Thomas Crowell, 1973), pp. 32-33.

3. Thucydides, *History of the Peloponnesian War,* trans. by Richard Crawley (London: J.M. Dent, 1910), pp. 121-124.

4. Aristotle, *Politics and Poetics*, trans. by Benjamin Jowett and S.H. Butcher (New York: Heritage Press, 1964), pp. 80-81

5. Ibid., p. 5.

6. Ibid., p. 251.

7. Ibid., p. 267.

8. Ibid., p. 268.

9. Nisbet, *Social Philosophers*, p. 36.

10. Ibid., pp. 121-123.

11. Ibid., p. 125.

12. Robert R. Palmer, *The Age of the Democratic Revolution; A Political History of Europe and America, 1760-1800* (Princeton, N.J.: Princeton University Press, 1959).

13. Ibid., pp. 4-5.

14. Nisbet, *Social Philosophers*, p. 399.

15. Palmer, *The Age of the Democratic Revolution*, p. 29.

16. See, for example, Bernard Bailyn, *The Ideological Origins of the American Revolution* (Cambridge, Mass.: Harvard University Press, 1967); Gordon S. Wood, *The Creation of the American Republic, 1776-1787* (Chapel Hill, N.C.: University of North Carolina Press, 1969); Stephen G. Kurtz and James H. Hutson, eds., *Essays on the American Revolution* (Chapel Hill, N.C.: University of North Carolina Press, 1973); Ralph Ketcham, *From Colony to Country: The Revolution in American Thought, 1750-1820* (New York: Macmillan, 1974); Clinton Rossiter, *The American Quest, 1790-1860: An Emerging Nation in Search of Identity, Unity, and Modernity* (New York: Harcourt Brace Jovanovich, 1971); Robert R. Palmer, *The Age*

of the Democratic Revolution; A Political History of Europe and America, 1760-1800), 2 vols. (Princeton, N.J.: Princeton University Press, 1959, 1964); and Bernard Bailyn, David Brion Davis, David Herbert Donald, John L. Thomas, Robert H. Wiebe, and Gordon S. Wood, *The Great Republic: A History of the American People* (Boston: Little Brown, 1977), (especially Part II by Gordon Wood).

17. Palmer, *The Age of the Democratic Revolution*, pp. 518-520.

18. Jean Jacques Rousseau, *The Social Contract and Discourses*, trans. by G.D.H. Cole (New York: Dutton, 1950), p. 52.

19. Nisbet, *Social Philosophers*, pp. 145-158.

20. Palmer, *The Age of the Democratic Revolution*, pp. 119-121.

21. Ibid., p. 127.

22. Rousseau, *Social Contract*, p. 15.

23. Francis Newton Thorpe, comp., *The Federal and State Constitutions, Colonial Charters...*, vol. 3 (Washington, D.C.: Government Printing Office, 1909), p. 1889.

24. Wood, *The Creation of the American Republic*, p. 465.

25. Kurtz and Hutson, *Essays on the American Revolution*, p. 22.

26. *The New York Times Book Review*, 26 October 1969.

27. I use the lower-case "federalist" to refer to the constitutional debates surrounding the adoption of the Constitution 1787-1789 (Madison was a "federalist" in this usage), but "Federalist" with an upper-case F refers to the emerging political party of the late 1790s that coagulated in opposition to the Jeffersonian Republican Party of 1800 (Madison was definitely *not* a Federalist). Recent historical scholarship sees no easy connection between "federalist" and "Federalist," or between anti-federalist and Republican. All professed loyalty to the Republic and thus were republicans.

28. Joseph Gales, ed., *Annals of Congress*, vol. 1 (Washington, D.C.: Gales and Seaton, 1834), p. 451.

29. Palmer, *The Age of the Democratic Revolution*, pp. 228-229.

Chapter 3

Historical Perspective on Citizenship Education in the United States*

F or two hundred years the American people have struggled with the dilemma of politics and education. On one hand, they believe that education is fundamental to the health and vitality of a democratic community, but, on the other hand, they do not believe that schools in a democracy ought to be involved in something called "political education." We have gone to enormous lengths to provide universal, free, compulsory, common schools in response, at lease in part, to the rhetoric that civic education should be available, even required, of all students; yet we draw back from the precipice of political indoctrination or inculcation of political ideas.

The horns of the dilemma are clear for all to see: We believe that schools should educate for democratic citizenship, yet "political" education in democratic values is often viewed as undemocratic or as unnecessary. We believe in education for national unity (especially in times of crisis), but we also believe in pluralistic freedoms of belief and action. We expect the schools, above all the public schools, to serve both causes. The danger is that they will serve neither *Unum* nor *Pluribus* as well as they might.

I believe that the reasons for this dilemma can best be understood by viewing the history of the civic role of public education as a product of the tensions arising from the interplay of three persistent themes in American life: 1) the cohesive value claims that undergird the overall democratic political community, 2) the differentiating value claims of pluralisms that give identity to various groups in the society, and 3) the modernization process that has been gathering strength throughout the world for two centuries.[1]

For the convenience of discussion, I identify four ingredients of each of these themes that serve as building blocks of the civic role of public education.

1) The cohesive value claims of the democratic political community and the long-range constitutional order:

---

*Portions of this chapter are based upon and drawn from my discussion in National Task Force on Citizenship Education, *Education for Responsible Citizenship* (New York: McGraw-Hill, 1977).

- Liberty
- Equality
- Popular consent
- Personal obligation for the public good

2) The differentiating value claims of pluralisms that give identity to diverse groups or segments in American society:
- Religion
- Ethnicity
- Race
- Localism or regionalism

3) The worldwide drive toward modernization that has wrought deep changes in rural, agricultural, and traditional societies all over the world for two centuries:
- Mobilization and centralization of power of the national state
- Industrialization and the technological production of goods, whether under capitalism or socialism
- Urbanization arising from the magnet of city life
- Secularization of knowledge and intellectual life stemming from modern science and empirical approaches to society

Proponents of citizenship education in the schools have almost always appealed in their rhetoric to the cohesive value claims of democracy as the rationale for a basic civic role for schooling. Sometimes this was wrapped in the authority of a particular religion (say Protestant), or ethnicity (Anglo-American), or race (white superiority), or localism or regionalism (states' rights). In these cases, one segment sought to use the public schools to promote its particular version of democratic political values. When other segments of pluralism grew strong or resistant, they might seek to break away from the cohesive values and form their own schools to promote *their* values as the basis for building their own kind of community. When the pluralistic elements seemed to threaten the cohesion of the overall political community, the claims of modernization (in the form of national unity, national strength, or economic development) often injected an overweening emphasis on patriotic loyalty into the citizenship education programs of the schools that sometimes led to a conformism that stifled any dissent.

The urge to promote citizenship education through the schools has arisen most insistently in times of real or fancied crisis, when the threats to national unity seem to be most critical or when drastic social changes seem to threaten social or political stability. The threats, however, have been viewed from very different perspectives, and the prescriptions for renewed unity have led to quite different conclusions.

One approach has stressed the need for greater cohesion and mobilization of disparate groups in order to achieve social or political reforms, in Robert Wiebe's terms, to achieve "a new social integration, a higher form of social harmony," releasing "powerful feelings of liberation from an inhibiting past and great expectations for a dawning new era."[2] Such were the expectations of the Revolutionary, Jacksonian, early Reconstruction, Progressive, New Deal, and New Frontier/Great Society periods. In these cases the call has been for citizenship education to stress the unifying democratic values of liberty, equality, justice, and obligation of the individual to the public good.

Another approach has stressed the need for citizenship education to reinforce the traditional or conservative cohesive values of the American past, its national destiny, its devotion to individualism and free enterprise, its attitude of superiority to other peoples and nations. Further, it was felt necessary to stem the tide of change and to rally the people around a particular version of the "American way of life," so as to protect it from threats of massive immigration, militant or subversive radicalism, hot wars, or cold wars. Sometimes, of course, the motivations or the prescriptions of these two approaches cannot be easily distinguished. Sometimes liberals and conservatives agreed in their rhetoric, but more often they contested for a priority place in civic education programs. The complexity of the periodic efforts to reform citizenship education increases the dilemma.

As a result of this persistent three-way pulling and hauling among the claims of a democratic polity, of segmental pluralisms, and of an unrelenting technological modernity, the civic education programs of the past have seemed to recent historians to vacillate between didactic approaches that ranged between two extremes: those motivated by strong moral, national, or nativist fervor that gave civic education a tone of preachy or pugnacious patriotism; and those that would at all costs avoid political controversy in the schools, and thus turn civic education into pedantic, pallid, platitudinous, or pusilanimous exercises.

No wonder, then, that professionals and the public alike often try to ignore or avoid or suppress the civic role of schooling by stressing other purposes of education in the hope that "politics" will be served *indirectly* by prescriptions for academic quality (the stress on "excellence"), achievement ("back to basics"), development of the individual ("personalized learning" or "individualized instruction"), vocational competence ("career education"), or cultural pluralism ("multicultural education" or "ethnic studies").

But the need for a better civic education keeps bubbling to the surface in troubled times. It may be seen as a response to foreign threats or to fundamental changes in domestic life marked, for example, by cynicism about or alienation from political institutions; increasing crime and violence in the streets; corruption in high places; disruption in family and community life; decline in religious, sexual, and moral virtues; oppressive conformity imposed by the mass media and popular culture;

53

or a pervasive retreat to the privatism and personal ego satisfaction of "doing one's own thing." While this list may sound like a description of the present era (and it is), it also has a familiar ring out of a past that has periodically led to calls for the schools to improve their civic role. It all began with the founding of the Republic itself.

The questions that history poses for the profession and the public at this time are: What kind of period shall we now enter? Shall it be a new period of liberal reform to which civic education should contribute? Or is it to be a reaffirmation of conservative traditions to which civic education should be anchored? Or should we ignore the whole thing in our preoccupation with privatism in politics and pluralism and alternatives in education? Our answers to these questions will help to shape the kind of civic education we decide we need for the future.

The Revolutionary Ideal: Unum, 1770s-1820s

As the founders of the Republic viewed their revolution primarily politically rather than economically or socially, so they viewed the kind of education needed for the new Republic largely in political terms rather than as a means to academic excellence, individual self-fulfillment or job preparation. They talked about education as a bulwark for liberty, equality, popular consent, and devotion to the public good, goals that took precedence over the uses of knowledge for self-improvement or occupational preparation. Over and over, leaders of the time, both liberal and conservative, asserted their faith that the welfare of the Republic rested upon an educated citizenry and that free, common, public schools would be the best means of educating the citizenry in the cohesive civic values, knowledge, and obligations required of everyone in a democratic republican society.

The principal ingredients of a civic education, most agreed, were literacy and the inculcation of patriotic and moral virtues; some added the study of history and the principles of republican government itself. The founders, as was the case with almost all of their successors, exhorted the value of civic education, but they left it to the textbook writers to distill the essence of those values for school children. Texts in American history and government appeared as early as the 1790s. And the textbook writers, who turned out to be very largely of conservative persuasion, more likely Federalist in outlook than Jeffersonian, almost universally agreed that political virtue must rest upon moral and religious precepts. Since most textbook writers were New Englanders, this meant that the texts were infused with Protestant and, above all, Puritan outlooks.

Noah Webster's spellers, readers, and grammar exemplified the combination of faith in literacy (Americanized), didactic moral instruction, patriotism, and Protestant devotion to duty. Immediately following the Revolution the textbooks began to celebrate the values of

54

national cohesion, love of country, and love of liberty. All things American began to be glorified. Even the staid *New England Primer*, from which generations of Puritans had learned the alphabet by Biblical injunctions, changed its couplet for the letter "W" from "Whales in the Sea, GOD's Voice Obey" to "Great Washington brave, His Country did save." Indeed, Washington became the object not only of extravagent praise but of virtually religious devotion. Ruth Elson quotes a 1797 textbook as saying of Washington: "The most unexceptionally, the most finished, the most Godlike human character that ever acted a part on the theatre of the world."[3]

In the first half-century of the Republic's life the most influential carriers of civic education in the schools were the spellers and readers. Their paramount theme was to "attach the child's loyalty to the state and nation. The sentiment of patriotism, love of country, vies with the love of God as the cornerstone of virtue: 'Patriotism...must be considered as the noblest of the social virtues.' "[4]

A less flamboyant but real faith in the study of history as a preparation for the duties of citizenship was expressed by Jefferson. In reviewing the reasons for his 1779 proposal of a Virgina law to establish public schools Jefferson stated:

> ...of the views of this law none is more important, none more legitimate, than that of rendering the people the safe, as they are the ultimate, guardians of their own liberty. For this purpose the reading in the first stage, where *they* will receive their whole education is proposed, as has been said, to be *chiefly historical.* [italics added] *History* by apprising them of the past will enable them to judge of the future; it will avail them of the experience of other times and other nations; it will qualify them as judges of the actions and designs of men; it will enable them to know ambition under every disguise it may assume; and knowing it, to defeat its views. In every government on earth is some trace of human weakness, some germ of corruption, and degeneracy, which cunning will discover, and wickedness insensibly open, cultivate and improve. Every government degenerates when trusted to the rulers of the people alone. The people themselves therefore are its only safe depositories. And to render even them safe their minds must be improved to a certain degree. This indeed is not all that is necessary, though it be essentially necessary. An amendment of our constitution must come here in aid of the public education. The influence over government must be shared among all the people.[5]

In addition to the study of history, the study of civil government was advocated as a basic element in civic education, but it was generally reserved in this early period for college students, those expected to be the rational citizen-leaders devoted to the public service. It was generally assumed that *they* were the ones most in need of the study of government. Washington put it this way in his final message to Congress in 1796:

...the common education of a portion of our Youth from every quarter, well deserves attention. The more homogeneous our Citizens can be made in these particulars, the greater will be our prospect of permanent union; and a primary object of such a National Institute should be, the education of our Youth in the science of *Government*. In a Republic, what species of knowledge can be equally important? And what duty, more pressing on its legislature, than to patronize a plan for communicating it to those, who are to be the future guardians of the liberties of the Country?[6]

While Washington was never to see his dream of a national university realized, a similar emphasis upon the study of government motivated Jefferson in his successful efforts to establish the state University of Virginia. His first two purposes as stated in 1818 were:

To form the statesmen, legislators and judges, on whom public prosperity and individual happiness are so much to depend;

To expound the principles and structure of government, the laws which regulate the intercourse of nations, those formed municipally for our own government, and a sound spirit of legislation, which, banishing all arbitrary and unnecessary restraint on individual action, shall leave us free to do whatever does not violate the equal rights of another....[7]

Jefferson urged that two of his 10 proposed schools for the new university be devoted primarily to civic education: a school of government and a school of law. Weary from the violent drumbeat of Federalist-Republican partisanship of 30 years, Jefferson was adamant in wanting his professor of government to expound Republican doctrines and ideals in order to counteract the Federalist biases of most of the colleges of the day. He thus raised one of the most tenacious and perplexing aspects of civic education. Should teachers indoctrinate by advocating a particular political point of view? Should teachers be selected on the basis of their political beliefs as well as their academic competence? Can political teaching be value-free or is it inevitably value-laden? In any case, Jefferson did not get his school of government, possibly because of conservative opposition in the state.

In the first half-century of the Republic, civic education put pre-eminent stress upon the inculcation of civic values, relatively less on political knowledge as such, and made no discernible attempt to develop participatory political skills. Learning to participate was left to the incipient political parties, the town meetings, the churches, the coffee houses, and the ale houses where men gathered for talk and conviviality. The press probably did more to disseminate realistic as well as partisan knowledge of government than did the schools, as the *Federalist Papers* demonstrated. The stated goal of civic education was to achieve a higher form of *Unum* for the new republic.

The commitments to liberty, equality, and popular consent proclaimed as the binding elements of the political community were usually viewed in the textbooks as perfectly enshrined in the constitutional regime and, for that matter, in the authority figure of Washington. Seldom were other authorities of goverment ever mentioned by name (except for the heroes of the Revolutionary War), nor were their actions or performance in office studied or evaluated.

No particular account was taken of differences in student backgrounds. The major stress was upon a common program of literacy, moral values, and inculcation of patriotism for all children who came to school. Despite the call for free public schools, little was achieved outside New England in this respect until the mid-nineteenth century. In fact, the trend toward a voluntary approach to education through private schools for those who could afford it, separate religious schools for the respective denominations, and charity schools for the indigent poor, had increased in the late eighteenth century. It was not until the Jacksonian period that the push for common public schools took the form of a campaign for civic education itself, harking back to the founders' affirmation of the political goal of *Unum*.

The Middle Years: The Contest Between Unum and Pluribus, 1820s-1870s

In the middle half of the nineteenth century the political values inculcated by the civic education program of the schools did not change substantially from those celebrated in the Republic's first 50 years. To the resplendent values of liberty, equality, patriotism, and a benevolent Christian morality were now added the middle class virtues (especially of New England) of hard work, honesty and integrity, the rewards of property and even riches for individual effort, and obedience to legitimate authority. Ruth Elson sums up hundreds of textbooks this way:

> Unlike many modern schoolbooks, those of the nineteenth century made no pretense of neutrality. While they evade issues seriously controverted in their day, they take a firm and unanimous stand on matters of basic belief. The value judgment is their stock in trade: love of country, love of God, duty to parents, the necessity to develop habits of thrift, honesty, and hard work in order to accumulate property, the certainty of progress, the perfection of the United States. These are not to be questioned. Nor in this whole century of great external change is there any deviation from these basic values. In pedagogical arrangements the schoolbook of the 1790s is vastly different from that of the 1890s, but the continuum of values is uninterrupted. Neither the Civil War nor the 1890s provide any watershed of basic values.[8]

While Elson gives short examples from hundreds of texts to support her generalization, a single longer quotation from the pre-eminent American historian of the day epitomizes beautifully the set of values the school texts echo and re-echo. An ardent Jacksonian Democrat,

George Bancroft wrote the following introduction to his projected 10-volume *History of the United States* in 1834. He saw no reason to change it in the succeeding editions and revisions for the next 40 to 50 years. This quotation is taken from the six-volume edition of 1879; a final revised edition was published in 1883:

The United States of America constitute an essential portion of a great political system, embracing all the civilized nations of the earth. At a period when the force of moral opinion is rapidly increasing, they have the precedence in the practice and the defense of the equal rights of man. The sovereignty of the people is here a conceded axiom, and the laws, established upon that basis, are cherished with faithful patriotism. While the nations of Europe aspire after change, our constitution engages the fond admiration of the people, by which it has been established. Prosperity follows the execution of even justice; invention is quickened by the freedom of competition; and labor rewarded with sure and unexampled returns....Every man may enjoy the fruits of his industry; every mind is free to publish its convictions. Our government, by its organization, is necessarily identified with the interests of the people, and relies exclusively on their attachment for its durability and support. Even the enemies of the state, if there are any among us, have liberty to express their opinions undisturbed; and are safely tolerated, where reason is left free to combat their errors. Nor is the constitution a dead letter, unalterably fixed: it has the capacity for improvement; adopting whatever changes time and the public will may require, and safe from decay, so long as that will retains its energy.... Religion, neither persecuted nor paid by the state, is sustained by the regard for public morals and the convictions of an enlightened faith. Intelligence is diffused with unparalleled universality; a free press teems with the choicest productions of all nations and ages. There are more daily journals in the United States than in the world beside. A public document of general interest is, within a month, reproduced in at least a million of copies, and is brought within the reach of every freeman in the country. An immense concourse of emigrants of the most various lineage is perpetually crowding to our shores; and the principles of liberty, uniting all interests by the operation of equal laws, blend the discordant elements into harmonious union. Other governments are convulsed by the innovations and reforms of neighboring states; our constitution, fixed in the affections of the people, from whose choice it has sprung, neutralized the influence of foreign principles, and fearlessly opens an asylum to the virtuous, the unfortunate, and the oppressed of every nation....[9]

Of all the political values that the textbooks extolled, liberty was pre-eminent. Whenever they attempted to explain why children should love their country above all else, the idea of liberty took first place. Now this was undoubtedly of prime importance in promoting unity in an increasingly diverse and pluralistic society. Yet the loyalty to liberty was more in affective terms of feeling than in analytical terms of knowledge.

Elson puts it this way:

> All books agree that the American nation politically expressed is the apostle of liberty, a liberty personified, apostrophized, sung to, set up in God-like glory, but rarely defined. To discover what liberty means in these books is a murky problem. The child reader could be certain that it was glorious, it is American, it is to be revered, and it deserves his primary loyalty. But for the child to find out from these books what this liberty is would be astonishing.[10]

As the Civil War approached, the textbooks began to speak of the dangers of disunion and, being Northern in origin, began to become more outspoken about the evils of slavery. Still, in the ante-bellum period the South continued to use the Northern textbooks, and even after the War, never did produce textbooks to equal the quality of Northern texts. In fact, the Confederate books that were written and published revealed political attitudes not much different from those that continued to flow from the North, except on the subject of slavery. A common custom was for the Southern teachers simply to excise the Northern discussion of the Civil War and Reconstruction by pinning the pages together so the young readers would presumably skip them in favor of the truth delivered by the teacher. To make up for these gaps, the Southern books and teachers could easily expand on the Southern heroes in the Revolutionary War with Washington brooking no competition.

While Bancroft may have been a Jacksonian Democrat, the predominant tone of the school textbooks of the nineteenth century was Federalist and conservative:

> Although schoolbook authors consider themselves guardians of liberty, they can be more accurately described as guardians of tradition. On social questions the tenor of the books is consistently conservative. The United States is always indentified with freedom, but this freedom is best identified as that established in 1783 after separation from Great Britain. The nineteenth-century child was taught to worship past achievements of America and to believe in the inevitable spread of the American system throughout the world. But contemporary problems are conspicuously absent, and reform movements which would have profound social or political effects are either ignored or derided. While Jeffersonian and Jacksonian democracy agitated the adult world, the child was taught the necessity of class distinctions. Nor are Jefferson and Jackson ever ranked as heroes;...in the schools Hamilton and Daniel Webster governed the minds of the children.[11]

While the textbook writers seemed to have no compunctions about taking sides in behalf of patriotic virtue, Republican devotion to liberty, or Federalist devotion to property, the school people in the 1830s and 1840s began to face the difficulties posed by pluralism in the burgeoning modernization of the new nation.

No one was more eloquent than Horace Mann himself on what he candidly called "political education." In 1848, summing up his 12 years as secretary of the State Board of Education in Massachusetts, Mann began with the assumption that citizens of the Republic must "understand something of the true nature of the government under which they live." He spelled out a civic education program in terms that will sound familiar to all teachers of civics since that time:

> ...the constitution of the United States and of our own State, should be made a study in our Public Schools. The partition of the powers of government into the three co-ordinate branches,—legislative, judicial, and executive—with the duties appropriately devolving upon each; the mode of electing or of appointing all officers, with the reason on which it was founded; and, especially, the duty of every citizen, in a government of laws, to appeal to the courts for redress, in all cases of alleged wrong, instead of undertaking to vindicate his own rights by his own arm, and, in a government where the people are the acknowledged sources of power, the duty of changing laws and rulers by an appeal to the ballot, and not by rebellion, should be taught to all the children until they are fully understood.[12]

By now the distinction between the basic ideal values of the political community and the actual operation of the system began to be apparent even to the educators. Caught in the swirl of contesting forces in Massachusetts occasioned by the immigration of Irish and Germans of Roman Catholic faith and by the changes in urban life attendant upon the industrial factory system, Mann knew all too well that "if the tempest of political strife were to be let loose upon our Common Schools, they would be overwhelmed with sudden ruin." He recognized that many would object to *any* study of political matters in the schools because the constitution was subject to different readings. He saw the dangers of political partisanship in the appointment of teachers on the basis of their political fitness in the eyes of the local school committee or of the majority in the community:

> Who shall moderate the fury of these conflicting elements, when they rage against each other; and who shall save the dearest interests of the children from being consumed in the fierce combustion? If parents find that their children are indoctrinated into what they call political heresies, will they not withdraw them from the school; and, if they withdraw them from the school, will they not resist all appropriations to support a school from which they derive no benefit?[13]

Mann could not admit that the public schools should avoid political education altogether, nor could he risk the destruction of the public schools by urging them to become "theatres for party politics." His solution was similar to that which he proposed for religious controversies; the schools should teach the common elements that all agreed to, but skip over the controversial:

> Surely, between these extremes, there must be a medium not difficult to be found. And is not this the middle course, which all

sensible and judicious men, all patriots, and all genuine republicans, must approve?—namely, that those articles in the creed of republicanism, which are accepted by all, believed in by all, and which form the common basis of our political faith, shall be taught to all. But when the teacher, in the course of his lessons or lectures on the fundamental law, arrives at a controverted text, he is either to read it without comment or remark; or, at most, he is only to say that the passage is the subject of disputation, and that the schoolroom is neither the tribunal to adjudicate, nor the forum to discuss it.

Such being the rule established by common consent, and such the practice, observed with fidelity under it, it will come to be universally understood, that political proselytism is no function of the school; but that all indoctrination into matters of controversy between hostile political parties is to be elsewhere sought for, and elsewhere imparted. Thus, may all the children of the Commonwealth receive instruction in the great essentials of political knowledge,—in those elementary ideas without which they will never be able to investigate more recondite and debatable questions....[14]

Thus would Mann stress the transcendant values of the political community, but pass over controversial ideas about the constitutional order and omit critical judgments about the actual operation of the system. Political knowledge should concentrate upon the formal structure of the governmental institutions, but the skills of participation should be delegated, along with the controversial, to the nonschool agencies of party, press, and caucus of adults.

Mann was so intent upon getting common schools established for an ever wider range of the potential school population that he would not risk the failure of the common school idea in order to bring political controversy into the schools. Thus it came about that the emerging public schools were largely satisfied with a civic program that initiated the poor, the foreigner, and the working class children into the political community by literacy in English, didactic moral injunctions, patriotic readers and histories, and lessons that stressed recitations of the structural forms of the constitutional order.

Up to the centennial celebration of 1876, the children of the "unincorporated" were still largely blocked from the public schools and thus from the civic education offered by those schools. The Reconstruction reforms had visualized extension of the public school system to the Southern states, but these were largely dissipated by the 1870s. And Northern states were slow to admit blacks to common schools, often preferring to establish separate schools for white and black. These evident failures of the educational system itself to put into practice the stated values of the political community helped to widen the gap between ideal and reality. Millions of immigrants were being assimilated by civic education, despite the patronizing and often hostile ethnic images that textbooks portrayed of the Irish and immigrants from southern Europe; but millions of racial minorities born in the U.S. were still not provided any form of citizenship education. In the face of mounting cultural pluralisms, the goal of civic education embraced rapid assimilation to an *ideal* American political system.

Aggressive Modernization and Progressive Reform, 1870s-1920s

In the 50 years straddling the turn of the twentieth century, the character of civic education programs began to undergo much more searching examination than they had for the first 100 years of the Republic. While the basic values constituting the political community did not change radically, there were three significant alterations in civic education resulting from the rapid social transformations of a half century of modernization. First, the earlier stress on love of a grand, free country became a more shrill and passionate devotion to a great and powerful nation. The ideas of manifest destiny, winning of the West, overseas expansion, and making the world safe for democracy led to exaltation of the U.S. as the superior nation of the world, imbued with the mission to lead all the rest and thus deserving, nay demanding, a loyalty to "my country, right or wrong." All this contributed to an increasingly nationalistic and strident tone to civic education.

Not only did the Spanish-American War and World War I stimulate a nationalistic and even militaristic fervor and flavor to civic education, but the massive immigration going on during this period added a second alteration, the demand for instant Americanization of immigrants, who seemed to many conservatives and liberals alike to pose a basic threat to the commitments of the democratic political community, to the stability of the constitutional order, and to the functioning of governing authorities. They could point to ghettos in the cities, crime in the streets, bloody strikes in the factories, corruption in local governments, and the spreading of socialist, communist, and revolutionary doctrines by radical groups.

This long-present fear of the alien and foreign was exacerbated by the millions of immigrants who poured in from Southern and Eastern Europe and Asia. While civic textbooks might attribute this influx to the search for liberty and equality, the civic education programs of settlement houses, patriotic organizations, and nativist associations began to turn more and more to Americanization programs that stressed not only didactic instruction in praise of the historic values but also demanded outward signs of loyalty from the new citizens as well as the old in the form of the public pledge of allegiance, salutes to the flag, loyalty oaths, patriotic songs and marching, required instruction in English, and attacks upon foreign language teaching in the schools.

A third shift in emphasis in civic education was the prominent role given to the image of self-made men, the self-reliant individuals who had shifted from pioneering in the West to pioneering an industrial-business system that was rapidly modernizing America with a producing and consuming capacity well ahead of all the other nations of the world. The political implication of this image was, of course, that it had all happened under auspices of a free enterprise system free from government controls.

But liberal reactions to the social and political results of an unbridled industrial, capitalistic economy led to the Progressive movement dedicated to political reforms in the electoral systems and civil service; social reforms in cities, prisons, and sweatshops; passage of child labor laws; and the enfranchising of women. Underlying the Progressive reforms was a belief in the collective efforts of government to control rampant business enterprise, protect the rights of people, and bring about good government through honest and efficient civil service, responsive bureaucracies, and regulatory agencies.

Conflicting political values began to reveal themselves in different approaches to civic education as educators responded to the ebullient modernization of America's polity and economy. They had to face the problem of what to do about the massive increases in school enrollments as more of the population began to realize that education was a prime means to get ahead in American society and as compulsory attendance laws aimed at abolishing child labor brought and kept more children in school. The problems were especially acute at the secondary school level as the schools tried to cope with a non-college-bound majority.

One response of the academically minded educators in the 1880s and 1890s was to strengthen the study of history (and thus reduce the emphasis on civics) by introducing more rigorous scholarly knowledge into history texts and courses. In the early 1890s the Madison Conference on History, Civil Government, and Political Economy made such proposals, which became a part of the overall re-examination of the entire secondary school curriculum undertaken by the Committee of Ten of the National Education Association, whose report was published in 1893.

The main assumption of the Committee of Ten headed by president Eliot of Harvard was that all courses in high school should provide the same strong mental discipline for the non-college-bound majority as for the college-bound minority. The teaching of history was thus not primarily to develop good citizenship and love of country but to teach high school students to think like historians.

For two to three decades the academic orientation of the Committee of Ten dominated curriculum thinking and curriculum making in the civic education programs of the secondary schools. In history the emphasis was upon the use of primary sources to develop in pupils a historic sense and to train them in the search for historical materials, the weighing of evidence, and the drawing of conclusions. In the effort to get children to think like historians, it was hoped the flamboyant nationalistic and patriotic history of the previous century would be toned down. In 1899 a Committee of Seven of the American Historical Association urged the use of primary sources to supplement the textbook. The *History Teachers Magazine* (founded in 1909) and the work of Henry Johnson at Teachers College, Columbia University, both contributed to the new movement to stress historical problem solving and reasoned judgment in a laboratory or workshop setting.

Another approach came from a Progressive upsurge of interest in the study of civil government in the early 1900s as new ideas about civic education began to appear among proponents in political science, economics, and sociology. In 1916 a committee of the American Political Science Association, reflecting the Progressive reform movements, argued that the standard courses in civil government should be restructured. Instead of starting with the study of the U.S. Constitution and a description of the formal structure of government and then proceeding to a similar study of state constitutions and governments, the procedure should be reversed. The committee endorsed the study of "community civics," assuming that political affairs nearest to home were the most important and should be considered first. The Progressively-inspired Municipal League promoted this idea.

Another, but far less popular, response was the effort by Progressive educators and social settlement workers of a liberal/humanitarian persuasion to urge that civic education should not view the ethnic heritage of immigrants as an ancestral bondage that should be quickly and thoroughly removed through assimilation, but rather should be honored and utilized in the process of Americanization. Jane Addams and John Dewey thus criticized the public schools for insisting upon a one-way Anglo-conformity that blatantly denationalized the immigrant children.

In the long run, however, the most influential force was the rising movement to make citizenship education the special province of the "social studies," which would pervade the elementary as well as the secondary school curriculum. This movement took place under the auspices of the NEA's Commission on the Reorganization of Secondary Education whose final report, *Cardinal Principles of Secondary Education*, was published in 1918. From 1913 to 1916 the Committee on Social Studies was at work preparing its report for the overall Commission. Again reflecting the Progressive views of reform, the Committee stated more explicitly than it had ever been stated before that citizenship was the social responsibility of the secondary school. In a preliminary statement in 1913 the chairman of the Committee, a sociologist, revealed the social reform intent to make civics much more than a study of government:

> Good citizenship should be the aim of social studies in the high school. While the administration and instruction throughout the school should contribute to the social welfare of the community, it is maintained that social studies have direct responsibility in this field. Facts, conditions, theories, and activities that do not contribute rather directly to the appreciation of methods of human betterment have no claim. Under the test the old civics, almost exclusively a study of Government machinery, must give way to the new civics, a study of all manner of social efforts to improve mankind. It is not so important that the pupil know how the President is elected as that he shall understand the duties of the health officer in his community. The time formerly spent in the effort to understand the process of passing a law over the President's veto is now to be more profitably used in the observation of the vocational resources of the community. In line with this emphasis the committee recommends that social studies in the high school shall include such topics as the following: Community health, housing and homes, public recreation, good roads, community education, poverty and the care of the poor, crime and reform, family income, savings banks and life insurance, human rights versus property rights, impulsive action of mobs, the selfish conservatism of tradition, and public utilities.[15]

In the final report of the Committee the term "social studies" was used to include not only history, civics, and government but also concepts from sociology and economics that related directly to the organization of society and man as a member of social groups. History still held a major place in the course proposals for grades 7 through 12, but a "problems approach" was to infuse the whole program. Civics was proposed for the junior high school years as well as a new course in "problems of democracy" for the twelfth grade.

Hazel Hertzberg summarizes the influence of the Committee's report this way:

> Instruction in the social studies should be organized around concrete problems of vital importance to society and of immediate interest to the pupil rather than on the basis of the formal social sciences....The social studies should contribute directly to the "social efficiency" of the student, helping him "to participate effectively in the promotion of social well-being" in the groups of which he is a member, from his own community to the "world community"....The skills to be learned by pupils were those of good citizens participating in the building of an invigorated society, not those of historians carefully interpreting evidence, developing criticism, and arriving at synthesis....

> The Report of the Committee on Social Studies had a significant impact on the direction of educational reform. It represented many of the deepest, most pervasive, and most characteristic viewpoints of the Progressive period. No doubt it would have been exceedingly influential in any case, but the circumstances that it was issued just

before American entry into World War I created a climate favorable to its concern with personal and social immediacy and utility and what is today referred to as "relevance."[16]

While the general impact of the final, overall Commission Report in the *Cardinal Principles* of 1918 was great indeed in making citizenship one of the cardinal goals, especially of the social studies, and while it tended to reduce emphasis upon abstract academic material in favor of live problems, it also tended to reduce the *political* concerns of civic education in favor of social and economic and practical personal problems. Note the withdrawal from "constitutional questions" in the pursuit of good citizenship:

> While all subjects should contribute to good citizenship, the social studies—geography, history, civics and economics—should have this as their dominant aim. Too frequently, however, does mere information, conventional in value and remote in its bearing, make up the content of the social studies. History should so treat the growth of institutions that their present value may be appreciated. Geography should show the interdependence of men while it shows their common dependence on nature. Civics should concern itself less with constitutional questions and remote governmental functions and should direct attention to social agencies close at hand and to the informal activities of daily life that regard and seek the common good. Such agencies as child welfare organizations and consumers' leagues afford specific opportunities for the expression of civic qualities by the older pupils.[17]

At last, however, the skills of civic participation began to be touched upon as social studies teachers were attracted to progressive education's new stress on projects, units, and activities in the classroom in order to promote the habits and outlooks appropriate to a democracy. The *Cardinal Principles* found valuable:

> ...the assignment of projects and problems to groups of pupils for cooperative solution and the socialized recitation whereby the class as a whole develops a sense of collective responsibility. Both of these devices give training in collective thinking. Moreover, the democratic organization and administration of the school itself, as well as the cooperative relations of pupil and teacher, pupil and pupil, and teacher and teacher, are indispensible.[18]

While this approval of the study of problems and "socialized recitation" in classrooms may seem to be a modest proposal to modern teachers, it by no means swept the profession off its feet. Teaching by the book, lecturing, note taking, question-and-answer recitation, memorizing, essay writing, and examination passing continued to be the prime activities of history and civics classrooms. And venturing out into the community was still more radical, especially if a zealous civics teacher actually ran up against the local politicians. In this case the study of "remote governmental functions" could actually be conducted more freely than treading on local political toes.

But at least the idea of participation could now take its place alongside the inculcation of values and political knowledge as the main ingredients of a civics program in the schools. And the way was being prepared for comparing the stated values of the political community with the actual operation of the governmental authorities by the stress upon critical thinking, scholarly sources of knowledge, and firsthand study of the actual functioning of government, at least at the municipal level of community civics.

Above all, it was recognized that the high schools had to deal with a very different kind of population from that of the secondary schools of the first 100 years of the Republic, i.e., the non-college-oriented students. However, assimilating vast numbers of foreign immigrants, both youth and adult, nearly engulfed the schools and exhausted teachers' energies. In many cases teaching English and the rudimentary structure of government were all that teachers accomplished. So in spite of all the protestations of the progressives, the national committees, and teacher educators, the courses in American history, civics, and civil government, which might have been engrossing to countless thousands of adult immigrants, were boring to millions of high school students who went through expanding cycles of social studies: communities in the third and fourth grades, civics in the ninth and twelfth grades, American history in the fifth, eighth, and eleventh grades, with geography, state history, and European or world history sandwiched in, probably in the seventh and tenth grades.

The ensuing fifty-year period witnessed many kinds of attempts to reform and break out of the social studies cycles on behalf of a better civic education, and belatedly to incorporate at last the minority and disadvantaged groups in society who had long been "outsiders" to the mainstream of American political and educational life.

Recurring Calls for Reform of Civic Education, 1920s-1970s

The outpouring of proposals and projects for more effective civic education programs during the past half-century would take volumes to relate. Yet there is repetitiveness in the lists of goals and objectives set forth by one commission after another. After the brutal realities and disillusionments of Vietnam and Watergate, some of the earlier statements seem grimly super-patriotic and others exude the bland optimism of Pollyanna herself. All that can be done here is to suggest the range of political outlooks that seemed to motivate some of the major approaches to civic education.

In the wake of World War I, citizenship education programs in the schools, the textbooks, and the teachers themselves were subjected to continuing campaigns at the hands of conservative civic and patriotic

67

organizations whose views today seem particularly narrow-minded in their anti-foreign, anti-pacifist, anti-immigration, anti-reform outlooks. In the 1920s, the American Legion led the campaigns to get Congress and the state legislatures to require civic education, flag salutes, military training, and loyalty oaths. The dominant mood of civic education in the 1920s was to rally 'round the flag, extoll the merits and successes, and say nothing derogatory about the greatest country on earth. Of course, other nations were doing the same thing in their programs of civic education, which were so well documented in the 10 volumes produced between 1929 and 1933 under the leadership of Charles E. Merriam, professor of political science at the University of Chicago.

In contrast, the 1930s witnessed a social reformist outlook sparked by the economic depression, the New Deal, and the onset of totalitarianism in the world. One of the most impressive examples of educational response was the Commission on the Social Studies of the American Historical Association, which was funded by the Carnegie Foundation from January 1929 to December 1933 and which issued 17 volumes between 1932 and 1937. The dominant tone of the most widely read volumes (such as those by Charles A. Beard, George S. Counts, Bessie L. Pierce, Jesse H. Newlon, and Merle Curti) was set forth in the *Conclusions and Recommendations of the Commission* (1934): the age of individualism and laissez-faire in economics and government was closing and a new collectivism requiring social planning and governmental regulation was emerging. The arguments struck notes that sound startlingly familiar today: deprivation in the midst of plenty, inequality in income, spreading unemployment, wasted natural resources, rising crime and violence, subordination of public welfare to private interest, and international struggle for raw materials. A particular curriculum was not promulgated, but it was hoped that this view of life and this political/economic framework would guide curriculum designs for civic education programs. The clear implication was that youth should be inculcated with the values of economic collectivity and interdependence in place of economic individualism, while continuing to promote personal and cultural individualism and freedom.

Like-minded proposals were stemming from George S. Counts, John Dewey, Harold Rugg, William H. Kilpatrick, John L. Childs, and other social reconstructionists. Counts' *Dare the School Build a New Social Order?* came out in 1932; and as editor of *The Educational Frontier* in 1934, Counts specifically endorsed the American Historical Association's *Conclusions and Recommendations* as policy for the new journal.

Naturally, the social reformers set the profession on its ears and elicited vigorous and shrill counterattacks. But the major professional organizations responded, on the whole, positively as far as giving renewed attention to civic education. The National Education Association and the American Association of School Administrators jointly sponsored the Educational Policies Commission in 1935, enlisting Counts, along with several more conservative administrators, to membership. The pronouncements of the Educational Policies Commission softened the social reconstructionist economic views, but they did emphasize over and over again the relationship of education to democracy. Charles A. Beard wrote the first draft of the Commission's historical volume, *The Unique Function of Education in American Democracy* in 1937; education for citizenship was the central theme.

And when *The Purposes of Education in American Democracy* was published in 1938 (written by William G. Carr, NEA executive secretary), the Seven Cardinal Principles had been reduced to four objectives, but "civic responsibility" was one of the four. The stated objectives of civic responsibility do not sound particularly daring today; there was little emphasis upon liberty or equality or due process, but for all the bland language, there was scope for realistic civic studies if teachers or communities had the stomach for them:

Social Justice. The educated citizen is sensitive to the disparities of human circumstance.

Social Activity. The educated citizen acts to correct unsatisfactory conditions.

Social Understanding. The educated citizen seeks to understand social structures and social processes.

Critical Judgment. The educated citizen has defenses against propaganda.

Tolerance. The educated citizen respects honest differences of opinion.

Conservation. The educated citizen has a regard for the nation's resources.

Social Applications of Science. The educated citizen measures scientific advance by its contribution to the general welfare.

World Citizenship. The educated citizen is a cooperating member of the world community.

Law Observance. The educated citizen respects the law.

Economic Literacy. The educated citizen is economically literate.

Political Citizenship. The educated citizen accepts his civic duties.

Devotion to Democracy. The educated citizen acts upon an unswerving loyalty to democratic ideals.[19]

The effort to make civic education more realistic, while at the same time not embracing the extremes of radical-sounding reconstructionism or reactionary radical-baiting, led civic educators back to the basic ideals of democracy, à la Horace Mann, and to activities that would involve students in community participation but no controversy. World

War II broke into this movement with its emphasis upon mobilizing the schools for the war effort and served to reassert the values of patriotism as the basis for national unity.

Following World War II, the idea of projects in civic education began to entice many school systems to give special attention to citizenship education. Among the early ones in the late 1940s were those associated with the schools in Detroit; Cambridge, Mass.; and the state of Kansas; and those associated with Syracuse University, Tufts University, and Teachers College, Columbia University.

Then, in the 1950s, education for good citizenship became popular in schools systems all over the country. Much of this movement attempted to show that the schools were not radical and not subversive, but were supporting the basic principles of political democracy and the basic economic values of the free enterprise system. This was a response to the Cold War crusades against Communism in the world and a defense against the onslaughts of McCarthyism at home. The hope was that children could be taught the values of consensus on political/economic matters, reflecting the spirit of accommodation and good will of the Eisenhower presidency.

One volume admirably reveals these twin drives—a fierce opposition to Communism in the world and a hope that good will, cooperative actions, and positive democratic attitudes would strengthen democracy at home. Sprinkled with photographs of smiling, clean, well-dressed groups of white pupils and teachers, the Thirty-Second Yearbook of the American Association of School Administrators, produced by its Commission on Educating for Citizenship, had this to say in 1954:

> At his best, the American citizen has always sought to realize the nation's historic ideals. Now, when communist imperialism threatens all security, he feels a new appreciation for the old ideals as a stable element in a shaky world. The public schools are the means on which the American leans most heavily to make sure that all children carry forward the American heritage. So now, even more urgently than in the past, the citizen demands that the schools educate for citizenship.[20]

In the book's first chapter, "The Threat Is Total," the Commission argues that the Russian communist dictatorship not only threatens our way of life throughout the world, but it is a political threat to democratic freedoms and "drives directly at our moral and spiritual ideals" and "our religious and ethical standards." So the schools should develop the knowledge, the attitudes, the problem-solving ability, and the skills of working with others for the general welfare. This conception of citizenship would not be limited to the political scientists' narrow view of citizenship. Rather, echoing the *Cardinal Principles* of 40 years earlier, the Commission opted for a much broader concept of citizenship education that would include "all the mutually helpful social relationships with others which democracy assumes should be characteristic of human life and living."

By thus opening still wider the door of citizenship education to all kinds of social and personal relationships, the Commission forecasted what often did happen in social studies programs. "Problems of democracy" courses often drifted off to "problems of democratic living" involving the behavior and psychology of adolescents, their personal, marital, and family problems, vocational interests, and personal values. As the social reconstructionists had stressed the economic side of civic education, so the social conception of citizenship often became so broad and so social that in the process it became watered down and neglected the basic political questions of power, influence, and decision making.

This was, of course, not true of all proposals or projects having to do with citizenship education in the 1950s. The Twenty-Second Yearbook of the National Council for the Social Studies in 1951 listed 24 characteristics of the good citizen, reflecting the composite thinking of 300 public figures as well as educators. The first 13 stressed the values of equality, liberty, basic human rights, the law, and other political competencies; the other 11 had to do with economic, family, community, and international matters.

One project in the 1950s that focused upon the concept of liberty was the Citizenship Education Project (CEP) at Teachers College, Columbia University. It stressed the values and knowledge appropriate to the free individual, the free government, the free economy, and the free world. It documented from the Constitution and law in great detail the premises of liberty under each of these headings. It was a most useful undertaking at the time, making available solid political knowledge and reversing the usual subordination of the political so common in other approaches. What was probably even more interesting to professional educators, however, was its stress on the skills of participation, which it identified by the neutral term "laboratory practices," perhaps in the hope that it would divert charges of being politically controversial. Hundreds of laboratory practices detailed how teachers and students could engage in action-oriented problem solving in the schools and in the community. Workshops and training programs were conducted across the country for hundreds of schools and thousands of teachers during the 1950s.

If taken seriously, the suggestions coming out of CEP could have led to much more than bland good will between the school and community, e.g., studying the local congressional district to see if it provides fair representation of minority groups, making a tax map of the community to see if tax assessments are equitable, getting young people to join political clubs, helping to get voters to register and to cast ballots accurately, providing citizens with nonpartisan political information, informing the community how candidates stand on issues, actually campaigning for candidates, drafting a real and not a sham school

71

constitution, and the like. Unfortunately, the CEP had to combat a political neutralism and caution among educators during the McCarthy era; its funds ran out just before the rise of political activism of the 1960s; and it never was well incorporated into the mainstream of teaching and research at Teachers College—the fate of so many special projects of the past and a warning for new ones in the future.

In the 1960s a curious coincidence of forces led to general relaxing of explicit calls for a more and better civic education. Both the "new social studies" movement and the rise of student unrest and activism undercut patriotism as an argument for civic education. Responding to the calls for a "new math" and "new science" stimulated by Sputnik and funded so generously by NDEA, the National Science Foundation, and the private foundations, the "new social studies" took on the patterns of the social science disciplines: cognitive analysis, systematic acquisition of organized knowledge, conceptual analysis, inquiry learning, discovery method, and in general a stress upon thinking like a social scientist, reminiscent, as Hazel Hertzberg points out, of the primary sources movement in history teaching of the 1880s to 1900.

It may be too early to make judgments about the relative value of various projects that could come under the heading of the "new social studies," but it is clear that the revived disciplinary approach to knowledge tended not only to belittle "soft" or superficial programs of social studies in the schools, but also to downgrade explicit citizenship education as a proper goal of the school curriculum. One of the most forthright and explicit statements of this "hard-headed" disciplinary view was made by the executive director of the American Political Science Association and his wife in 1962:

> There is a long-standing tradition according to which secondary-school instruction in political science, or instruction based upon the knowledge political science provides, has as its main objective the making of good citizens. This tradition appears to be based on the belief that instruction in government, politics, the political process, and the important issues of public policy will produce citizens who will discuss, act, and vote rationally and intelligently and that we may thereby achieve a sane and effective democratic society. Without asserting that education in the field of government, politics, and public policy has no role to play in helping form better citizens, we feel required to state at the outset, in the interests of clarity, that we regard this tradition and the beliefs upon which it is based as mistaken and misleading: first, because it is based on a distorted conception of how citizens are made; second, because it is based on a distorted conception of democracy; and, third, because it is based on a misconception of political science.[21]

In other words, citizens are made by the total process of political socialization outside the schools; democracy must rest upon the expert knowledge of specialists; and political science is a complicated

72

intellectual discipline about political behavior, not a set of maxims about good citizenship. Caught in the middle by such disciplinary views from one extreme, and the raucous non-negotiable demands for *relevance now* from militant student activists at the other extreme, the traditional programs of civic education seemed pale, irresolute, and outmoded. Whether the new social studies could provide the answer was in doubt.

It is surely true that many of the curriculum development projects of the 1960s were more realistic, more sophisticated, more analytical, and more attuned to the claims for equality made by the unincorporated minorities and their struggles for civil rights than was the civic education of the 1950s. Yet they did not seem to "pay off," according to the test results regarding political knowledge and political attitudes. It is instructive to observe, for example, that of 26 major curriculum centers and projects reported on and analyzed in *Social Education* in 1972, only seven or eight seemed to put special stress upon citizenship objectives.[22]

This listing in *Social Education* did not include projects that had just recently closed down or that had recently begun. In the former category was the Center for Research and Education in American Liberties at Columbia University and Teachers College, which began in 1966 at the crest of the wave of the curriculum reform movements of the Great Society and at the beginning of the violent unrest on the college campuses. Its stress on liberty, on political values, knowledge, and skills held great promise, but it succumbed as special government funds for curriculum development began to wither at the beginning of the 1970s. The Center at Columbia heralded a growing concern for law-related civic education which, however, was overshadowed during the 1960s by the massive outpouring of the more general, and less politically oriented, social studies materials.

This rapid survey of principal trends in citizenship education brings us to the 1970s and the predicaments of the present. But, first, let me summarize what I believe we might learn from this historical perspective. This was the subject of a colloquium in April 1978 sponsored by Research for Better Schools in Philadelphia. The interesting thing about the colloquium was the difference in interpretation between my reading of the history and that of three "revisionist" historians.[23] All three were pessimistic about *any* kind of civic education in the schools, because they felt it was bound to impose middle-class, capitalistic values upon the lower classes, and it would further strengthen the class hierarchy status quo.

Clarence Karier of the University of Illinois reads the history of citizenship education as the steady victory of the totalitarian state over individual freedom, with the schools being partly responsible for this victory of the state. Karier thinks the schools should not teach loyalty to the government or the Constitution. He is pessimistic about the role of schooling in citizenship education. Marvin Lazerson of the University of British Columbia finds that citizenship education has not permitted root differences among cultural groups to be accepted as legitimate differences, so he is pessimistic that citizenship education can be reconceptualized unless the state itself is reconceptualized. I take this to mean that the historic liberal state must be reconceptualized along socialistic lines. And Michael B. Katz of the University of Pennsylvania finds the essence of our history to be a conflict of social classes with the schools always on the side of the upper classes, imposing *their* values upon a reluctant lower class. So Katz believes the schools should be value-neutral and simply teach the basic academic skills. He is not in favor of deliberate programs of civic or moral education, because they are bound to be used to maintain the present exploitive, class-based status quo. The pessimism of the radical historians and their proposals for schooling parallel in large part those of neo-conservative pluralists mentioned in Chapter 1.

In contrast, I find that political *Unum* is still a desirable goal for civic education, and that the schools should do their best to regenerate a sense of democratic political community in each new generation of citizens. Despite the failures and inadequacies of civic education in the past, I believe that the welfare of the Republic does rest on an educated citizenry, as the founders argued. I believe that the prime purpose, the highest priority, for a genuinely public education is the political goal of empowering the whole population to exercise its rights and to cope with the responsibilities of a genuinely democratic citizenship.

But we also should learn from history that society and government, and thus the nature of citizenship, have changed drastically in the past 200 years. So we cannot be content with the prescriptions for a civic curriculum that were produced in the late eighteenth or early nineteenth centuries. Simple competence in reading, writing, and arithmetic for elementary school white boys is obviously not enough. Simple history as proposed by Jefferson or the elements of civil government as proposed by Washington are not enough. Vague preachments on the glories of liberty as described by Ruth Elson are not enough. Didactic appeals to the moral, spiritual, or political virtues are not enough, and partisan indoctrination of particular economic or ideological platforms is not appropriate. Textbook writing should not be left to socially or politically conservative authors.

Yet, somehow, the schools do have a responsibility for doing all they can to teach the values, the knowledge, and the participation skills required of a modern democratic citizenry. Such ingredients should not be left to the political parties, the newspapers, the ministers, or the coffee houses as they were in the Revolutionary period; nor to modern business or labor leaders or television commentators or special interest pleaders as they are so often today.

In reexamining the stated purposes used to justify the development and spread of the common public school in the middle decades of the nineteenth century, I believe that the citizenship argument is still valid. The highest priority for a genuinely public school is to serve the public purposes of a democratic political community. The "back to basics" people should be reminded that citizenship is the basic purpose for universal literacy. If the fundamental purposes of schooling are preparing for a job, or preparing for college, or developing individual talents, these might be achieved in private schools that select students for particular destinies. But I share the faith of the common school reformers that civic tasks can best be performed by public schools characterized by a public purpose, public control, public support, public access, and public commitment to civic unity.

Now, it is obvious that the public school reformers did not fully achieve these goals. I believe that Horace Mann was on the right track when he argued for the necessity of what he candidly called "political education," but I believe that he fell short of what is needed (then as well as now). While he stressed understanding the constitutional regime and knowledge about civil government, he backed away from the discussion of controversial political or constitutional questions in the schoolroom. He thus helped to establish the tradition that the schools are not legitimate forums in which to discuss politically sensitive matters. This was a difficult issue for Mann, but he concluded that it was better to have "neutral" public schools than to have none, a dénouement he feared would come about if the schools became "theatres for party politics." I think we can and must find a way to surmount Mann's difficulties.

A second thing we should learn from the middle decades of the nineteenth century is that there were at least two lines of thought that influenced the civic role of public education with regard to the assimilation of the immigrants, who began to come in large numbers prior to the Civil War. It is undoubtedly true that a growing nativism in the period from the 1830s to the 1850s sometimes gave the public school movement an anti-Catholic, anti-radical, and Anglo-superiority tone. But we should remember, as John Higham points out, there were also some proponents of the public schools who argued that they should become a humane assimilative force.[24] In the 1860s and 1870s ethnic rivalries declined, nativism was muted, modernization welcomed enormous new pools of manpower, and a Christian belief in the brotherhood of man was still alive and well. All these influences flowed into what Higham calls "The Age of Confidence," i.e., confidence in the capacity of the Republic to accept great diversity and pluralism as a basic characteristic of the democratic political community. And the public schools could contribute to this cosmopolitan view of assimilation. Bilingual public schools in several states during the

75

nineteenth century exemplified this faith.

The main lesson we should learn from the Gilded Age and Progressive Era is that there were two major pressures influencing citizenship education. The first and the most influential through most of this period emanated from the business-oriented and nationalistic nativism associated with the burgeoning modernization of the nation. Three significant trends in civic education already noted reflect these pushes to conformity: 1) the shrill and passionate patriotism that accompanied an expanding and powerful nation; 2) the demand for instant Americanization of the millions of immigrants who flooded into the U.S. from the 1880s to the 1920s; and 3) the glorification of the self-made man who labored (and prospered) on behalf of free enterprise unhampered by government regulations. These trends were amply illustrated in textbooks in American history and civil government.

But, as Robert Wiebe so well points out, there was a second source of influence in the new middle-class professionals who were social service progressives.[25] Their concern was the use of liberal government on behalf of social reform (in prisons, sweatshops, child labor practices, and temperance legislation) as well as political reform (civil service, electoral innovations, women's suffrage, and compulsory attendance on behalf of universal education). This stream of progressive endeavor resulted in a number of efforts to reform citizenship education in the schools. These included: strengthening of history teaching by basing it on primary sources and thus combating excessive chauvinism; developing a community civics to replace a sterile study of constitutional structures; and the "new civics" embodied in the social studies movement and in the Seven Cardinal Principles. Some progressives even tried to reorient the Americanization process so that assimilation could be accomplished with a sympathetic and respectful concern for immigrant cultures and traditions. Thus was "cultural pluralism" born.

I hope that we never have to return to the excesses of super-patriotic conformity that marked the aggressive modernization period in the U.S. I hope that schools can take seriously the "problems-approach" to social, economic, and political issues. But one result of the reform movement of the Progressive era was a reduction of *political* concerns in history and social studies. There was a withdrawal from a study of the basic ideas of the political community. While the general civic education curriculum has seldom dealt with the fundamental concepts of liberty, equality, justice, and obligation for the public good, I gain considerable hope from increased attention to these basic ideas, examples of which will be described in Chapters 4 and 5.

The Present Predicament of Citizenship Education

While the nation and especially the youth were engaging in some of the most extreme political activism in our history during the later 1960s and early 1970s, the results of citizenship education in the schools seemed to leave much to be desired. I mention only two kinds of evidence: nationwide testing of political knowledge and attitudes and surveys of curriculum trends in the social studies and textbooks widely used in the schools.

The most extensive data we have on citizenship and social studies is that reported by the National Assessment of Educational Progress, (NAEP), which tested political knowledge and attitudes of 9-year-olds, 13-year-olds, and 17-year-olds between 1969 and 1976.[26] The startling result was not that the test scores in general declined, but that the test scores on citizenship and social studies declined *more* than those in reading, writing, and science. And the declines for 17-year-olds were by and large greater than those for 9-year-olds and 13-year-olds.

One could speculate at length as to the reasons for the decline and take little encouragement about the future of the Republic from the level of knowledge revealed by some of the test items. At a time when the U.S. was facing one of its most serious crises of confidence, the section of the test dealing with the "structure and function of government" showed the greatest average decline from test scores of 13- and 17-year-olds between 1969 and 1976; and the scores of 17-year-olds, who were eligible to vote in the year following their taking of the test, declined more than did those of the 13-year-olds. Less than half of the 17-year-olds and less than one-fourth of the 13-year-olds knew that the Senate must approve an appointment to the Supreme Court; this at a time when one of Richard Nixon's appointees was turned down by the Senate. Only two-thirds of the 13-year-olds could even *name* the Senate as the "other part of Congress." Most disturbing in this section was the fact that fewer than half of 13-year-olds and only about three-fourths of 17-year-olds could give *any* word or phrase (let alone a sentence) that could remotely be termed an explanation of the basic concept of democracy.

In the section on "political process," similar declines were recorded in the students' understanding of and willingness to participate in the political process. In 1976 less than 20% of 13-year-olds and about a third of 17-year-olds could tell how a Presidential candidate was selected, and that was in the year of nominating conventions. Similarly, low scores and declines characterized the ability of students to name any senator or representative from their state.

One could argue that merely knowing factual items is not a good measure of citizenship, but even if this were granted, it is sobering to learn that so few students could recognize some of the basic constitutional rights. Only a half to two-thirds agreed that it was all right for a person who did not believe in God to hold public office, or that a magazine or newspaper had the right to criticize a public official, or that people had the right of peaceable assembly, even for unpopular causes. Some comfort could be taken from the fact that the most dramatic increase in scores had to do with the rights of the accused in a criminal case—credit for which might be attributed to TV police shows and law-related education programs.

Finally, the items on "respect for others" showed less decline than other topics and even some improvement on some items. In general, both 13-year-olds and 17-year-olds increased in their stated willingness to have persons of other races participate in such activities as living in their neighborhoods or voting in elections, and the tests also measured an increase in students' understanding of problems of the poor. This can be attributed, no doubt, to the change in attitudes attendant upon the civil rights movement and possibly the expansion of teaching about multicultural pluralism, but declines were still marked in matters of constitutional rights of freedom of religion, assembly, expression, and press. While 13-year-olds increased in their replies on understanding the need for law, 17-year-olds declined on that item; and one-third said they would not report to the police if they saw a stranger slashing the tires of a car. At the bottom of the list stood an almost unnoticed item recording the greatest decline of all: only a half of 13-year-olds and two-thirds of 17-year-olds could think of *any* way in which universal education helps the nation.

The reasons for the decline in achievement are many and complex. In December 1977 I was one of three persons asked to consult with NAEP officials in the effort to interpret the results. The others were Anna Ochoa, professor of education at Indiana University and president-elect of the National Council for the Social Studies; and Celeste Woodley, program development specialist for the Boulder Valley (Colorado) Schools. The following summary of our observations is, I believe, a useful explanation.

> The results [of the NAEP tests in citizenship] are, to these consultants, "disappointing, but not surprising." The assessments spanned a turbulent era in American political history—including the Vietnam war, campus riots, and the erosion of confidence in political institutions and persons, culminating in the Watergate scandal—and these events undoubtedly affected student political knowledge and attitudes.

> However, considering all that transpired in 1969 and 1976, it is encouraging that students' valuing of constitutional rights and their respect for others did not decline substantially. The basic beliefs which underlie our constitutional system still appear to be valued by most students.

> The most encouraging news is in the area of respect for others. Most young people appear to respect the rights of people of other races, to understand the need for laws, and to recognize some problems faced by different groups of people.

> The decline in knowledge about the structure and function of

government and the essential concepts underlying democracy is most disappointing and should be the cause for a hard reassessment of the social studies curriculum. Results may reflect changes in curricular emphasis. Also, some of the facts assessed by the tests do not really constitute "essential" knowledge. It is more important to understand the basic concept of democracy, for example, than to remember that the Senate is the body that approves Presidential appointments.

Students' declining political participation may reflect the attitudes of the adult society. The 1970s have seen an increasing preoccupation with personal goals, a general disillusionment with the political process, and a trend toward conservatism. It is not surprising that youths have been influenced by these tendencies.

Students have improved in their understanding of ways to avoid future wars and to peacefully settle disputes between nations. This situation, probably a direct result of the national concern with the Vietnam war, may be an encouraging indication that students are becoming more aware of global interdependence.

Possible Factors in the Decline in Achievement

During the 1970s, declines have occurred in funding for the social studies, in consultant support at the state and local levels, and in the extent to which students take courses dealing with political knowledge. Dr. Ochoa cited a study by John Patrick of Indiana University which revealed that many social studies consultants are being eliminated or asked to turn to more general consulting tasks and that required course offerings have decreased. For example, only 26 states currently require students to take a unit in state government ....

The curriculum in the social studies has undergone changes in emphasis since 1969. In the 1960s social studies curricula tended to focus upon the separate disciplines. In the 1970s there has been more stress on the intellectual processes—understanding how to construct hypotheses, how to evaluate evidence, how to differentiate between facts and opinions, and so forth. This aspect of the social studies has for the most part not been evaluated by current testing efforts.

Students seemed to improve on facts and concepts which were reinforced by events reported in the media and to do less well on those which were not externally reinforced. For example, knowledge about the State Department improved during a period when Henry Kissinger was covered extensively by the media. However, knowledge about the Senate's role in approving treaties may well have declined because few controversial treaties were in the news.

Textbooks in the area of civics and government are often uninspiring. A review of several studies of textbooks presented by the American Political Science Association Committee on Pre-Collegiate Education in 1971 found that texts tended to emphasize "dreary descriptions" of such things as the powers and duties of government departments and officials and the step-by-step process by which a bill becomes law. Texts often presented an idealized view of the working of American democracy. The realities of the American political system were largely untreated, although students are certainly aware, through the media, that the system does not always work in an ideal fashion.

Teacher training in the social studies is far from uniform across the nation, and tends to neglect a basic study of the political and moral foundations of civic education. For instance, National Education Association data on social studies certification show that it would be possible to become a secondary social studies teacher with little or no training in government. Typically, social studies teachers major in one of the social science disciplines and then take courses in educational methods. Too often they are not prepared to teach inquiry skills and do not have an opportunity to develop a personal or professional philosophy of education appropriate to revitalized citizenship education....

The schools espouse concepts of democracy but often are run as autocratic communities where the students have little or no voice in decisions affecting them. The contrast between the "hidden curriculum" of the schools—implied through teacher attitudes, administration attitudes, methods of conducting school affairs—and the concepts taught in the social studies curriculum may affect student attitudes.

Schools appear to do fairly well in areas concentrated upon by teachers. For example, from 1971 to 1975, a time period roughly corresponding to that covered by the Citizenship and Social Studies assessments, the number of states having statewide projects in law-related approaches to citizenship education increased from six to 26, and the number of active projects jumped from 150 to 400. Performance did improve on many law-related items included in the assessment.[27]

Whatever the reasons for the declines as revealed by the NAEP tests, the general judgment of scholars in political science and in social studies was that in the 1960s students in the schools were alienated by the prevailing content, methods, and textbooks employed in the field of social studies.

In 1971, the Committee on Pre-Collegiate Education of the American Political Science Association reported on its survey of curriculum materials and textbooks in elementary and secondary school civics and government. Its major conclusions were that much of the material

• transmits a naive, unrealistic, and romanticized image of political life that confuses the ideals of democracy with the realities of politics

• places undue stress upon historical materials [a customary political science view], legal structures, and formal institutional aspects of government and fails to transmit adequate knowledge about political behavior and processes; and ignores or inadequately treats such traditionally important political science concepts as freedom, sovereignty, consensus, authority, class, compromise, and power, but also such newer concepts as role, socialization, culture, system, decision making, etc.

- reflects an ethnocentric preoccupation with American society and fails to transmit to students an adequate knowledge about the political systems of other national societies or the international system
- fails to develop within students a capacity to think about political phenomena in conceptually sophisticated ways; an understanding of, and skill in, the process of social science scientific inquiry; or a capacity to analyze systematically political decisions and values
- fails to develop within students an understanding of the capacities and skills needed to participate effectively and democratically in politics
- and, in conclusion, the sociopolitical organization of American schools, in conjunction with the formal curriculum in civics and government, combines to produce a situation where democratic theory has been so divorced from practice that students are skeptical of both and unable to develop an understanding of the skills necessary for meaningful participation in the political life of the society.[28]

Lest these views be taken solely as the supercilious judgments of academic scholars looking down on the schools, the general malaise in the social studies field at large has been amply documented, albeit from somewhat different orientations. For example, Richard E. Gross, professor of education at Stanford, conducted a survey of the changes taking place in the social studies across the nation during the years 1970 through 1975.[29] With his interest in history he did not interpret the situation exactly as the political scientists did, but their combined views do not lend encouragement to the civic role of the schools. Such views may help to explain some of the reasons for the general decline in political knowledge as measured by the NAEP tests.

Gross found a tendency for secondary schools to follow the lead of many colleges in permitting students to take almost any courses they wanted to take in grades 9 through 12. American history and U.S. government remain the dominant courses, but enrollments in both have markedly declined while enrollments in world history, world geography, civics, and problems of democracy have declined even more precipitously. There is no longer anything like a standard curriculum in the social studies. Some of this has to do with loosening of state requirements, but even more with the substitution of new social science courses, above all, psychology, which is the fastest growing course, but also economics, sociology, anthropology, ethnic studies, and the like. The popularity of psychology is undoubtedly related to the Yankelovich survey findings on the rise of interest in privatism with its strong focus on self.

As for the elementary schools, Gross found teachers backing away from the social studies, especially encouraged by the "back to basics" mania and minimum competency testing. To make matters worse, the newer teachers seemed even less interested in social studies than the older ones, and states were becoming more permissive in allowing local districts to interpret the state mandates. According to Gross, there seems to be a lack of interest in or even an active movement against the social studies by grassroots community groups. He comments somewhat pessimistically:

> This is a development which social studies teachers and organizations ought to be able to meet and thrust off if we are properly united, professionally active, and really believe in what we are doing. I am convinced, unfortunately, that a major force in the decline of the social studies is our own lack of conviction and persuasiveness as to the import of the field.[30]

In a study that followed hard on the heels of Gross's, John Jarolimek, professor of education at the University of Washington, Seattle, conducted intensive case studies of the social studies programs in six areas of the country: Boston, three cities in Ohio, an agricultural center in South Dakota, suburban San Francisco, San Antonio, and Birmingham. His basic finding was the astonishingly great diversity in social studies programs. His conclusion is particularly germane to the civic role of public education:

> It would seem that such diversity and lack of apparent effort to attend to critical elements of the common culture will have serious consequences for citizenship education unless this trend is reversed. Perhaps the only reason there is any similarity in programs at all is because schools everywhere continue to rely heavily on the content and teaching strategies suggested by nationally marketed textbooks.[31]

The importance of the textbook in social studies was reemphasized by several more surveys in the late 1970s. Three massive studies sponsored by the National Science Foundation have been usefully summarized by James P. Shaver, O.L. Davis, Jr., and Suzanne W. Helburn insofar as they apply to the social studies.[32] The findings reinforce the oft-stated proposition that the teacher is the key to what happens to the students in the classroom, no matter what a stated curriculum may say; the textbook is the dominant source of knowledge, tool of instruction, and focus of testing; whatever uniformity in social studies curriculums there may be across the country is mainly furnished by the publishers' textbooks, which exhibit great uniformity; and the impact of the "new social studies" of the 1960s projects has been relatively slight (approximately 10% to 20% of teachers reporting that they have used such material).

Of particular interest to me, also, is the evidence that social studies teachers consider their goals to include not only the teaching of knowledge about history, government, and geography, but that they should instill in their students positive feelings and attitudes about American society. They believe that part of their purpose in preparing students for good citizenship is developing what Shaver calls "emotive commitment" to the basic political values of American democracy. The problem, however, is twofold: Those teachers and parents who believe that basic values should be taught do not agree on what those values are; and the academic, scholarly community is wary of anything that sounds like indoctrination or inculcation of beliefs. The result has often been, as this chapter indicates, that teachers, administrators, and textbook publishers and writers have tried to avoid the controversial or the seamy side of American history or politics.

Another survey of a quite different sort was the widely acclaimed analysis of history textbooks written by Frances FitzGerald for *The New Yorker* and later published as a book.[33] In her telling fashion she describes how the texts reflected different moods in American society at different times in our history. Sometimes they adopted preachy, moralistic tones; sometimes they were bland and uncontroversial; sometimes they responded, as in the period prior to 1960, to pressures that came from political and economic right-wing groups; and more recently, they have responded to the pressures of single-issue groups. So that now the newest texts are full of racial diversity, ethnic pluralism, multicultural art work, and mention of some social "problems" that somehow seem to exist in a disembodied way with little sense of hard conflict and little sense of any kind of consensus.

At the annual convention of the Association for Supervision and Curriculum Development in Atlanta in March 1980, FitzGerald concluded her analysis of the history textbooks with the query "What shall be done?" She said that the lack of consensus and lack of a "common mythology" in the texts was not a bad thing: We should teach history as the story of the past, not to "develop values" or impose a "catechism." History teaching should be put back where it belongs—with the teacher.

But I wonder. Is it fair to pass over the basic ideas of the American democratic constitutional order as a "common mythology"? Or the development of common civic values as simply "preaching a catechism"? I do not believe we can leave it at that. In the face of the resurgence of a New Right in politics, economics, and religion; in the face of the growth of what Common Cause calls the "special-interest state" and single-issue politics; in the face of the prospect of a turning point in international affairs arising from the Islamic revolution in Iran and the Communist revolution in Afghanistan, we must reexamine once again the fundamental questions about education and citizenship.

So, as we are swept into the swirling educational rapids of the 1980s, how do we avoid on the one hand the Charybdis whirlpool of nationalistic jingoism, of religious fervor calling for Holy War at home and abroad, of authoritarian witch-hunting, or of pugnacious patriotism; and on the other hand the rock of Scylla: apathy, indifference, self-indulgence, blandness, and nervousness about dealing with controversy in the schools? And, finally, how do we cope with a third set of currents that buffets us in the middle of the channel, that is, the preoccupation of profession and public alike with the numerous riptides concerning the purposes and practices of education? They bubble up all around us in the form of "alternatives," "student centeredness," "reality therapy," "individual learning styles," "behavioral objectives," "fulfilling student needs," "teacher centering," "a parenting curriculum," "competency-based teacher education," and the multifaceted enticements of a curriculum smorgasbord. Now I do not mean to imply that all of our scattered and fragmented efforts to make the school curriculum flexible and diverse and innovative and relevant are unimportant. Far from it. But let me try to make my point as clearly as I can.

Several major professional education organizations have drawn up and circulated a statement called *Organizations for the Essentials of Education*, which they have collectively endorsed. The organizations include the Association for Supervision and Curriculum Development, the National Council for the Social Studies, the National Council of Teachers of English, the International Reading Association, the National Association of Elementary School Principals, the National Science Teachers Association, and the organizations serving teachers of mathematics, art, music, foreign languages, speech, health and physical education. I take it the major purpose of such a statement by these main-line organizations interested in the school curriculum is to resist easy formulas or pressures for back to the basics, minimal competency testing, and simplistic emphasis upon survival skills. They are arguing that American society must reaffirm the value of a balanced education resting upon the interdependence of skills and subject matter content of all the essential studies in the school curriculum. Let me quote three key sentences:

> What, then, are the essentials of education? Educators agree that the overarching goal of education is to develop informed, thinking citizens capable of participating in both domestic and world affairs. The development of such citizens depends not only upon education for citizenship, but also upon other essentials of education shared by all subjects.

I think that this is an excellent short statement. I hope that educators do agree. But note what I would underline: the *"overarching goal"* is developing *"informed, thinking citizens."* The opening sentence of the 1979 revised curriculum guidelines of the National Council for the Social Studies is very similar:

> The basic goal of social studies education is to prepare young people to be humane, rational, participating citizens in a world that is becoming increasingly interdependent.[34]

The *overarching* goal; the *basic* goal. That is why I argue that education for citizenship is the primary purpose of universal education; it is not solely nor primarily to serve the self-fulfillment of individuals, or to develop the mind for its own sake, or to get a job, or to get into college. These latter purposes have come to be important goals of education in the U.S., but the fundamental reason that some of the founders of this Republic called for public schooling was that the education of all the people was *essential* for the achievement and maintenance of a republican form of government. This purpose has been paramount in much of the subsequent efforts to establish a truly universal, free, common system of public schools, as I tried to show in Chapter 3.

Let me come back to the previously mentioned statement, *Organizations for the Essentials of Education*. After the general proposition that the overarching goal of education is to develop informed, thinking citizens, this is how the statement defines the essentials:

> More specifically, the essentials of education include the ability
>
> - to use language, to think, and to communicate effectively;
> - to use mathematical knowledge and methods to solve problems;
> - to reason logically;
> - to use abstractions and symbols with power and ease;
> - to apply and to understand scientific knowledge and methods;
> - to make use of technology and to understand its limitations;
> - to express oneself through the arts and to understand the artistic expressions of others;
> - to understand other languages and cultures;
> - to understand spatial relationships;
> - to apply knowledge about health, nutrition, and physical activity;
> - to acquire the capacity to meet unexpected challenges;
> - to make informed value judgments;
> - to recognize and to use one's full learning potential;
> - to prepare to go on learning for a lifetime.

Now I think this is an excellent short statement of the essentials for the educated *person*. It should appeal to the vast majority of the educational profession. But what happened to the overarching goal of developing *citizens*? All of these "essentials" will surely stand citizens in good stead, but I do not see that this statement, or any number of other curriculum guides I have seen, tries to make explicit what the meaning of citizenship is or should be, what explicit roles public citizens (as distinguished from private persons) should play in social and political

85

life. I do not find much clue as to what our "informed, thinking citizen" should be informed or think about in his or her role of *citizen*. I find no hint as to what kind of society or government it is that this citizen is being prepared to participate in.

I am quite prepared to admit that it may be unfair to criticize this short statement for not doing what it possibly did not intend to do. But I think it is fairly representative of many, many other curriculum statements about the goals of education. While it does lay claim to education's primary goal of preparing citizens, my argument is that we must now, more than ever, take seriously our claim that we are preparing citizens. This goal may not monopolize all of what we try to do in the schools, but it should come as the highest priority throughout the years of schooling. Many professional education associations are "person-oriented," and this is surely to the good. But now I think they should become more concerned about the person-as-citizen.

The basic ideas and values of citizenship should become the core of knowledge, thinking, and participation that make up the curriculum design for the educated citizen. I do not mean simply the moralistic preachments that FitzGerald makes fun of. Indeed, I would not mock the good intentions of those in the past who identified good citizenship in the schools with the effort to make good little boys and girls. This is not what I mean. Nor do I mean the long lists of general goals and purposes, or behavioral objectives, or specific competencies, or learning activities, or process skills that typically make up the scope and sequence plans drawn up by state or local curriculum committees.

I mean that the fundamental ideas and values upon which our constitutional order is built should be the core of sustained and explicit study, based upon realistic, scholarly knowledge, and searching criticism carried on throughout the school years from kindergarten through high school and the years of liberal general education in college. Now it is perfectly clear that there will not be universal agreement as to what these key ideas and values are, and it is clear that there will not be and should not be a single curriculum design imposed upon all schools in the nation. But I think that the profession should be trying much more rigorously and vigorously to become sophisticated and explicit about the substantive concepts and ideas that form the common core of American citizenship. In Chapter 4 I outline some significant movements toward this goal. In Chapter 5 I have used the term "democratic civic values" to define what I believe should be the core of citizenship education in the schools.

Chapter 3 Notes

1. For a full-scale discussion of this historical framework of analysis, see R. Freeman Butts, *Public Education in the United States: From Revolution to Reform* (New York: Holt, Rinehart and Winston, 1978).

2. Robert H. Wiebe, *The Segmented Society; An Historical Preface to the Meaning of America* (New York: Oxford University Press, 1975), pp. 124-125.

3. Ruth Miller Elson, *Guardians of Tradition; American Schoolbooks of the Nineteenth Century* (Lincoln, Nebr.: University of Nebraska Press, 1964), p. 195.

4. Ibid., p. 282.

5. Thomas Jefferson, *Notes on the State of Virginia*, 2nd American ed. (Philadelphia: 1794), pp. 215-216.

6. John C. Fitzpatrick, ed., *The Writings of George Washington, from the Original Manuscript Sources, 1745-1799* (Washington, D.C.: Government Printing Office 1940, vol. 35), pp. 316-317.

7. Saul K. Padover, *The Complete Jefferson* (New York: Duell, Sloan & Pierce, 1943), p. 1098.

8. Elson, *Guardians of Tradition*, p. 338.

9. George Bancroft, *History of the United States of America from the Discovery of the Continent*, 6 vols., vol. 1 (Boston: Little, Brown and Company, 1879), pp. 1-3.

10. Elson, *Guardians of Tradition*, p. 285.

11. Ibid., p. 340.

12. Lawrence A. Cremin, *The Republic and the School; Horace Mann on the Education of Free Men* (New York: Bureau of Publications, Teachers College, Columbia University, 1957), p. 93.

13. Ibid., p. 95.

14. Ibid., p. 97.

15. Taken from Daniel Calhoun, ed., *The Education of Americans: A Documentary History* (Boston: Houghton Mifflin, 1969), p. 495.

16. Hazel W. Hertzberg, *Historic Parallels for the Sixties and Seventies: Primary Sources and Core Curriculum Revisited* (Boulder, Colo.: Social Science Education Consortium, Publication #135, 1971), pp. 11-12.

17. National Education Association, Commission on the Reorganization of Secondary Education, *Cardinal Principles of Secondary Education*, U.S. Bureau of Education, Bulletin #35 (Washington, D.C.: Government Printing Office, 1918), p. 14.

18. Ibid., p. 14.

19. Educational Policies Commission, *The Purposes of Education in American Democracy* (Washington, D.C.: N.E.A. and A.A.S.A., 1938), p. 108.

20. American Association of School Administrators, *Educating for American Citizenship* (Washington, D.C.: A.A.S.A., 1954), p. 5.

21. Erling M. Hunt et al., *High School Social Studies: Perspectives* (Boston: Houghton Mifflin, 1962), pp. 99-100.

22. *Social Education* 36 (November 1972).

23. Research for Better Schools, *History of Citizen Education Colloquium* (Philadelphia, Winter 1978).

24. John Higham, *Strangers in the Land; Patterns of American Nativism, 1860-1925* (New York: Atheneum, 1974), Chapter 2.

25. Robert H. Wiebe, *The Search for Order, 1877-1920* (New York: Hill & Wang, 1967), pp. 154-155.

26. National Assessment of Educational Progress, *Changes in Political Knowledge and Attitudes, 1969-1976* (Denver: Education Commission of the States, March 1978).

27. Ibid., pp. 59-62.

28. American Political Science Association, Committee on Pre-Collegiate Education, "Political Education in the Public Schools: The Challenge for Political Science," PS 4 Newsletter of the American Political Science Association (Summer 1971). The general findings are characteristic of other writings in political socialization and political science. See, e.g., Frederick M. Wirt and Michael W. Kirst, *The Political Web of American Schools* (Boston: Little, Brown, 1972).

29. Richard E. Gross, "The Status of the Social Studies in the Public Schools of the United States: Facts and Impressions of a National Survey," *Social Education* (March 1977): 194-200 and 205.

30. Ibid., p. 199.

31. John Jarolimek, "The Status of Social Studies Education: Six Case Studies," *Social Education* (November/December 1977): 575-576.

32. James P. Shaver, O.L. Davis, Jr., and Suzanne W. Helburn, "An Interpretive Report on the Status of Pre-college Social Studies Education Based on Three NSF-Funded Studies" (Washington, D.C.: National Council for the Social Studies, 1978). For a brief summary of this report, see Shaver et al., "The Status of Social Studies Education: Impressions from Three NSF Studies," *Social Education* (February 1979): 150-153. For further comment, see Gerald Ponder, "The More Things Change...: The Status of Social Studies," *Educational Leadership* (April 1979): 515-518; and Donald O. Schneider and Ronald L. Van Sickle, "The Status of the Social Studies: The Publishers' Perspective," *Social Education* (October 1979): 461-465.

33. Frances FitzGerald, "Onward and Upward with the Arts: Rewriting American History," *The New Yorker* (26 February 1979; 5 March 1979; and 12 March 1979); see also *America Revised; History Schoolbooks in the Twentieth Century* (Boston: Atlantic-Little, Brown, 1979).

34. See *Social Education* (April 1979): 262.

Chapter 4

Signs of Revival

I n the 1970s a revival of interest in citizenship education began to sprout in a number of important places. Some key professional associations, a few private foundations, an increasing number of chief state school officers and school administrators, some politicians and officials in state and federal governments, some old and some new voluntary organizations, and a growing number of professionals and authors began to attack the problem from a variety of approaches.

Individual schools, school systems, and special projects run by universities and independent agencies began to try in one way or another to think through and do something about improving citizenship education in schools and communities.

I cannot possibly present here a thorough or systematic description of the revival momentum. I shall simply mention some of the major groups that have been involved. As I go along, I shall mention some of the key reports or documents that spell out in some detail the general trends or particular activities. This is more a personal report than an exhaustive survey. Several useful surveys of the "state of the art" have already been undertaken.[1] I would like to refer first to developments initiated by several professional associations, private foundations, and government agencies and then to outline some of the principal innovative approaches to civic education.

The Gathering Momentum

Among professional associations I found three that seemed to me to be most active during the past decade. The first is the American Political Science Association (APSA), which reversed its fairly long-standing position of ignoring the lower schools by appointing its Pre-Collegiate Committee in 1970. I have already mentioned its survey of civic and government programs in the elementary and secondary schools. Supported by a grant from the National Science Foundation, the Committee began its Political Science Course Content Improvement Project. It sponsored investigations of the political learning processes of elementary school children and the development of curriculum and teaching materials on the decision-making process. This was done at the

Mershon Center at Ohio State University under the direction of Richard C. Remy. Similarly, it sponsored the research and writing of a new textbook aimed at the high school government course. This undertaking was carried on at the Social Studies Development Center at Indiana University, which had produced a new government textbook in 1971 by Howard Mehlinger and John Patrick, *American Political Behavior*. The newer project, *Comparing Political Experiences*, was written by Judith Gillespie and Stuart Lazarus, with contributions from Mehlinger, Patrick, and others. Remy and Patrick have written *Civics for Americans* in a similar vein, stressing decision making in the political behavior of citizens.

These projects represent one very significant approach to reforming citizenship education, i.e., bringing up-to-date knowledge, concepts, and evidence from the discipline of political science into existing elementary and secondary school courses in civics and government. The projects are developed on the assumption that most teachers still rely heavily upon textbooks as the staple of their teaching and hoped-for learning. Thus, the APSA, through these projects, has been trying to remedy some of the glaring inadequacies of courses in the schools that its survey of 1971 revealed. In addition, the Pre-Collegiate Committee is in the process of sponsoring a book of readings on political education that promises to be an extremely valuable digest of research produced during the 1970s, mostly by political scientists, on such topics as the social and political functions of education; factors in political learning, such as learning theories, multi-ethnic backgrounds, and sex roles; the institutional context of political learning in schools, mass media, and families; the analysis of goals and outcomes of alternative as well as existing approaches to political instruction; and political education in worldwide perspective.

The second professional organization that renewed its interest in citizenship education in the 1970s was the National Council for the Social Studies (NCSS), which had published yearbooks on the subject in 1951, 1960, and 1967. In 1975 the NCSS governing board made a commitment to make citizenship education a top priority for discussion and action for the following three years. The presidents during this period were James P. Shaver of Utah State University, and Howard Mehlinger and Anna Ochoa, both of Indiana University. James Shaver issued the call in his presidential address in November 1976:

> If citizenship is the intended goal of social studies education, why not focus the National Council's attention on it?...There are organizations for historians *qua* historians, economists *qua* economists, psychologists *qua* psychologists, political scientists *qua* political scientists, and so on. Why not one organization in which we ask the subject matter specialists to join with those of us who are...social

studies specialists...to address the very significant question of what citizenship education should be in this society. The central query for NCSS should not be how to teach history, or economics, or political science better, but rather: What contribution does each have to make to citizenship education?[2]

So the NCSS gave a great deal of attention to citizenship education from 1975 to 1978 at its national and regional meetings, including workshops conducted by a variety of special civic education projects for teachers who were ready to undertake new approaches to the old task of citizenship education. These meetings became valuable gathering places for those who wished to bring together a fragmented series of separate projects into something like a coherent constituency. In 1977 the Council published a bulletin titled *Building Rationales for Citizenship Education,* edited by Shaver, and containing significant papers by Fred M. Newmann of the University of Wisconsin/Madison and Dan Conrad and Diane Hedin of the University of Minnesota. In 1980 NCSS, under the presidency of Todd Clark, moved even more vigorously to reaffirm that citizenship education was the basic goal of all social studies education.

The third professional association that had a major impact in the 1970s is the American Bar Association (ABA), which established in 1971, while Leon Jaworski was president, its Special Committee on Youth Education for Citizenship. The Special Committee consists of nine or 10 lawyers who are members of ABA along with an Advisory Commission consisting of a dozen educators who are especially concerned with citizenship education. The Committee has injected into current usage the term "law-related education" by which it means the effort to improve the citizenship knowledge, skills, and attitudes of American youth by promoting an understanding of law, the legal process, the legal system, and the fundamental principles and values upon which they are based.

Under the leadership first of Joel F. Henning and then of Norman Gross, the staff of the Committee has been very active in promoting conferences, holding meetings, publishing working papers, directories, and guidelines to stimulate school systems, individual schools, and teachers to try some form of law-related education.[3] It does not have a particular approach, curriculum, or methodology to promote, but tries to act as a facilitating and catalytic agent for innovation in the field. The number of projects, ranging from a few teachers in a single school to statewide programs, has mushroomed from around 100 in 1971 to something between 400 and 500 in 1978; and statewide programs have expanded from five or six states in 1971 to as many as 35 in 1978.

As a member of the ABA Advisory Commission since 1976, I can testify to the value of the regular interchange of ideas among lawyers and educators. The reciprocal teaching and learning that takes place in

91

an atmosphere of open, free, and critical discussion has been extremely useful for both professions. Especially useful in this connection has been the project funded by the National Endowment for the Humanities in which seven different projects have been attempting to design distinctive models for introducing and infusing law-related education through the humanities into elementary schools. These projects are described in *Synergy* (Winter/Spring 1979) and *Social Education* (May 1980).

Of the private foundations, the Danforth Foundation of St. Louis, Missouri, seemed to have the most consistent and effective record in supporting citizenship education activities during most of the 1970s. It has a long-standing interest in ethical education, especially at the collegiate level, and when it formally entered the precollegiate level in 1975, much of its concern moved toward citizenship education under the leadership of Gene L. Schwilck, president, and Geraldine Bagby, vice-president and chairperson of the Foundation's Pre-Collegiate Committee. In the 1960s major grants by the Foundation went to such agencies as the Lincoln Filene Center for Citizenship and Public Affairs at Tufts University, the American Heritage Foundation, the Council for Civic Education in Washington, D.C., and the Foreign Policy Association, New York City.

In the 1970s the Danforth Foundation gave partial support to several special projects that together represent three of the major approaches to citizenship education: 1) law-related education (Constitutional Rights Foundation, Los Angeles, and Law in a Free Society, Santa Monica, California); 2) moral development (Harvard, Boston, and Carnegie-Mellon Universities); and 3) community action programs for school-age youth (Minneapolis, Minnesota, and Madison, Wisconsin). I shall have more to say about each of these later, for I was fortunate enough to be able to gain some first-hand knowledge of these projects in 1977-1978 at the request of the Danforth Foundation. The Danforth Foundation has also cooperated with the Ford Foundation in several projects, especially through the efforts of Edward J. Meade, Jr., in the public education program at Ford. Danforth helped to sponsor the National Task Force on Citizenship Education from 1975 to 1977 in cooperation with the Kettering Foundation under the leadership of Samuel G. Sava, Kettering's vice-president for educational activities, and B. Frank Brown, director of information and services for Kettering's Institute for Development of Educational Activities. Brown acted as director of the Task Force. I served as chairperson of the meetings of the Task Force's Advisory Committee, whose report contained some key chapters about major directions for civic education.

The middle years of the 1970s also saw an awakened interest in citizenship education by some key persons in the federal government. Largely through the initiative of Frank Brown, a number of us were able to convince President Ford's staff assistant for the Domestic Council that a prospective White House Conference on Education should focus attention upon education for citizenship, a subject we thought highly appropriate in the wake of the Watergate scandal. But in the summer of 1975, Secretary of HEW Caspar Weinberger vetoed the idea of a White House Conference on Education, largely on the grounds that it would probably call for larger amounts of spending, which was contrary to President Ford's approach to government at that time.

Soon afterward, a new secretary of HEW was appointed, David Mathews, on leave from the presidency of the University of Alabama. Through the initiative of Geraldine Bagby, several of us were invited to meet with Mathews to talk about his concern to increase citizen participation in governmental affairs in general, as well as in education. So, in October 1975, Mathews invited Bagby, Schwilck, Brown, Sava, Stephen K. Bailey, then vice-president of the American Council on Education, and myself, along with Terence Bell, U.S. Commissioner of Education, and members of their staffs and consultants to attend a meeting in his office.

We did indeed find that Secretary Mathews was deeply concerned about education for citizenship, and had a deep interest in changing citizenship from a spectator sport to genuine participation in affairs of government, especially in the affairs of the HEW bureaucracy. At the meeting, Secretary Mathews asked Commissioner Bell to take steps to see what the Office of Education could do to promote citizen participation and citizenship education. Bell quickly appointed a citizen education staff to advise him and called a meeting of some 45 to 50 key persons to discuss what the federal government's policy should be. It was at that meeting in December 1975 that several of us presented working papers. In mine, I stated briefly the principles that should guide civic education in the schools (see Chapter 5).

A major national conference on education and citizenship was held in Kansas City in September 1976, sponsored jointly by the U.S. Office of Education and the Council of Chief State School Officers. The Kansas City conference brought together representatives of business, labor, community groups, voluntary agencies along with educators, and it did focus some national attention upon the problem. It may have done more good than a White House conference on Education, whose topics would have been dispersed over the whole range of problems of education and work. A direct outcome of the Kansas City conference was the organization of the Alliance for Citizen Education with headquarters at the Institute for the Study of Civic Values in Philadelphia under the leadership of Edward Schwartz. Labor, church, youth, and neighborhood groups make up its principal clientele.

The Citizen Education staff in the U.S.O.E., first under the leadership of Logan Sallada and then of Elizabeth Farquahar, shifted the emphasis somewhat away from a special interest in civic education in the schools and toward what came to be called "citizen education."

This term was used to convey the idea that all kinds of voluntary agencies have a role in the education of citizens along with the schools. Several conferences and several publications addressed the topics of just what these roles might be with regard, for example, to citizen education through the workplace, the mass media, and through all sorts of participation in voluntary and governmental agencies.[4]

A major sign that the U.S.O.E. staff was tapping a vital movement was the holding of the National Conference on Citizen Participation in September 1978, which attracted more than 650 persons representing hundreds of voluntary and governmental organizations. It was co-sponsored by the Lincoln Filene Center for Citizenship and Public Affairs, Common Cause, Interagency Council on Citizen Participation, League of Women Voters Education Fund, National Association of Neighborhoods, National League of Citizens, National Municipal League, United Way of America, and the Urban League. The featured speakers were Senator Edward Kennedy, Alvin Toffler, and Ralph Nader. Although citizenship education in the schools was a relatively minor theme, the conference gave wide notice to the importance of citizen participation in government and in public affairs.

While the U.S.O.E. Citizen Education staff was at work on citizen participation, another working group was established in U.S.O.E. to make recommendations concerning what the federal government should be doing in the field of law-related education. This study group was chaired by Steven Y. Winnick of the HEW General Counsel's office; its members included staff from the General Counsel's office, the National Endowment for the Humanities, the National Institute of Education, the Office of Juvenile Justice and Delinquency Prevention of the Justice Department, as well as the U.S.O.E. Its final report, submitted in September 1978, was based on consultations with a wide range of persons from the academic and professional worlds.

In the course of its deliberation between November 1977 and September 1978, I had some concerns that the study group would define the scope of law-related education too narrowly and thus become one more special-interest effort seeking federal government support, along with such categories as metric education, consumer education, environmental education, drug abuse education, and the like. I was concerned about fragmentation of effort. But by the time the study group's report was finished, I was convinced that it was an excellent statement and had probably gone as far toward my views as the realities of the political process would permit—and still result in some desirable action.

The Study Group defined law-related education as follows:

...education that is designed to give people an adequate base of knowledge and training about the law, the legal process, and the legal system that, as part of their *general* education, enables them to be

94

more informed and effective citizens. Law-related education includes education relating to government institutions and processes for making and administering laws [especially the Bill of Rights and other Constitutional law], the principles of freedom, justice, and democracy (as well as other values underlying the legal system), and laws influencing the daily lives of citizens [such as conflict and dispute resolution or avoidance; criminal, consumer, labor, administrative, environmental, and family law]. It also includes education about the role and limits of law in a democratic society [both past and present; issues of freedom, authority, enforcement, punishment and resolution of social and political issues]. For the Study Group's purposes, law-related education includes school programs for elementary and secondary school students and adult and community law-related education programs; it does not include direct training for careers in law.[5]

The report recommended that federal funds should be provided to enable the U.S.O.E. and other federal agencies to grant funds to state and local agencies to promote law-related education as defined above. The conclusions and recommendations were as follows:

• Law-related education should be recognized as an integral part of each person's basic education for becoming a knowledgeable and responsible citizen.

• Promoting the "legal literacy" of citizens safeguards our democratic institutions and is a national interest which justifies federal support of law-related education.

• There is need at this time for O.E. support to build upon the rich diversity of programs and materials in law-related education among educators, and to provide training in law-related education for teachers and administrators....

• O.E. should work closely with other federal agencies such as the Justice Department's Law Enforcement Assistance Administration and the National Endowment for the Humanities, which should continue their support of law-related projects.

• O.E. should establish a discretionary program (under the Special Projects Act) to fund grants and contracts to support law-related education activities.

• In addition, O.E. should provide technical assistance and information to state and local educational agencies and other potential applicants to promote use of other O.E. funds to support law-related education. Training should be provided for O.E. employees to increase their understanding of law-related education and its relationship to their program responsibilities.[6]

In the course of the Study Group's deliberations, I wrote a letter expressing my hopes regarding what it would recommend. My preference would be federal funding to help the states and local districts to improve what they are already mandated to do with regard to education for citizenship, i.e., prepare the young to appreciate the

95

historic values of American democratic institutions, to understand the realistic workings of the basic constitutional order and political processes, and to take informed and responsible part in the civic affairs of local community, state, and nation.

My point was that law-related education as defined in the study group report was only one approach to better citizenship education for children and youth. The recent report of the National Task Force on Citizenship Education, *Education for Responsible Citizenship*, sponsored by the Danforth and Kettering Foundations, outlined several other approaches. Among these are efforts to improve instruction in the academic disciplines that undergird citizenship (especially history, the humanities, and the social sciences); to focus attention in social studies courses upon the pressing social issues that face policy makers in our domestic and foreign affairs; to promote critical analysis of ethical issues and moral dilemmas that face citizens in their various stages of moral development; and to enhance the quality of students' participation in the affairs of their schools and communities as a means of learning to become effective citizens.

I believe that federal funding, if and when it comes, should be available for state and local agencies of education to experiment with and develop programs that will include this variety of approaches to civic education in addition to the law-related approach. I believe that significant and creative work is being done in each of these approaches; that each needs the stimulus of federal funding for research, development, dissemination, and teacher training; and that state and local school systems should be allowed to select among them significant ways to meet their varying circumstances. This has been our historic solution to the dilemma posed by the need to achieve political and social cohesion while at the same time serving the pluralistic values of diversity.

If I had been writing the study group report or the subcommittee's legislative proposals, I would have opted for strengthening the overall civic role of the schools as the "first of the basics." I would have stressed the fact that the original purpose of universal public education as viewed by the founders of the American Republic was to prepare all persons for their roles as citizens in the new representative democracy. The basic purpose for teaching everyone to read and write was not so that they could get a job, or get into college, but so that they could perform the duties of citizenship. I would remind the present enthusiasts for "back to basics" that perhaps they have forgotten the most basic reason for the basics of literacy.

I would have argued for a broader conception of civic education and for the need to revitalize and strengthen the several approaches to it. Although my views on the broader conception of civic education were not fully accepted by the study group, I was persuaded that law-related education was finally defined broadly enough so that it could include my concerns for instruction in the basic political, philosophical, and moral values of American democratic citizenship. I believe that the study group's reference to the values and principles upon which the legal system is based embraces the definition of the goals of law-related education as given by Paul Freund, university professor of law at Harvard. He designated three goals. The second and third were understanding the functions of law and acquiring information about the law, but his *first* goal was the most important:

> First of all, there is the goal of learning moral reasoning or ethical analysis by continued practice in reaching decisions and having to justify them. I put this goal first because if I am right in thinking that some facility in moral reasoning is a product of the introduction of law into the schools, then the result is not limited to the knowledge of the law. It can pervade the entire educational process for the student who has learned the art. It carries over, in other words, throughout his active life.[7]

There were several other references in the report to the principles of freedom, justice, and democracy underlying the legal system and its operation that led me to believe that the "law" was being interpreted to embrace virtually the entire political system and the overall political community in their broadest senses, as well as the more narrowly construed constitutional regime and day-to-day political process.

I realized that the study group's mandate was to deal with law-related education, and it therefore could not readily broaden the topic to civic education in general. I recognized that the realities of the political process in Congress were such that a large number of influential senators and representatives (who are lawyers) would be impressed by the term "law-related education." I realized that there is a good deal of ambivalence and ambiguity among educators over the meaning and importance of the term "citizenship education." And, I realized the tactical importance of getting *something* into the legislation that would promote the improvement of civic education in schools across the nation.

But I urged the study group to do at least two things, assuming that it could not change the term itself from "law-related education" to "civic-related education" (as I would prefer):

1. Define law-related education in the much broader context of civic education so that any funding that might come along would not be narrowly confined to a particular approach but would unmistakably embrace the variety I have mentioned.

2. Recommend that Congress and the U.S.O.E. consider the study group's proposals for law-related education as simply a first step leading to a broader initiative in citizenship education. While the study group did not come out for the broader initiative, I still believe that the

process of improving the overall civic role of American education should be promoted in a variety of ways, so long as all of them are based upon sound scholarship and valid pedagogy. I would not like to see a narrow conception of law-related education locked into the legislative enactments or into the federal funding guidelines and regulations.

Congress approved in the summer of 1978 an amendment as Title III, Part G, to the Elementary and Secondary Education Act that authorized the U.S. Commissioner of Education "to carry out a program of grants and contracts to encourage state and local educational agencies and other public and private nonprofit agencies, organizations, and institutions to provide law-related education programs." While no funds were recommended by the Carter administration and no funds were appropriated by this Law-Related Education Act of 1978, the first major legislative step had been taken along the general lines recommended by the study group. Section 347 of Title III defines law-related education as "education to equip nonlawyers with knowledge and skills pertaining to the law, the legal process, and the legal system, and the fundamental principles and values on which these are based."

Thus, through the efforts of the Study Group on Law-Related Education and the Citizen Education staff of U.S.O.E., some excellent groundwork had been laid by early 1980 that could provide the basis for a federal role in promoting civic education in the schools. Whether the political clout could be mustered to move forward remained to be seen. I hope that Judge Shirley Hufstedler's role as Secretary of Education will include strong advocacy for civic education in the new Department.

Meanwhile, the states were responding with considerable alacrity to the political demands that something ought to be done about citizenship education. Most states already had on their books a considerable body of mandates that, one way or another, related to citizenship education in the schools. A comprehensive study of such mandates made by the Special Committee on Youth Education for Citizenship of the American Bar Association summarized the situation as of 1974-1975:

• Statutes in 45 states prescribe the study of constitutions (41 of both federal and state constitutions and four of the federal constitution only).

• Statutes in 43 states require the study of American history (33 of both state and nation and 10 of nation only).

• Statutes in 38 states require study of civics and government in some form.

• Every state has one or more of the above statutes on its books.

• 41 states prohibit graduation from high school for any students who have not taken the required courses on constitution or history or government.

• Statutes in 38 states require inculcation of various kinds of values or attitudes. These range from morality, piety, truth, benevolence, sobriety, frugality, moderation, and temperance to civic virtues, loyalty, and patriotism.[8]

The Special Committee's study found that the enforcement or implementation of such laws and the regulations following upon them varied greatly. Many social studies teachers were not even aware of such mandates, while others assumed that suggested state curriculum guidelines were compulsory and were to be followed explicitly. In general, most educators thought that some kind of mandate was desirable, so long as it did not prescribe curriculum or methods too closely and did not involve indoctrination of students or political advocacy by teachers.

Since the data for the ABA Special Committee's study were gathered, several new trends in state legislation and regulations have been observed, as reported by LeAnn Meyer in her analysis for the Education Commission of the States. She reports that since 1973, about one-half of the states have taken action of some kind related to citizenship education, usually requiring a course or a unit on some topic. As many as eight states have moved to require the study of the "free enterprise system" sometimes in connection with "government" or "Americanism." The use of this phrase in legislation usually implies a positive position will be taken in teaching about the private economic sector and the free market. A second trend that Meyer reports is the recent legislative stampede to require tests of minimum competency in the basic skills for high school graduation. Of the 36 states that have initiated such programs, a research study by Chris Pipho of the Education Commission of the States indicates that 10 states have included citizenship as one of the subjects to be tested.[9]

A third trend in the state initiatives that may be related to civic education is what is often referred to as "values education" or "moral education" or "ethical-citizenship education." The latter term is used by Research for Better Schools in Philadelphia. A well-publicized Gallup poll in 1976 revealed that two-thirds of those polled believed that schools should be more active in shaping desirable moral behavior of school children. Pursuing this theme, Mark Blum of the University of Louisville conducted for Research for Better Schools a survey of the several state departments of education to see what they said they were doing or planning to do in this field. Blum reports that all 46 states that responded were planning to integrate the values and principles identified with the history of democratic institutions in the U.S. into any new civic education effort; and that 31 states had begun major revisions in their citizenship education programs since 1970.[10]

Blum points out that the vast majority of state department of education responses agreed that ethical and moral values should somehow be related to civic education, whether in the curriculum content or skills

99

development; whether in regular courses or in special projects; whether in curriculum guides or teacher training activities; whether in the humanities or the behavioral sciences. Blum then classifies the major efforts of the states into nine categories of ethical-citizenship education and tabulates the number of states involved:

1. Values education
   a. Values clarification (38 states)
   b. Concrete values necessary for every citizen,
      e.g., liberty, equality (39 states)
2. Moral reasoning (mostly Kohlberg) (14 states)
3. Personal development (eight states)
   a. Deliberate psychological education
   b. Family therapy
   c. Self-enhancing education
   d. Life-skills education
4. Prosocial behavioral training,
   e.g., behavior modification, especially for delinquents (four states)
5. Law-related education (30 states)
6. Community education (seven states)
7. School-community education (25 states)
8. Economic-political practicum education (five states)
9. Consumer education (21 states)[11]

I have considerable difficulty sorting out the bases of classification in this analysis. I have even more difficulty including within the rubric of citizenship education such activities as values clarification, personal development, prosocial behavior modification, school-community education, and work-study plans (unless they are defined carefully), or consumer education. It seems to me that such an all-inclusive approach to civic education is likely to lead to yet another laundry list of "competencies" or "values" or "behaviors," each of which may have some intrinsic usefulness but which provides no coherent or consistent framework by which to judge what civic education is or ought to be.

Major Approaches to the Reform of Civic Education

A much more useful analysis, to my way of thinking, is that of Fred Newmann of the University of Wisconsin/Madison as published in the report of the National Task Force on Citizenship Education. He lists eight approaches to citizenship education that may indeed not be mutually exclusive but that are usually identifiable:

Academic disciplines (history and the social sciences). This approach tries to teach facts, concepts, and generalizations about social phenomena (past and present and across cultures) as such knowledge has been generated through scholarship in the academic disciplines, especially history and the social sciences. In the last 15 years special attempts have been made to teach not only the findings of these

100

disciplines, but also the methods of inquiry employed by the practicing scholar [the "new" social studies of the 1960s]. Rather than focusing on specific problems that the citizen might face, the approach assumes that mastery of developed scholarly systems will help the citizen understand unforeseeable, particular problems in civic matters as they arise.

Often, the teaching of the disciplines is not advocated on grounds of direct relevance to the exercise of active citizenship. Instead, it has been argued that disciplined scholarship reveals the best thinking educators have to offer in the human search for truth. In spite of a plethora of proposals to relax the dominance of history and social science in citizenship education, these disciplines remain the staple, prevailing approach in secondary curricula and in the preparation of teachers.

Law-related education. The earliest forms of law-related education emphasized the Constitution, the Bill of Rights, the structure of federal, state, and local government—often in a ninth-grade civics course or a later course in American government. More recently a major national effort, supported by such groups as the American Bar Association and the Constitutional Rights Foundation, has tried to revitalize and expand the teaching of fundamentals of legal process. The movement offers diverse projects on legal concepts—particular controversies arising out of the Bill of Rights, the system of juvenile justice, techniques of legislative lobbying, judicial reasoning in case law, laws that apply particularly to youth, problems of law enforcement agencies, and other topics. The projects produce curriculum that can be inserted into existing courses as well as materials that stand on their own as separate courses in legal process. Projects vary in depth, detail, self-sufficiency, and the extent to which they encourage students to adopt a critical posture or one of unquestioning obedience and respect. In contrast to the disciplines approach, the goal of law-related education could be characterized not as a search for truth and understanding but as an effort to preserve and make more just the role of law in a democratic society.

Social problems. This approach concentrates on particular social issues of current or predicted importance in the students' lives, such as war, crime, discrimination, poverty, pollution, drugs, and energy [the "new" social studies of the 1970s]. The knowledge from the disciplines and about legal process may be used to clarify such problems, but the problem (not the discipline or the legal material) is the focus of study. The assumption here is that to deliberate adequately on social problems, the citizen needs practice in grappling with the specifics of actual social issues. (How should consumers be protected? What alternatives to welfare are available? What are the effects of racial busing?) This approach has been adopted in Problems of Democracy courses, and more recently in separate, discrete courses on problems like those just mentioned.

Critical thinking. Like democracy and motherhood, critical thinking in citizenship education is endorsed by almost everyone. The critical

101

citizen is portrayed as someone who cannot be deceived or manipulated by leaders and the media but who reaches autonomous conclusions and can rationally justify them to others. He is aware of basic assumptions in his own position, the possibility of bias or selective perception, and incompleteness of information. To arrive at this point, the citizen needs to learn a thinking process that helps distinguish among different types of issues, a process that offers a method for testing and evaluating empirical claims, logical inferences, definitional statements, value judgments, and so on.

Separate courses on critical thinking are rare; the requisite skills, if taught at all, are taught usually in connection with a particular subject such as history, economics, or social problems. The teaching of inquiry skills in the social sciences often is equated with critical thinking, but some scholars have suggested that the specific intellectual operations required for critical thinking about citizenship differ in important ways from those of other kinds of critical thinking. In this sense the critical thinking approach has as much potential for diversity as any of the approaches reviewed thus far.

Values clarification. To the extent that civic problems result from confusion over values, educators might relieve personal and social stress by helping individuals clarify their own ultimate values. The goal of values clarification is to help people to become "purposeful, enthusiastic, and positive," and to direct their lives autonomously through a process of deliberate "choosing, prizing, and acting." Students try to discover what they value by making their own decisions in various dilemmas and trying to determine whether their decisions were actually freely arrived at, with due consideration of alternatives. They try to determine whether they prize their decision, would proclaim it publicly, and would act on it consistently. Values clarification exercises may be added to existing courses or taught in special courses on values. The issues called up for scrutiny in this approach can include, but need not concentrate upon, problems of public policy.

Moral development. Kohlberg and associates see moral development not as preaching but as progress along a naturally occurring psychological path, which leads from the lower "preconventional" to "conventional" to the higher "principled" forms of moral reasoning. It is alleged, for example, that the principles enunciated in the Declaration of Independence, the Constitution, and the Bill of Rights can be understood only by people who have attained higher stages in cognitive development. Kohlberg argues that the higher, principled types of reasoning are ethically and epistemologically better than the lower stages. The higher stages signify a concern for social contract, equal liberty, and more generally the principles of justice that a democracy presumably aspires to attain.

In this approach students are presented with moral dilemmas (such as a man trying to decide whether to steal an overpriced drug to save his dying wife), and are asked to reason with each other about the morally right solution....According to the theory, students will discover inadequacies in their reasoning as they confront persons who reason at higher stages. The desire to resolve conflicts and move toward a consistent position will lead to adoption of more sophisticated reasoning patterns. In contrast to values clarification (suggesting a relativistic, nonjudgmental philosophy in which all student responses are supported by the teacher), moral development recognizes certain types of reasoning as universally better than others and seeks to advance students from the lower to the higher levels.

Community involvement. All six approaches above call for instruction in the school and a style of learning based largely on abstract analysis and verbal communication. Concerned that such curricula tend to isolate students from experience in the "real world," advocates of community involvement try to move students into the nonschool community in order to observe social process as it occurs, to make surveys on community needs and problems, to render volunteer service to social agencies, to create new youth-operated programs, to participate in electoral politics and community organization, and to participate in other forms of direct citizen action. Involvement and participation are emphasized not as substitutes for study and reflection, but as insurance that study and reflection will be directed toward social realities and participation skills.

Community involvement curricula can reflect different ideologies. Volunteer service in social agencies could be promoted, for example, as an attempt to build altruistic behavior, as a way to give students a sense of worth and to enhance self-esteem, as a technique for raising student consciousness about contradictions and injustice in society, or as a method of pacifying and co-opting youth rebellion. All the ideologies have in common a belief in "learning by doing," "experiential learning," or dealing with concrete "here and now" realities.

Institutional school reform. The structure and general quality of life in school may have more impact on citizenship than does the official curriculum or course content. Critics who agree that the "hidden curriculum" is educationally dysfunctional may differ as to the appropriate direction for institutional reform. Liberal critics claim that one cannot teach democracy in an authoritarian institution and that the school should, therefore, be reformed to give students full rights of citizenship. This would include a meaningful role (not necessarily unilateral power) in the governance of the institution, and the right to all the constitutional protections afforded adult citizens. In exercising responsibility for their own education and resolving inevitable conflicts in governing a public institution, students would learn better how to function responsibly in the society.

Conservative critics, on the other hand, claim that formal education implies an authoritarian structure. Students are required to attend school precisely because they are judged incompetent to perform the role of responsible adult citizens. One should not mislead students into believing they have full rights of citizenship, but should teach them to obey and to respect the authority that legitimately governs them until they gain their citizenship rights (by either earning a diploma or reaching the age at which the society judges them "mature" enough to participate). While some conservatives might endorse expansion of students' rights to due process in disciplinary matters, they would be unlikely to relinquish authority to students for governing the school or for prescribing educational practice.[12]

I agree with Newmann that the approaches that seem most promising for a revival of the civic learning are law-related education, moral development, and community involvement. I would also include what he calls institutional school reform, if it involves deliberate efforts to democratize the school community. I will try to explain later my reasons for emphasizing these four approaches. The need to be more rigorously concerned about the distinctive political meaning of citizenship education is further illustrated by one more composite list of content areas or approaches that are presumed to be associated with citizenship education. Drawing upon several sources, LeAnn Meyer identifies the following:

1. Academic disciplines—history and political science
2. Social problems
3. Critical thinking; decision making
4. Values clarification and skills; concrete values
5. Ethics; moral development
6. Community involvement; action skills; community education
7. Law-related education
8. Economics; free enterprise education
9. Global perspectives education
10. Family-related education
11. Multi-ethnic education; pluralism
12. Personal development and social skills; prosocial behavioral training.[13]

This does not include other social studies concerns, such as the academic disciplines of sociology and psychology, career awareness/ development, consumer education, and environmental and energy education—although some persons would include one or more of these items on the list also.

This may not even be the complete laundry list, but it will do to illustrate the "overload" that has been heaped upon schools by concerned public and professional interests. From my perspective and experience in the past five years, I see more hope for civic education in projects that now come under the heading of moral development, law-related education, and community involvement than in the others. I also see great value in those aspects of the academic disciplines, the study of pressing social problems, decision making, global perspectives, and multi-ethnic education that stress the public and political issues involved in them. The test I would use is whether or not the content and approach deal *primarily* with issues of political policy. Much interesting and valuable knowledge may be achieved in the other approaches, but it may or may not be properly focused upon citizenship education. I see little point in trying to stretch the scope of civic education to include such private activities as values clarification, family-related education, or personal development and social skills. Again, these may be perfectly useful, interesting, and personally rewarding activities, but I think we should concentrate on the prime *political* purposes of civic education. We should not dilute it with an array of efforts directed at what Newmann calls the "economic mission" of schooling (concentrating on the virtues of the free enterprise system or on the student as producer and consumer of goods and services), or the "psychological mission" (facilitating individual cognitive-affective growth), or the "cultural mission" (transmitting broad aspects of the human search for truth, beauty, and goodness).[14]

I believe that the main burden of civic education is covered in three chapters in the previously mentioned National Task Force report, those by Stephen K. Bailey on the enveloping polity; by Howard D. Mehlinger on the crisis in civic education; and by Isidore Starr on the necessity to come to terms with five basic political ideas: liberty, justice, equality, property, and power.[15] These writers' statements are good examples of fundamental assumptions underlying a law-related approach to citizenship education.

For my own part, I have found one of the most important examples of this approach to be the Law in a Free Society project, under the direction of Charles Quigley. It is a civic education project sponsored by the State Bar of California and principally funded by the National Endowment for the Humanities and the Danforth Foundation. The project's affiliation with the State Bar of California is a powerful aid in attracting widespread public recognition to its potential significance. At the same time, its executive committee of lawyers and educators has been able to maintain intellectual and ideological autonomy from special interest intervention because of its respect for high standards of scholarship in the fields of political science, history, law, philosophy, and literature.

The Law in a Free Society resources include lesson plans, case books, course outlines, teachers' guidelines, and multimedia instructional materials organized around eight basic concepts that lie at the heart of a free society: authority, justice, freedom, participation, responsibility, diversity, privacy, and property. These fundamental ideas of a democratic political community are used as the basis for helping students realize the values and the knowledge necessary for effective citizenship.

The Law in a Free Society project has produced and disseminated highly literate curriculum materials that have been extensively field-tested in schools in California and elsewhere. They have been organized into five-week units designed to be used in regular social studies courses from kindergarten through twelfth grade.

Inservice courses for teachers have been conducted in many parts of California and elsewhere. Lawyers, judges, and criminal justice personnel as well as other community members often take part in these workshops. I am greatly attracted to the concepts and the supporting materials. They are exceptionally well organized, clear, and meaningful. Their influence on my own views will be evident in Chapter 5.

There are other examples of excellent and creative materials being developed by law-related education projects. I have a high regard for the Constitutional Rights Foundation in Los Angeles under the leadership of Vivian Monroe and Todd Clark, and for its quarterly periodical *Bill of Rights in Action* and its volumes on "living law," *Criminal Justice* and *Civil Justice.* There are still other projects that appeal to students because of their practical relevance to the juvenile justice system and to legal matters that affect youth and their families. Some of the better known are the Institute for Political and Legal Education in New Jersey, the Citizenship Development Program at the Mershon Center at Ohio State University, and the National Street Law Institute in Washington, D.C.

In addition to the Law in a Free Society project, I have had the opportunity to become personally acquainted with several civic education projects using an approach generally referred to as moral development and associated with the work of Lawrence Kohlberg of Harvard University. It is a part of a renewed public and professional interest in the teaching of values, but it is to be distinguished from the "values clarification" movement that gained widespread popularity in the late 1960s and early 1970s under the impetus especially of Sidney B. Simon at the University of Massachusetts. Like many others, I find the values clarification approach largely a matter of self-revelation and self-understanding but of little import for civic education.

Quite different is Kohlberg's theory of moral development, whose research on the sequential stages of moral development has particular relevance to civic education. He has personally been involved in applying his theory to civic education at the high school in Cambridge, Mass.; and variations on the theme have been carried out by Ralph Mosher of Boston University at the high school in Brookline, Mass., and by Edwin Fenton of Carnegie-Mellon University at several high schools in the Pittsburgh area, in Bakersfield, Cal., and elsewhere. While visiting schools in Cambridge, Brookline, and Pittsburgh, I became acquainted with the principal consultants and several of their staff members and teachers.

In each case Kohlberg's stages of moral development provide the theoretical foundation for an effort to reform the curriculum in social studies and English. Using hypothetical and real moral dilemmas with discussion-centered teaching, the goal is to establish a democratic community for the students and teachers by dealing with actual problems that involve the rules and regulations that guide their public lives. Kohlberg's theory of the stages of moral development has attracted enormous attention in the academic world, and it is not without its critics. But if it contributes to actual changes in curriculum and in school governance, it may turn out to be an important catalyst in the revival of civic learning in the schools.

Kohlberg's stages of moral development are not intended to be taught to students or to be used as a test of their individual development. For an excellent analysis of Kohlberg, I recommend the chapter by Edwin Fenton in the Task Force report.[16]

According to Kohlberg, at stages 1 and 2 (pre-conventional level) people tend to think about and act on moral issues on the bases of fear of punishment, or desire for reward, or exchange of favors. In stages 3 and 4 (conventional level) they think and act on moral issues on the basis of maintaining the expectations held out for them or duties imposed upon them by authorities for the sake of the good of the order. In stages 5 and 6 (principled level) people think and act on the basis of moral principles genuinely accepted by the individual rather than on the basis of simply conforming to the authority of the group. Stage 5 is the stage of the social contract and human rights (for example, the Declaration of Independence and the U.S. Constitution); and stage 6 is the stage of universal ethical principles pertaining to liberty, equality, and justice. Advocates of Kohlberg's theory argue that the most effective teaching of values can be undertaken by direct confrontation of moral decisions in open discussions among teachers and students. Such a process, conducted in the setting of a "just community," will move students from lower levels to higher stages of development.

Much of the criticism of Kohlberg's stage theory has to do with the claim that people in all societies move sequentially from a lower stage to a higher stage in moral reasoning.[17] The universality of application of the theory to all cultures is questioned, as is the assumption that the higher stages are morally "better" than the lower ones. Philosophers and psychologists have widely debated the theory. Kohlberg himself has eased some of the criticism by announcing in August 1978 at the National Conference on Civic Education held in Marina del Rey, California, that he had removed stage 6 for lack of empirical validation. I do not believe that the removal of stage 6 destroys the usefulness of the stage theory for civic education, since stage 5 is the level to be sought in most matters dealing with citizenship.

Whether or not Kohlberg's stage theory holds for all cultures or whether all individuals progress from one level to another in rigid sequential order, it seems to me that the theory provides a reasonable and useful intellectual framework for teachers, who should be advocates of democratic rules and moral norms and not just "knowledge dispensers" or "process facilitators." I believe that teachers should be able to recognize that students at lower stages of moral development are essentially ego-centered and self-centered, and at the middle stages they are small-group centered (family, peer, neighborhood) but that the *goal* of civic education is to move students toward the value claims of democracy based upon the principles of justice, equality, freedom, and the like. These are among the basic goals of civic education. I try to spell them out a bit more in Chapter 5.

The Cluster School at Cambridge High School began in 1974 as an alternative school that attempted to implement Kohlberg's theory. At the request of parents, Kohlberg was asked to be a consultant. The curriculum consisted of a core program of studies in the social studies and English during half of each day. The curriculum was structured around discussion of moral dilemmas while "community meetings" were devoted to solving immediate problems arising from the self-governance of the Cluster School. The school had some 60 students and five teachers in grades 9 through 12, and each student and each teacher had one vote in the community meetings. The students were about 50% inner-city blacks, 30% intellectual types from academic households, and 20% whites from working-class homes.

Kohlberg relates that the community meetings in the first year were almost pure chaos and anarchy as the group faced continuing "rip-offs." The community finally made rules against stealing, but there was very little trust during that first year. In the second year some students recognized that the stealing was their fault and that they ought to help each other to do better. By the third year the stealing had virtually disappeared as the process of "community building" took effect. And by the fourth year a constitution and bill of rights were formulated that set out the rules and behavior of a "just" community. There were, to be sure, some who still refused to sign the contract (the extreme privatists) and some who still argued that each person or small group should make up individual constitutions (the extreme pluralists). But on the whole, there was a great deal of movement in thought and action from the lower stages of self-interest and disregard for others to the higher stages of community concern. I had the good fortune to visit the school in the spring and again in the fall of 1977 (the third year). Even in that short period of time I could see the evidence of an increase in orderly participation in the meetings and greater commitment of the students to the decisions made.

Planning by the Cambridge superintendent of schools and his staff began in 1978 to reorganize the new high school into "house" plans that might incorporate many of the self-governance ideas of the Cluster School, including special attention to community meetings and a revitalized and genuine student government system: a steering committee to meet regularly with the principal and superintendent, a campus life committee, a fairness committee, a guidance committee, and the like. If adopted, this plan could make the Cluster School even more of a model for democratizing schools than it now is.

The School Within a School at Brookline (Massachusetts) High School, an alternative program of some 90 students and four staff members, has adopted Kohlberg's community meeting idea, but is distinctive in that it reflects the guidance and counseling orientation of the chief consultant, Ralph Mosher, developmental psychologist at Boston University. Much emphasis is put upon democratic governance through the regular community meetings. After two years the students themselves voted to make attendance compulsory.

Great stress has been put upon the development of materials by the English and social studies teachers and by the guidance counselors (rather than by central office staff) to make the curriculum and the discussions lively and significant for the moral development of students. I was particularly impressed by the syllabus, "American History in Modern Dress," which gave special attention to moral dilemmas to be discussed in class. (If you had been on the U.S. Supreme Court, how would you have voted in the *Dred Scott* decision or the Pullman strike case?) I observed a "constitutional convention" in which each delegate first represented his colonial constituency as close to the historical record as possible, and then the clock was turned forward and each was to judge how he or she would vote today and why. One of the teachers in the middle school was developing study materials on the holocaust long before it became a matter of wide public involvement.

The project relies heavily on the counseling role of Mosher and his participant-observer assistants and has the backing of the central office administrators (superintendent, director of social studies, director of guidance, and director of personnel services), as well as the teachers both inside and outside the School Within a School. The teaching is remarkably lively and engrossing; the staff are keen to train other teachers, and they have had remarkable success in conducting workshops for other school systems. Of particular interest is the effort to extend the moral development approach and participatory governance to the middle grades (6 through 8). There has been much consultation and interconnection with the Cambridge Cluster School project.

Under the leadership of Edwin Fenton, professor of history and social studies at Carnegie-Mellon University, five high schools in Pittsburgh and two in Bakersfield, California, have established alternative programs called Civic Education Schools. Fenton is an enthusiastic supporter of the Kohlbergian theories of moral development and democratic school governance. The three elements in the civic education programs are social studies, English, and community meetings.

Fenton's tilt as a historian is toward systematic knowledge, which is revealed in the curricular materials used in all participating schools. The tenth-grade courses in social studies stress sociological concepts, and the eleventh-grade curriculum focuses on American history. Both attempt to combine rigorous scholarship with moral dilemma discussions. Similarly, the tenth-grade English course stresses the moral and ethical concerns revealed in world literature, with emphasis upon a growing sense of community as a central theme. Special efforts are made to show connections with the social studies curriculum. The eleventh-grade English curriculum attempts the same approach in American literature, with the central theme being the search for justice in the U.S.

One of the most distinctive elements in Fenton's approach is the staff development workshop conducted for 15 weeks for 60 to 70 persons who are or will be teachers in the several civic education units. Administrators, students, and interested colleagues also join in the program of reading, lecture, discussion, and demonstration that focuses upon his five goals of civic education: participating skills, personal development, basic intellectual skills, development of democratic values (Kohlberg's stages), and acquisition of knowledge. The Carnegie-Mellon project has the unique opportunity to judge the relative values of the approach for a variety of communities, ranging from middle- and upper-class public high schools to working-class neighborhoods served by Catholic as well as public high schools.

Fenton reports that most adult Americans think at the middle stages 3 and 4 of conventional thought (conforming to group expectations), and only a small minority (5% to 10%) attain full stage 5 thought, i.e., the level of thought required to understand and act upon the principles of the Declaration of Independence, the Constitution, and the Bill of Rights. The transition to stage 5 takes place, if at all, when people are in their late teens or early twenties. If American youth are ever to reach the higher stages of moral development, then a liberal education should include deliberate efforts to develop a civic morality among *all* high school and college students—not simply "clarifying one's values," not simply acquiring a breadth of political knowledge, not simply acquaintance with the history and structure of government in the past. If we are to continue to have mass secondary and higher education, and I think we must, there must be a common civic core to it. If we are to continue to have a democratic political community, the schools and colleges must give priority to their civic task.

Although I have not visited the project called the Ethical Quest in a Democratic Society in the Tacoma (Washington) Public Schools, I have found their materials developed by local teachers most interesting

110

and challenging. The Tacoma project is perhaps the largest moral education program in the country, enlisting some 100 teachers from all grade levels and supported by the National Endowment for the Humanities since 1975. It has benefited from the work of Ralph Mosher at Boston University and of Norman A. Sprinthall at the University of Minnesota. The project, under the leadership of Paul J. Sullivan, director, and Mary Dockstader, resource coordinator, has concentrated on the moral issues that arise in the existing curriculum in the English, social studies, and health courses. One of the instructive lessons to be learned from the Tacoma project was its success in achieving broad community support when it was charged in its early days by conservative religious and political groups with irreligion and radicalism. The board of education, the advisory committee, and religious and community groups all came to the support of the project.[18]

The third major element in the revival of civic education is what I prefer to call "citizen participation," although the terms "citizen involvement," "community participation," and "citizen action" are also commonly used. Whatever the term, authorities agree that there has been an almost explosive expansion of citizen effort to influence public policies during the past decade or two involving thousands of grassroots neighborhood organizations and block associations, hundreds of national public-interest and special-interest groups, and consumer groups. Here I find Stuart Langton's definition and distinctions useful:

> Citizen participation refers to purposeful activities in which citizens take part in relation to government.[19]

This emphasis upon participation in affairs related to *government* gives a limitation that helps to keep the meaning of citizenship education within reasonable bounds and defines a range of activities for which education should prepare citizens. Langton classifies four types of citizen participation:

> 1. *Citizen action*, which is initiated and controlled by citizens for purposes that *they* determine. This category involves such activities as lobbying, public advocacy, and protest.
>
> 2. *Citizen involvement*, which is initiated and controlled by *government* to improve and/or gain support for decisions, programs, or services. This category involves such activities as public hearings, consultation with advisory committees, and attitudinal surveys.
>
> 3. *Electoral participation*, which is initiated and controlled by government according to law in order to elect representatives and vote on pertinent issues. This category involves such activities as voting and working for a political candidate or in support or opposition to an issue.
>
> 4. *Obligatory participation*, which involves the mandatory responsibilities that are the legal obligations of citizenship. This category includes such activities as paying taxes, jury duty, and military service.[20]

[I would add compulsory school attendance.]

This categorization of citizen participation provides a useful framework in which new programs for schools and communities could be carried out. A fine example of citizen education through participation is a program in the public schools of Minneapolis called Affirming Our City Together (ACT), under the direction of Diane Hedin and Dan Conrad at the Center for Youth Development and Research at the University of Minnesota.[21] The fundamental assumptions of the project are that young people are *citizens now*, not merely people preparing for citizenship. As citizens, adolescents can contribute significantly to the welfare of their communities, ideally by performing tasks that both the community and the students find worthwhile in solving social problems. Youth benefit from the opportunity to participate as citizens; learning requires action; schools should facilitate youth participation in community affairs in a number of ways, including political action but also through active volunteer service and community projects (health, United Way, Red Cross, Chamber of Commerce, and the like). Youth participation should be a central ingredient in civic education.

An effort is made to infuse action learning practices into a wide range of courses in many (or all) junior and senior high schools in Minneapolis. The student activities range from volunteer service on an intermittent basis to longer term internships that carry academic credit. The interns I met performed a variety of tasks: working in a nursing home for the poor, working with deaf children, working as an aide to a mathematics teacher in a parochial school, working as a laboratory assistant at the Veterans Administration. I was told by the city attorney that he regularly took his intern to court with him and sought his advice in selecting jurors and on other matters. In some cases, whole new courses on action learning and community involvement have been established. Timely activity, enthusiasm, and widespread involvemet are the hallmarks of the Minneapolis action learning program.

Although the Minneapolis program is the only one I have had the opportunity to observe firsthand, I also recommend the approach to citizenship education through involvement in the real public affairs of communities as set forth by Fred Newmann of the University of Wisconsin/Madison in his book, *Education for Citizen Action*. He argues persuasively that "state-supported, publicly financed education ought to work for the maintenance and enhancement of democratic political process" by improving the ability of high school students to exert influence in public affairs, i.e., those "issues of concern to groups of people to which institutions of government should respond."[22] Newmann outlines a general secondary school curriculum that he believes would have the social/political objective of strengthening the whole democratic consent system rather than working toward specific social goals such as the elimination of poverty or improved medical care.[23]

As director of the Citizen Participation Curriculum Project at the University of Wisconsin/Madison, Newmann has introduced a comprehensive year-long course on competence in citizen action (for eleventh- or twelfth-grade volunteers) in one of the Madison high schools. The new program is described at length in a book titled *Skills in Citizen Action*, by Newmann and two of his doctoral students.[24]

They combine aspects of all the major approaches to civic education into a structured, nearly full-time English and social studies program for high school juniors and seniors. The three elements of the first semester are a course in political/legal process, a communication course, and a community service internship. In the second semester students take an action-in-literature course, participate in a citizen action project, and prepare a "public message" summarizing the meaning of the citizen action projects in which they have participated. This approach is a fascinating one, well worth the close attention of educators. Newmann is something of a gadfly, and as such is an outstanding analyst and clarifier of the new civic education movement.

One final point. Participation by students in real life public issues can become a delicate, sensitive, and even explosive problem for the schools in some communities. Even studying about controversial issues can be difficult for teachers and administrators in the face of aggressive pressure groups. If the school appears to be siding with one special interest against another, it may get caught in the middle. The situation may be compounded if "action" to influence public issues becomes the goal beyond simply "studying about" issues. But the effort should be made if civic education is to be revitalized. A distinction that appeals to me between "issue politics" and the "public-interest movement" is made by David Cohen, president of Common Cause:

> Issue politics is the practice of organizing around issues, no matter what values are involved. The public-interest movement—consumer, environmentalist, government reform, institution-related professionals—deals with those questions that are not ethically, radically, sectionally, economically, or occupationally dominant.... .
> The public-interest movement is basically an attempt at restoring representational balance in our public institutions. It strives to change our system by building a place for those voices that are often unheard.... Public-interest organizations are often defined as groups that seek "common, collective, or public goods" that do not exclusively, materially, or selectively benefit their members. Open government, clean air, and freedom of information are examples of collective goods.[25]

In Cohen's terms it seems to me that the public schools should be seen as an integral part of the public-interest movement, should draw upon it for support, and should contribute to it by preparing young citizens to

take part in and improve the political system toward openness, respon-
siveness, diffusion of power, majority actions, and minority rights. I like
his stress on the need for professionalism and professional skills in
promoting open government:

> The lessons of recent years suggest that a healthy political system
> requires an open decision-making process and well-organized,
> effective citizen action as a bulwark against a government that is
> dominated and influenced by a variety of special interests that have
> mastered the rules and procedures and often have exclusive access to
> certain public officials.... Because the structure of our pluralistic,
> democratic form of government strongly favors special-interest
> policies over holistic policies, the public-interest constituency has a
> vital role to play. As an agenda setter and watchdog, it must continue
> to press government to take a comprehensive approach to policy
> setting while working toward active and appropriate participation by
> citizens.[26]

I can find few accounts that provide a better statement of the goals and
setting in which civic education of the schools should function:

> Our most urgent challenge is to seek to build a society motivated
> by a sense of public purpose; a society based on hope, vision, and
> confidence; one that reflects its institutions and is proud of them; a
> society that shares values and has a sense of the greater good.[27]

The foregoing states admirably what I have been trying to say for the
past half-dozen years. When Carey McWilliams, then editor of the
Nation, telephoned me at Teachers College in 1972 and asked if it was
about time that I addressed myself once again to the predicament of the
public schools, I agreed to do a piece on public education. I concluded
that article in the spring of 1973 with the argument that the prime goal
of public education was to serve the public purpose:

> A public school serves a public purpose rather than a private one. It
> is not maintained for the personal advantage or private gain of the
> teacher, the proprietor, or the board of managers; nor does it exist
> simply for the enjoyment, happiness, or advancement of the
> individual student or his parents. It may, indeed it should, enhance the
> vocational competence, or upward social mobility, or personal
> development of individuals, but if that were all a school attempted, the
> job could be done as well by a private school catering to particular
> jobs, or careers, or leisure-time employment.
>
> Rather, the prime purpose of the public school is to serve the
> general welfare of a democratic society, by assuring that the
> knowledge and understanding necessary to exercise the responsi-
> bilities of citizenship are not only made available but actively
> inculcated. "If," said Thomas Jefferson, "a nation expects to be
> ignorant and free, in a state of civilization, it expects what never was
> and never will be."
>
> Achieving a sense of community is the essential purpose of public
> education. This work cannot be left to the vagaries of individual
> parents, or small groups of like-minded parents, or particular interest

groups, or religious sects, or private enterprisers, or cultural specialties. Thus, when the population became ever more heterogeneous after the mid-nineteenth century, the need for compulsory education became increasingly apparent to the lawmakers of the states and of the Union.

...[Public] schools have a commitment to elevate the civic goal of unity above the particularist goals of special and self-serving interests in the society. This is one of the most sensitive and complicated of all the tasks of public education, for it is extremely difficult to draw the line between the values of diversity (which a democratic society prizes) and of divisiveness (which may threaten the very society itself). Most modern school systems in the world are torn by two conflicting drives: On the one hand, to help build national unity out of diverse racial, cultural, ethnic, religious, and linguistic groups, and, on the other, to honor the drive of particularist groups that demand their own schools for the teaching of different languages, religious beliefs, ethnic customs, or regional aspirations....

I believe that there must be a mobilization to insist that the public schools concentrate as they never have before on the task of building a sense of civic cohesion among all the people of the country. This should become the chief priority for educational planning, curriculum development, organization, research, and experimentation. I am not calling for a new patriotism of law and order, nor for loyalty oaths, nor a nationally imposed curriculum in "civics," nor flag salutes, nor recitation of prayers or pledges of allegiance. But I do believe that we require the renewal of a civic commitment that seeks to reverse and overcome the trend to segmented and disjunctive "alternatives" serving narrow or parochial or racist interests.

Our people are badly divided and dispirited, if not demoralized, by trials they underwent in the late 1960s and early 1970s. They badly need a spark to rekindle the sense of community. That is what the French meant when they coined the term *civisme* to denote the principles of good citizenship, the attitudes, virtues, and disposition devoted to the cause of the French Revolution of 1789. It was from a similar urgency that the founders of this country argued that a new republic needed an appropriately republican education to assure the stability and success of a democratic government and democratic society. The nation and the world are drastically different nearly 200 years later, but that is only the more reason to concentrate on what the new civism should be and what the public education system should do.

I believe the chief end of American public education is the promotion of a new civism appropriate to the principles of a just society in the United States and a just world community. We have forgotten or simply mouthed these goals; now we must advance them in full seriousness as the first order of business for the future.

Whatever else the general guidelines of the new civism should be, they will be found by renewing the principles of justice, liberty, and equality summarized in the Bill of Rights of the Constitution and applied to the states by the Fourteenth Amendment. So far, the federal courts have seen this fact more clearly than have the legislatures or the politicians or the organized teaching profession itself. They have been more faithful to the basic meaning of public education than have the profession, the critics, the reformers, or the local or state boards of education.

We must take the judicial doctrines seriously. While the social scientists argue and wrangle over their empirical data, the people of America must preserve their public school system by concerted political action so that there will be something to improve. We can no more dismantle our public schools, or let them be eroded, than we can dismantle our representative government, or our courts, or our free press. This is not to say that important changes are not necessary; it is to say that undermining free public education is tantamount to undermining the free society itself. In this respect the radicals are correct: The question is whether the government and the society are worth saving. It is my opinion that they are. Therefore, I believe that public education must be rejuvenated.

It is a task worth the best efforts of all concerned citizens—professional organizations, political parties, voluntary groups, Common Cause, and all other good-government organizations. If we mean to maintain and improve a cohesive and just society based upon liberty, equality and fraternal civism, there is no alternative to the public schools.[28]

In the years following Watergate, I returned to this theme in lectures at the Seventy-Fifth Anniversary Forum of the College Entrance Examination Board in the fall of 1975 and at the fourth annual George S. Counts lecture at Southern Illinois University in the winter of 1976. Despite the similarity of statements, I believe the conclusion of the Counts lecture is worth quoting. It provides a useful setting and introduction to the final chapter of this book:

We well know that didactic moral instruction and outward expressions of patriotism through enforced pledges of allegiance, loyalty oaths, or flag salutes have lost their savor among academics. We well know, too, the danger of attempts to use the schools for self-serving patriotism, manipulative propaganda, or partisan politicization. Yet, somehow, the schools must promote a strengthened sense of the importance of civic morality and political integrity—if you please, a revitalized civism devoted to the political virtues of constitutional self-government that have sustained us at our best, that we have ignored or desecrated at our worst.

In renewing a sense of political community, embodied above all in the Bill of Rights and successor amendments, a liberal civic education should help to build social cohesion without resort to coercion, without slavish adherence to a narrow party line, without succumbing to witch hunts against the deviant, without silencing the unorthodox, and without dwelling upon an ethnocentric preoccupation with American society to the neglect of the interdependence of the peoples of the world. A liberal civic education must rely upon scholarly knowledge and research without becoming bloodlessly intellectualized or rigidly circumscribed by the arbitrary boundaries of the separate and specialized academic disciplines, and without degenerating into random discussions or enticing games. We must protect the rights of privacy without retreating into the privatism of purely personal experience as the norm of public morality.

In a desirably pluralistic society, civic education must honor cultural *Pluribus*, but it must also strength political *Unum*. Somehow, civic education must promote and protect the right of all persons to hold a diversity of *beliefs*, but it must also develop a commitment to *actions* that uphold the common bonds of a free government as the surest guarantee of the very holding of a pluralism of beliefs. It must, in Jefferson's words, render "the people the safe, as they are the ultimate guardians of their own liberty."

On a recent occasion[29] I argued that after all we have been through as a nation in the past decade I should think we could now face frontally and frankly the proposition that American education does have a political role to perform in achieving our historic ideals of political community. Such a proposition may well be criticized from the conservative right as being an effort to impose leftist ideology. If so, let conservatives say candidly where they oppose equality (as Nathan Glazer has just done in *Affirmative Discrimination*). It may well be criticized from the radical left as merely imposition of middle-class capitalist values or simply as wishy-washy liberalism. If so, let radicals openly say where they oppose the constitutional freedoms and due process. It may well be criticized by empirical social scientists or socially neutral scholars on the grounds that schools cannot effect social change; schools simply follow the dictates of society. If so, let them say to what agencies they *would entrust* deliberate efforts to build and generate a sense of democratic political community.

I would argue that if the teaching profession of two to three million persons took seriously the authority of the enduring ideals, sentiments, and moral commitments of our historic political community at its best, as embodied in the constitutional regime and especially in the Bill of Rights, the schools and colleges of this country *could* mobilize the majority of people on behalf of putting into practice our professed democratic ideals. This could indeed amount to a basic social change. But it would take the combined efforts of liberals in the legal profession, the scholarly and public service professions, the reform-minded wings of the political parties, labor, and the media, the good citizen groups, the civil rights and civil liberties organizations, the students, the civic-minded women's and ethnic groups.

In response to George Counts' challenge of nearly 50 years ago, the education profession by and large did *not* dare to build a new social order based upon economic collectivism. The thought was too new and the profession was too timid. Today the challenge is different; the thought of collective interdepence is no longer new, and the profession is surely more militant. The challenge today is even more political and cultural than it is economic. The challenge is to achieve

117

what we proclaim to be our historic political goals: freedom, equality, justice, and community.

The issue once again is what can and should the schools do to meet *this* challenge. No one argues that the schools can do it all or do it alone. What I *am* arguing is that the prime contribution of the schools is not to preach specific *economic* solutions favored by laissez-faire capitalism or revolutionary socialism; it is to enhance as far as possible the political capabilities of students to think and act as citizens who will support and improve the liberal political community, so that it will be the context within which the economic decisions will be made. This leaves open for study such questions as whether in the future the economic system of the United States and of the world should tip in favor of capitalism or socialism, economic planning by government or free rein for the market system, state ownership or private ownership or mixed ownership of essential industries, centralized control and regulation or decentralized autonomy or world-order coordination of economic affairs, hierarchical management by governmental or corporate bureaucracies or participatory decision making by worker-owners. All of these topics should be considered, studied, and discussed at appropriate levels in the schools and on the basis of the best scholarship obtainable, scholarship that ranges across the full spectrum from left to right. But what the schools should do above all is to try to build positive commitments in thought and action to the democratic values of the liberal political community and to the liberal political processes of the democratic constitutional order.[30]

Chapter 4 Notes

1. National Task Force on Citizenship Education, *Education for Responsible Citizenship* (New York: McGraw-Hill, 1977).

   Elizabeth Farquhuar and Karen S. Dawson, *Citizen Education Today* (Washington, D.C.: U.S. Office of Education, 1979).

   Le Ann Meyer, *Programs and Problems: The Citizenship Education Issue* (Denver: Education Commission of the States, 1979).

   Byron G. Massialas and Judith V. Torney, *Behavior Variables Related to Citizen Education Objectives* (Philadelphia: Research for Better Schools, 1978).

   Mary Jane Turner, *Who Teaches Citizenship? A Survey of Documents and Resources* (Boulder, Colo.: ERIC Clearinghouse and Social Science Education Consortium, 1977).

   Byron G. Massialas, "Education and Political Development," *Comparative Education Review* (June/October 1977): pp. 274-295.

2. James P. Shaver, "A Critical View of the Social Studies Profession," *Social Education* (April 1977): p. 302.

3. Useful publications include *Law-Related Education; Guidelines for the Future* (St. Paul, Minn.: West Publishing Co., 1975); *Teaching Teachers About Law* (Chicago: American Bar Association, 1976); *Directory of Law-Related Education Projects,* 3rd ed. (Chicago: American Bar Association, 1978); *Update, On Law-Related Education,* published three times a year; and Lynda Falkenstein and Charlotte Anderson, *Daring to Dream; Law and Humanities for Elementary Schools* (Chicago, ABA, 1980).

4. The titles published by U.S.O.E. in 1978 were:
   - Ann Parker Maust and Lucy Knight, *An Analysis of the Role of the U.S. Office of Education and Other Selected Federal Agencies in Citizen Education*

   - Larry Rothstein, *New Directions in Mass Communications Policy: Implications for Citizen Education and Participation*

   - *Examining the Role of the Workplace in Citizen Education*

   - Nea Carroll Toner and Walter B. Toner, Jr., *Citizen Participation: Building a Constituency for Public Policy*

   - Robert H. Salisbury, *Key Concepts of Citizenship: Perspectives and Dilemmas*

   - Willis W. Harman, *Citizen Education and the Future*

5. U.S. Office of Education, "Final Report of the Study Group on Law-Related Education" (Washington: U.S. Government Printing Office, 1979), p. xiii.

6. Ibid., pp. xi-xii.

7. Paul A. Freund, "Law in the Schools: Goals and Methods," *Social Education* (May 1973), p. 363.

8. American Bar Association, Special Committee on Youth Education for Citizenship, *Mandate for Change: The Impact of Law on Educational Innovation.* Joel F. Henning, project director. Chicago, Illinois, 1979. See especially Chapter 3.

9. Le Ann Meyer, *Programs and Problems*, p. 33.

10. Mark Blum, *Ethical-Citizenship Education Policies and Programs: A National Survey of State Education Agencies* (Technical Report, Philadelphia: Research for Better Schools, Spring 1977).

11. Ibid., pp. 10-16.

12. National Task Force on Citizenship Education, *Education for Responsible Citizenship*, pp. 180-184.

13. Le Ann Meyer, *Programs and Problems*, pp. 25-26.

14. National Task Force, *Education for Responsible Citizenship*, p. 175.

15. Ibid., Chapters 3, 5, and 6.

16. Ibid., Chapter 7, pp. 98-99. See also Edwin Fenton, ed., et al., *The Cognitive-Developmental Approach to Moral Education, Social Education* (April 1976); and Lawrence Kohlberg, "Moral Development and the New Social Studies," *Social Education* (May 1973): pp. 325-369.

17. See, for example, Jack Fraenkel, "The Kohlberg Bandwagon: Some Reservations," *Social Education* (April 1976): pp. 216-222; Fenton and Fraenkel exchanged views in *Social Education* (January 1977): pp. 56-61.

18. Paul J. Sullivan, "Implementing Programs in Moral Education," *Theory into Practice* 16: pp. 118-123.

19. Stuart Langton, ed., *Citizen Participation in America* (Lexington, Mass.: Lexington Books, 1978), p. 17. See also, Commission for the Advancement of Public Interest Organizations, *Periodicals of Public Interest Organizations: A Citizen's Guide* (Washington: The Commission, 1979).

20. Ibid., p. 21.

21. See National Task Force, *Education for Responsible Citizenship,* Chap. 8.

22. Fred M. Newmann, *Education for Citizen Action; Challenge for Secondary Curriculum* (Berkeley, Cal.: McCutchan, 1975), pp. 41-46.

23. Ibid., p. 166.

24. Fred M. Newmann, Thomas A. Bertocci, and Ruthann M. Landsness, *Skills in Citizen Action; An English-Social Studies Program for Secondary Schools* (Madison: University of Wisconsin, 1977).

25. Langton, ed., *Citizen Participation in America*, pp. 56-57.

26. Ibid., pp. 61 and 63.

27. Ibid., p. 63.

28. R. Freeman Butts, "The Public School: Assaults on a Great Idea," *The Nation* (30 April 1973): pp. 554-555, 558-560.

29. R. Freeman Butts, "The Search for Purpose in American Education," *College Board Review* (Winter 1975/76): p. 18.

30. R. Freeman Butts, "Once Again the Question for Liberal Public Educators: Whose Twilight?" *Phi Delta Kappan* (September 1976): pp. 13-14.

Chapter 5

A Decalogue of Democratic Civic Values

I argued in Chapter 1 that the decade of the 1980s will present special challenges to the education of American citizens because of an escalating privatism in politics and pluralism in education. I would argue now that the decade of the 1980s is a particularly important time for a revival of civic learning in the schools. The time seems particularly appropriate for a revival of civic learning as we approach the 200th anniversary of the framing of the Constitution in 1787, its adoption in 1788, its operational beginning in 1789, and the adoption of the Bill of Rights in 1791.

Significantly, a special bicentennial celebration of the Constitution is being planned by a joint committee of the American Historical Association and the American Political Science Association called "Project 87." It is to be conducted in three stages. The first, from 1978 through 1980, is devoted to academic scholarships, fellowships, seminars, and conferences to study anew the Constitution's relevance and adequacy for the present. The second stage, beginning in 1981, will focus on improving teaching about the Constitution in elementary and secondary schools and in producing public television programs. The third stage, culminating in 1987, will engage the broadest possible public participation in discussions of the Constitution. Thus, this decade is a peculiarly strategic time to meet the challenges of political pessimism, alienation, and disaffection, and to reaffirm the primacy of the civic role of the schools, which was their oldest innovation and could again be their newest innovation.

When I speak of the revival of civic *learning*, I am purposely using multiple meanings of the word learning. In history we speak of the revival of classical learning of the twelfth and thirteenth centuries, a prelude to the Renaissance. Learning in this sense is a corpus of knowledge and scholarship that informs and challenges the highest reaches of the intellectual, moral, and creative talents of humankind. Thus, a revival of civic learning must be based upon the major disciplines of knowledge and research.

Learning also means the different processes whereby individuals acquire knowledge, values, and skills at different ages and stages of their development and in all the contexts of modern life. Thus civic learning includes all those skills and experiences relating to the political processes and the moral judgments that underlie the political system. Civic learning embraces the fundamental values of the political community, a realistic and scholarly knowledge of the working of political institutions and processes, and the skills of political behavior required for effective participation in a democracy.

I like the waý Charles Frankel put the matter in an article on the humanities called "The Academy Enshrouded":

> In every generation in which the humanities have shown vitality, they...have performed an essential *public, civic, educational function*: the criticism and reintegration of the ideas and values of cultures dislocated from their traditions and needing a new sense of meaning. This is what humanistic scholars did in fifth- and fourth-century Athens, in the thirteenth century...in the Renaissance, and in the nineteenth century. Can they perform this function now?[1]

In answering Frankel's question, I propose that *we* educators are indeed determined that the schools shall perform their "essential public, civic, educational function," and that we try to give a new sense of meaning to the ideas and values that have been dislocated from our traditional civic community.

My study of the history of citizenship education does not lead me to a sanguine belief that a genuine revival of the civic learning will be easy, nor is the long-term reform of civic education assured. But neither am I pessimistic or cynical about the prospects of a revival. The stakes are too great to justify either easy optimism or hard pessimism. One thing the record of innovation in education seems to show is that piecemeal efforts, the adding of a course, or the adoption of faddish methods, techniques, or hardware, seldom have long-term effects.

Now we must try a wholesale approach over a long period of time, embracing the curriculum, the teaching methods, the governance and environment of the school, and the interaction of teachers, administrators, students, parents, government, and community agencies. This generalization has been stated over and over again, but too often it is made without sufficient attention to formulating a consistent coherent framework to carry out the work and without clearly stated goals. A reform can attempt too much as well as too little. I have no illusion that my particular effort to state guidelines for the reform of civic education will meet with instant widespread consensus. But the effort must be made if we are to avoid doing nothing on one hand or to try unrealistically to achieve 176 discrete competencies or behavioral objectives on the other.

I believe that civic education should be focused upon education in relation to the political system. It should not try to encompass all urgent social, economic, or intellectual problems. Yet it must be broad enough to go beyond sheer information to include the political values and concepts, as well as political knowledge and political participation.

Of course, young children do not vote in national elections, but it is clear that much political socialization goes on during elementary school years. Civic learning in school and community environments begins very early, as the ABA projects in law and the humanities in elementary education so clearly demonstrate.

My general framework relies on a conceptual and normative approach to the basic principles of a democratic political community rather than the more directly practical considerations of "street law" or immediate problems of criminal or civil justice. These latter topics are undoubtedly of direct interest to many youth. This motivation should surely be drawn upon and harnessed as appropriate, but I believe that the long-term reform of civic education must go beyond the problems of getting into trouble with the "law."

In my guidelines for civic education I have not been able to encompass the vast and rapidly growing empirical evidence about how children learn political attitudes in and out of school through the process of political socialization.[2] Too much of it is equivocal to arrive at clear-cut generalizations that apply nationwide or worldwide; and some of the data collected 10 or 20 years ago surely is out of date in some respects. But a full-fledged rationale for civic education must take into account the best child developmental data that can eventually be gathered and relied upon concerning the acquisition of political attitudes. I have not been able to do that, so it must be left to a later enterprise.

All that I can do here is to outline in very broad and general terms a conceptual framework that may be useful in arriving at some principles with which the public and the profession may approach the reform of civic education in American schools.

My view is that the goal of civic education for American schools is to deal with all students in such a way as to motivate them and enable them to play their parts as informed, responsible, committed, and effective members of a modern democratic political system. This can be achieved in a number of different specific ways but should include the three basic aspects: political values, political knowledge, and the skills of political participation needed for making deliberate choices among real alternatives. Also, those who plan civic education must recognize that students come with different backgrounds, different interests, and different capabilities; but the goal is to achieve as much common understanding and common commitment to the democratic value claims as possible. See the diagram on page 124, "The New ABCs of Citizenship Education in the Schools," which presents a matrix showing the major elements in an efficacious civic education program. Following is a discussion of the matrix.

A. The Political System

I find it useful to follow the widely recognized analysis of three levels of the political system as set forth by David Easton, professor of political science at the University of Chicago: 1) the political community, 2) the long-range constitutional regime, and 3) the day-to-day governing authorities.[3]

The political community is the group of persons drawn together by their common participation in shared governing processes and bound together by a common frame of political values. In the U.S. the political community is symbolized by "We the People" who not only are the ultimate authority for the shared political structures and sets of political processes by which they seek to solve their problems in common, but who share a sense of community marked by feelings of mutual identity and distinctive belongingness, sentiments that support cohesion and solidarity, and commitments or obligations to the welfare of the total community, i.e., the public good. What makes a diverse people with conflicting interests into a "We" are the common moral commitments and the shared sense of distinctive identity and cohesion that are essential for building, maintaining, and improving the basic political structures of the long-range constitutional regime as well as the day-to-day processes of governmental decision making.

The political community is to be distinguished from other types of communities whose binding relationships are based upon kinship, race,

The New ABCs of Citizenship Education in the Schools

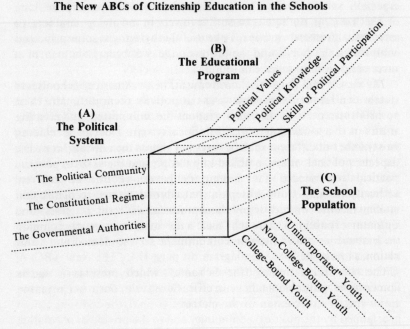

124

ethnicity, language, religion, social class, intellectual or professional interest, scholarly knowledge, or military power. The tensions and cleavages arising from the contending loyalties of these other communities make the building of political community a particularly difficult task. Since the founding of the Republic we have affirmed that the American political community should be committed to the democratic values of liberty, equality, justice, popular consent, and personal obligation for the public good.

The long-range constitutional regime. The second sphere of the political system is the long-term constitutional regime embodied in the fundamental law that flows from the sovereign authority of the political community. The fundamental law is codified into written constitutions and bills of rights that define the basic procedures, norms, and rules by which political demands and interests are aggregated, regulated, and channeled into authoritative decisions generally accepted by rulers and ruled alike. In addition to fundamental law, a vast network of formal and informal operations define the basic structure of institutions and their interrelationships: the legislative, executive, and judicial functions; their distinctive and separate powers; and the relation of different levels of government to one another. The fundamental rights and liberties of individuals and groups in the society are spelled out as guides to legislators, executives, bureaucrats and judiciary. Procedures are outlined for the orderly revision or amendment by the people of their basic constitutional order. The founders of the Republic, especially as revealed in *The Federalist Papers*, anticipated something of the ensuing political process involved in resolving conflicts of interests, pressure groups, parties, lobbying, negotiating, and compromising, but could not foresee the vast complications of a succeeding technological and bureaucratic society.

The day-to-day governing authorities. The third level of the political system consists of the persons who temporarily occupy the offices or positions of authority and who conduct the daily, ongoing, operating affairs of the political system. Their decisions are accepted as binding most of the time by most of the citizens, as long as the officials act within the limits of their roles as defined by the constitutional order and the political community. The temporary governing officials exercise authority ranging from those who have broad discretion in decision making in their conduct of governmental affairs (President, governors, legislators, judges) to those who have a narrower range of discretion in the bureaucracies and departments of public service at local, state, and national levels.

The number of public officials has expanded enormously as the functions of government have grown. Obviously, their performance varies greatly in the extent to which they live up to the enduring values proclaimed by the political community and to the principles of conduct undergirding the constitutional regime. A revitalized civic education should include study and analysis of all three levels of the political system. The fundamental values and concepts of the political community need to be critically scrutinized because they often come into conflict with one another; the constitutional regime must also be explored to see wherein it genuinely reflects the proclaimed values and wherein it may obstruct them; and the actual conduct and behavior of officials must be held up to scrutiny in order to make judgments about their political performance.

The most obvious example is Watergate: What was the "justice" the high officials were charged with obstructing legally, and what was the "freedom" they violated? What was the nature of the crisis of the constitutional regime occasioned by conflict of the powers of President, Congress, and Supreme Court? And which officials fully lived up to the value claims of the political community and the requirements of the constitutional order—and which did not? The sensitivity of such study at appropriate grade levels in the schools is obvious and most difficult to deal with. But what are the alternatives? Describe the values in platitudes? Talk about the separation of powers in abstract terms? Ignore the conduct of public officials and thus fail to hold them accountable? Study something else? No, I believe a candid, critical, scholarly, and fair-minded approach is the best way.

B. The Civic Education Program

An effective civic education program will include not only curriculum content and learning activities but will embrace the whole school system—its organization, administration, and governance; its climate and "hidden curriculum"; and its relation to the community agencies concerned with civic education. It will not only impart valid, reliable, and realistic knowledge, but it will exemplify democratic political values throughout its whole operation to help students to learn the skills of political participation.

No one would argue that the schools can perform the whole task of education for citizenship in a society influenced by mass media, peer culture, powerful voluntary interest groups, and the like. But some *do* argue that the schools cannot do very much in the face of all these other powerful educative influences. Yet, I would argue that the schools do have a distinctive role, one that should not be left to some other agency. That role has three parts: 1) providing continuing study of and commitment to the value claims of political democracy; 2) imparting realistic and scholarly political knowledge, and 3) teaching the participation skills required for the maintenance and improvement of the democratic political system.

Political value claims. For 200 years the values of political democracy

126

have been asserted and debated in the United States. The assertions range from the most eloquent and persuasive statements in the English language to endless pedantic and trite mouthings of unexamined phrases. Yet, when the crises arise or the fundamental values are challenged, certain key concepts emerge that lay claim to the beliefs, commitments, loyalties, and actions of American citizens. Without such support, no political system can maintain itself or reform itself short of violent revolution. And no political system can maintain itself without socializing each new generation to acquire its basic values.

I propose a set of 10 value claims in the form of a decalogue, which I believe should be used as an intellectual framework to guide the development of civic education programs in the schools. I make no claim for their originality. Too much has been thought and said about these values over too long a time to make any such claim. And each value often elicits wide differences of interpretation. But there may be a special merit of my decalogue in that it grows out of my analysis of the challenges of privatism in politics and pluralism in education.

For purposes of stimulating the revival of civic learning I have classified the 10 value concepts into two general types: 1) those that seem primarily to promote desirable cohesive and unifying elements in a democratic political community, and 2) those that primarily promote the desirable pluralistic or individualistic elements in a democratic political community. See the chart on page 128. There is a continuing tension, sometimes overt conflict, between the values of *Unum* and the values of *Pluribus*, but I believe that civic education must, just as American democracy must, honor and promote both. As a whole, they make up a decalogue of the civic values that schools should seek to promote.

The values in my decalogue are not lists of competencies or behavioral goals.* They are conceptions of the desirable elements in the political system that should be used as the criteria by which specific goals of behavior are chosen and judged. To put it another way, I believe that those in charge of programs of civic education should test the elements of their programs to determine to what extent they incorporate these concepts in their curriculum and practice.

These values are normative concepts, each with long histories of scholarly analysis, controversial interpretation, and conflicting practice. But they are the very stuff of political life, and I believe they should be confronted directly and explicitly in a manner appropriate to

---

*Significant progress has been made recently in developing such behavioral competencies. See, for example, Richard C. Remy, *Handbook for Basic Citizenship Competencies; Guidelines for Comparing Materials, Assessing Instruction and Setting Goals* (Alexandria, Va.: Association for Supervision and Curriculum Development, 1980). Subsequent handbooks will be addressed to administrators, parents, and school board members, prepared by Remy at the Mershon Center, Ohio State University, and Mary Jane Turner of the Social Science Education Consortium, Boulder, Colorado.

A Decalogue of Democratic Civic
Values for American Schools

(With apologies to Moses and Aristotle)

Corrupted Forms	True Forms of Unum	True Forms of Pluribus	Corrupted Forms
"Law and order"	Justice	Freedom	Anarchy
Enforced sameness	Equality	Diversity	Unstable pluralism
Authoritarianism	Authority	Privacy	Privatism
"Majoritarianism"	Participation	Due Process	"Soft on criminals"
Chauvinism	Personal Obligation for the Public Good	International Human Rights	"Cultural imperialism"

Cosmopolitan Civism   Stable Pluralism

Pluralistic Civism

the age and capacity of students. They are not the "new" social science concepts of role, status, stratification, socialization, political culture, decision making, and the like, as the American Political Science Association might prefer. But they appear in the highest reaches of political discourse and jurisprudence as well as in the ordinary language of governance in schools and communities, in political discussions and campaigns, and in the proceedings of courts, hearings, grievance committees, and policy councils. They require nothing less than a lifetime of consideration if they are to become more than sunshine symbols or crisis crutches. I shall have more to say about each concept, but first a word about the other two aspects of an effective civic education program.

Political knowledge. Knowledge, of course, is the stock in trade of schools. It includes all the various ways in which systematic information is transmitted through reading, thinking, writing, inquiry, discussion, and the nonverbal media of communication. Social scientists like to speak of the disciplines of knowledge, psychologists speak of cognitive skills, and humanists speak of analytical judgments and normative judgments. Whatever the scholarly discourse, the object is to make available knowledge based upon the most rigorous, critical, analytical, and realistic methods available to modern scholarship. The schools are the natural channels for making the efforts of scholarship available to the younger generation. History, political science, other social and behavioral sciences, languages, literature, philosophy, and other humanities should be plumbed for their contributions to the scholarly basis of the civic learning, to provide what my late colleague Lyman Bryson called a reliance upon "significant truth rather than plausible falsehood or beguiling half-truth."

As an example, the humanistic side of political philosophy and moral philosophy has received a renaissance in such diverse and influential works as John Rawls' *A Theory of Justice*, Robert Nozick's *Anarchy, State, and Utopia*, and publications of the Institute for the Study of Civic Values. From the behavioral, empirical, and philosophic approaches, there are new bodies of learning in political science that can influence civic learning in the schools.

There are signs that the other social sciences are also moving down from their lofty disciplinary perches of the 1950s and 1960s to apply theory to practice. Nathan Glazer has stressed this point:

> [The social sciences] have moved from a stance toward the world that emphasizes detached observation and analysis to a stance in which observation is increasingly mixed with participation, analysis with judgment and advice. The social scientist relates to institutions less as an uninvolved scholar seeking general truth than as a participant whose concerns are close to, intermixed with, the concerns of the practitioner.[4]

Presumably this is because they both share the same concerns in their general role of the citizen. Why has this shift of intellectual orientation among the disciplines taken place? Glazer gives three reasons: 1) the enormous expansion of government in many spheres; 2) radical changes in such institutions as schools, hospitals, prisons, and social work agencies; and 3) the fact that the growth and change in government and other institutions have become increasingly problematic, something to be questioned, challenged, and defended. This shift from theory to practice has affected both conservatives and radicals in sociology:

> Social change—seen in the past as consisting of such processes as technological change, cultural lag, social movements, and revolution—now is increasingly felt to result from change in the behavior and scale of government and in the service institutions that

had become so large a part of government activities.

And so today, schools, prisons, hospitals, housing, and public administration are now all considered as linked deeply to and implicated in the structure of society. *They reflect and shape its values, creating the world we all live in....* (Emphasis added)

I think a necessary adaptation of the social-science disciplines to a changing world is taking place, a world increasingly created by law, regulation, judgment, and large organization, as against the atomic action of individuals and small organizations.[5]

Similar points could be made with regard to history. Robert Kelley points out how historians are finding that the cultural politics of pluralism are more revealing than the older theories of class confict and economic materialism. And, above all, psychology has developed an enormously important approach to questions of moral development and civic responsibility, notably through the work of Lawrence Kohlberg at Harvard.

My point is that the world of scholarship now has more to offer the schools in a renaissance of civic learning than has been the case for 30 or 40 years. The disciplines are once more concerned in a way that they have not been since the New Deal and the Fair Deal of the 1930s and 1940s.

The skills of political participation. These skills should be the third part of a vital civic education program. They should be learned through realistic involvement of students in the public affairs of the community as well as in the schools themselves. This goes far beyond simply learning how to get out the vote, important as that is; it also involves firsthand practice of skills ranging from learning to speak effectively in an orderly committee meeting to the sophisticated arts of negotiation, compromise, use of power, and decision making. Since I have already discussed the participation process in Chapter 4 and will again in the final section of this chapter, I say no more here except to stress that participation as a mode of the learning process should always be accompanied by systematic study of the value claims and scholarly knowledge appropriate and relevant to the participant activity—just as the treatment of values, concepts, and knowledge should be linked to and enlivened by practice.

C. The School Population

I have already said a good deal in Chapter 1 about the state of political knowledge, political attitudes, and the cultural values of youth. An effective civic education program must take hold of students and involve them where they are, if it is to lead them to any kind of reasonable understanding of and commitment to the cohesive as well as the pluralistic values of political community. The program must deal with the total range of students to be served; their different cultural backgrounds; their socioeconomic status; their racial, ethnic, and sexual identities; and their particular learning styles. The National Assessment of Educational Progress tests of political knowledge make it clear that there are regional differences in achievement of political knowledge: Northeast and Central regions typically performed above the national level; the Southeast below, and the West at about the middle. The suburban regions around the large urban centers performed above and the big cities below the national average. The affluent sections of urban areas performed above and disadvantaged sections of urban areas performed below the national average. While there was little difference between the sexes, the higher educational level of parents was associated with higher scores on political knowledge tests. Taken at its face value such a finding should mean that the longer the present generation of children and youth stay in school, the better the chances *their* children will have of doing well on tests.

While all these test scores show the influence of social class and family backgrounds on achievement, evidence from the political socialization studies show that schooling in civic education has more influence on the political motivation and knowledge of lower-class children than it does on middle-class children. So civic education for non-college-bound children is probably even more important than for more affluent college-bound children of middle-class and professional families who will have continuing opportunities to acquire more political knowledge and participation skills in college. But civic learning is likely to be most important of all for the "unincorporated" youth who for one reason or another have been historically blocked from access to the mainstream of American political and social life: the disadvantaged minorities—the blacks and other ethnic groups—and the continuing poor.

The common foundation of civic learning is all the more reason for the children and youth not to be separated into special ability tracks or into separate private, parochial, or public schools. I believe that it is extremely important for pluralistic groups in our schools to learn about each other through study and participation *together*. The schools should be training grounds in acquiring the sense of community that will hold the political system together. At a time when black and Hispanic leaders are calling for strengthened public schools, I believe that the majorities should not pull away. I believe the goal for black youth stated by Benjamin Hooks, head of the National Association for the Advancement of Colored People, expresses the historic ideal of civic education in a nutshell: "a high school diploma in one hand and a voter registration card in the other." Our task, however, is to be sure that earning the diploma and the registration card requires a solid foundation of political knowledge and participation skills that can be exercised to make a reality of the basic values that the democratic political system proclaims.

As I have said, the value claims of a political democracy are not discrete or mutually exclusive; some often conflict with others; and they are subject to many different interpretations, as all really important ideas are. But I believe they provide significant guidelines to what should be taught in an effective program of civic education. I would not argue for a particular order in pedagogical treatment. Teachers may well start at different points or with different concepts, depending upon their appropriateness for the local situation, but it seems to me that a comprehensive civic education program will consider all of them at some point in the school's program.

Professional educators often proclaim that the overarching goal of education is to prepare informed, thinking citizens. I believe that we must take seriously this claim and that therefore the basic ideas and values of democratic citizenship should become the core of knowledge and participation that makes up a curriculum design for the educated citizen. I do not mean simply the long lists of general goals, or behavioral objectives, or specific competencies, or learning activities, or process skills that so often are set forth in curriculum guides or scope and sequence plans drawn up by state or local curriculum committees.

I mean that the fundamental ideas and values upon which our constitutional order is built should be the core of sustained and explicit study based upon realistic, scholarly knowledge and searching criticism carried on throughout the school years from kindergarten through high school and the years of liberal education. Although there will not be universal agreement as to what these key ideas and values are and there is no intent to impose a single curriculum design upon all schools in the nation, I think that the profession should be trying much more rigorously and vigorously to become sophisticated and explicit about the substantive ideas and concepts that form the common core of American citizenship.

I hope that this task will become a major part of the efforts now under way by the National Council for the Social Studies and the Social Science Education Consortium to work out new options for a national revision of the K-12 scope and sequence in social studies to replace the present pattern largely worked out in 1916-1917 and subsequent years. Several major professional organizations have recently and properly emphasized the importance of pluralistic, multicultural, and multi-ethnic values in the curriculum. I think it is now time to exert concerted effort to formulate the civic and cohesive values that major national organizations, both professional and public, could collectively endorse. The following decalogue is an attempt to promote this effort.

1. Justice

I start with the concept of justice for several reasons. The basic ideal of justice (that which is *fair*) is pervasive in most social contacts and at most ages. It can range from the kindergarten child who cries out to the teacher that it wasn't "fair" to be pushed out of a turn at the swing to the rampaging crowd before the city hall in San Francisco, who shouted "We Want Justice!" in response to the jury's verdict of manslaughter instead of murder for Dan White, the admitted killer of the mayor and a city council supervisor.

The idea of justice as fairness cuts across a wide range of society's activities—from making decisions that are fair to persons who are in conflict, or who have been wronged or injured, or who have been deprived of benefits to which they are entitled. The idea of justice thus encompasses the processes of civil justice, criminal justice, courts of law, juries, lawyers, punishments, prisons. I categorize issues of procedural justice and corrective justice under the heading of due process and issues of fair distribution of social benefits and burdens under the heading of equality.

I think of justice as the very moral basis of a democratic society, what John Rawls calls the "first virtue of social institutions." It is what must govern the conduct of persons in their relations to one another if the society is to be self-sufficient and well-ordered. Rawls speaks of a *public sense of justice* that produces a well-ordered society in which everyone accepts, and knows that others accept, the same principles of justice. This means that the members of a well-ordered society must develop strong moral sentiments and desires to act as the principles of justice require:[6]

> If men's inclination to self-interest makes their vigilance against one another necessary, their public sense of justice makes their secure association together possible. Among individuals with disparate aims and purposes a shared conception of justice establishes the bonds of civic friendship; the general desire for justice limits the pursuit of other ends. One may think of a public conception of justice as constituting the fundamental charter of a well-ordered human association.[7]

What the public sense of justice does is to establish the claims of what is *right* as prior to the claims of what is *good*, since what is good is defined differently by individuals and groups according to their particular life styles and personal desires. What is right or just thus puts limits on what are reasonable conceptions of what is good. A just social system thus defines the boundaries within which individuals and pluralistic groups may operate.

Rawls defines two principles of justice that set these boundaries, and the first principle must be satisfied before moving on to the second. The first principle is stated as follows:

> Each person is to have an equal right to the most extensive total system of equal basic liberties compatible with a similar system of liberty for all.[8]

The "equal liberties" of citizenship bear a close resemblance to those guaranteed in the Bill of Rights:

> The basic liberties of citizens are, roughly speaking, political liberty

(the right to vote and to be eligible for public office) together with freedom of speech and assembly; liberty of conscience and freedom of thought; freedom of the person along with the right to hold (personal) property; and freedom from arbitrary arrest and seizure as defined by the concept of the rule of law. These liberties are all required to be equal by the first principle, since citizens of a just society are to have the same basic rights.[9]

After the principle of equal political liberties is satisfied, then the second principle of justice should come into play:

Social and economic *in*equalities are to be arranged so that they are both:

(a) to the greatest benefit of the least advantaged...and

(b) attached to offices and positions open to all under conditions of fair equality of opportunity.[10]

Once the *political* principle of justice is satisfied, then a just society will move on to distribute income and wealth and develop a social structure that makes use of differences in authority and responsibility:

While the distribution of wealth and income need not be equal, it must be to everyone's advantage, and at the same time, positions of authority and offices of command must be accessible to all. One applies the second principle by holding positions open, and then, subject to this constraint, arranges social and economic inequalities so that everyone benefits.[11]

Rawls's total position cannot be adequately covered here, and of course it has been severely criticized by some philosophers and social scientists.[12] But his position points unmistakably to the priority of achieving a common civic community based on the principle of justice as the prime purpose of public education. This is in sharp contrast to the pluralistic views of Novak, Nisbet, Itzkoff, or Sizer. Rawls has not elaborated a full-scale philosophy of education based upon his underlying political and moral philosophy as Dewey did. Nor has he linked thought and action sufficiently or given as much attention to intuition or affect, as William Torbet charges. But I believe he has paved the way for the philosophers and practitioners of education to restore a profound civic, moral, and political basis to public education, if we but will.

Recapturing a sense of legitimacy and of moral authority for public education may well rest upon the success with which the education profession can bring about what so many of the American people have hoped for it for 200 years—establishing as a priority the vigorous promotion of the basic values of the American civic community— liberty *and* equality *and* justice. It may just be that not only is the future of public education at stake, but the future of the democratic community itself.

2. Freedom

What I like best about Rawls's theory of justice is his assignment of first priority to the idea of *equal basic liberties*. The just political community will then be committed to the idea of freedom as well as equality. I view freedom as having at least three elements relevant to civic education.[13] Freedom involves:

a. the right, opportunity, and ability of every human being to live his or her own life in dignity and security and to seek self-fulfillment or self-realization as a person or as a member of a chosen group without arbitrary constraint by others. This is the freedom of the person and of private action.

b. the right, opportunity, and ability of every human being to speak, read, inquire, think, believe, express, learn, and teach without arbitrary constraint or coercion by others, especially as a means for making deliberate choices among real alternatives on the basis of reason and valid and reliable knowledge. This is the freedom of the mind and of intellectual inquiry.

c. the right, opportunity, and ability of every citizen to take active part in shaping the institutions and laws under which he or she lives in common with others and to do this by making uncoerced choices and by participating through active consent in cooperation with one's fellow citizens; and to do it in such way as to promote justice, freedom, and equality for others. This is the freedom of the citizen and of public action.

These are the great freedoms especially protected by the First Amendment, but they obviously include more than that. I like the distinction that Alexander Meiklejohn made between public freedoms and private freedoms.[14] Public freedoms are those that inhere in the welfare of the democratic political community and which the liberal state is obligated actively to protect from coercive majorities in the community, despotic minorities in the community, or from the state itself. The First Amendment guarantees these freedoms of belief, expression, and public discussion to be virtually unlimited. They cannot be abridged, because they are indispensable for the public decision-making process that is essential for the maintenance and improvement of a free and democratic political community. Indeed, the liberal state is obligated actively to safeguard and promote the public freedoms of teacher, learner, and citizen from threats by either majorities or minorities in the community. On the other hand, private freedoms are those that inhere in the individual, but which *may* be limited for the public good under due process of law as guaranteed by the Fifth Amendment. These limitations can be applied under certain conditions and in the interests of justice to life, liberty, and property.

Tensions become readily apparent when one begins to inquire as to the limits that should be placed upon freedoms of action that threaten the freedoms of others. Freedom of speech is limited by penalties for libel and defamation of character; freedom to accumulate and dispose of property or advertise it falsely is subject to limitations of fines, taxation, and monopoly; freedom to produce goods is limited by threats to the public interest in protecting the environment; freedom to discriminate and segregate in public education is limited by the belief in equality and the equal protection of the laws.

I agree with Meiklejohn on the fundamental importance of the continuing study of the concept of freedom as basic to civic education. Just as we need a "public conception of justice" as the basis for a well-ordered society, so do we need a "public conception of freedom" that is held sufficiently in common to assure the vitality of a democratic political community. Meiklejohn puts it this way:

> ...[A] primary task of American education is to arouse and cultivate, in all members of the body politic, a desire to understand what our national plan of government is.... [This] is a challenge to all of us, as citizens, to study the Constitution. That Constitution derives whatever validity, whatever meaning it has, not from its acceptance by our forefathers..., but from its acceptance by us now. Clearly, however, we cannot, in any valid sense, "accept" the Constitution unless we know what it says. And, for that reason, every loyal citizen of the nation must join with his fellows in the attempt to interpret, in principle and in action, that provision of the Constitution [the First Amendment] which is rightly regarded as its most vital assertion, its most significant contribution to political wisdom. What do We, the People of the United States, mean when we provide for the freedom of belief and the expression of belief?[15]

And, speaking of "our forefathers," I believe it is wise to remember that Madison clearly had in mind that the bill of rights he was proposing would protect individuals not only from abuses by government but would mean that the government itself would protect individuals from abuses of their liberties by other individuals in the community, namely the majority. In his speech of 8 June 1789 before the Congress, Madison put it this way:

> But whatever may be the form which the several States have adopted in making declarations in favor of particular rights, the great object in view is to limit and qualify the powers of Government, by excepting out of the grant of power those cases in which Government ought not to act, or to act only in a particular mode. They point these exceptions sometimes against the abuse of the executive power, sometimes against the legislative, and, in some cases, against the community itself; or, in other words, against the majority in favor of the minority.... But I confess that I do conceive, that in a Government modified like this of the United States, the great danger lies in the abuse of the community than in the legislative body. The prescriptions in favor of liberty ought to be levelled against that quarter where the greatest danger lies, namely, that which possesses the highest prerogative of power. But this is not found in either the executive or legislative departments of Government, but in the body of the people,

operating by the majority against the minority.[16]

Here is a clear vision of the *positive* role of a free government in protecting the rights and liberties of individuals. Freedom is not merely something to be protected against invasion by government but is also something that liberal governments must protect against violation by one group or individual against others in the community. States should protect local minorities against local majorities. But, also, the federal government must protect minorities in a state against majorities in a state. And the logic of Madison's position would certainly apply this principle to protection of black minority rights against white majorities. The U.S. Supreme Court and federal courts in recent years have ruled against local and state majorities on questions of religion, segregation, loyalty oaths, and infringements on freedom of speech and belief. I think Madison would have approved.

The first principle of justice, according to Rawls, requires that each person has an equal right to basic liberties but only so far as such liberties are compatible with equal basic liberties for *all*. Thus we come to the idea of equality.

3. Equality

Along with justice and freedom, the idea of equality runs through the value claims of the American creed. "All men are created equal" is the first of the self-evident truths of the Declaration of Independence. It even comes before the inalienable rights of life, liberty, and the pursuit of happiness. We have noted in Chapter 2 how the idea of equality was a counterpoise in the eighteenth-century struggle for democracy against the tyrannies of privilege and the closed orders of aristocracy and hierarchy. Much of that discussion is pertinent here. But it is also true ever since then that there has been an almost constant contrapuntal discord between the claims of freedom and the claims of equality.

Equality was to be the remedy for the special privileges of the ruling elites whose snobbishness, arrogance, pretentions, and contempt for "the people" so infuriated the middle classes, the yeomen, the professionals, and the artisans of the American towns and countryside. Again, equality was an elusive term. Then, as now, it sometimes meant that all persons should have an equal chance or *opportunity* to develop their talents and not be handicapped by inherited status of family, property, or class. Sometimes it seemed to imply that a rough equality of *condition* would be a desirable thing, but seldom was there great stress on *economic* levelling. It was more often a determination that *political equality* was the goal, for it was widely believed that there were bound to be natural intellectual differences or distinctions based upon ability. The important thing was to keep the avenues of mobility open so that "artificial" differences of property or wealth or family status would not harden into political hierarchies and privileges as they had in the

137

regimes of Europe. The emphasis in the term "natural aristocracy" should be upon "natural" rather than upon "aristocracy." Rewards were to be made upon the basis of achievement and merit in a society in which equality of opportunity was kept open through the political process and especially through public educational systems, where all would have the opportunity to make the most of their natural talents.

No one would argue that the founders defined with exactitude what they meant when it was declared that "all men are created equal," nor that the amorphous dictum has been faithfully carried out in practice. But Edmund Morgan argues that the creed of equality achieved a kind of consensus during the Revolutionary period that has had a powerful and pervasive influence ever since:

Those who have claimed the benefits of equality in America have usually had to press their own claims against stubborn opposition. Men with power over other men have often affirmed their dedication to the principle while denying it by their actions, masters denying it to slaves, employers to workmen, natives to immigrants, whites to blacks, men to women.

Is it fair, then, to call this a point of consensus? Was it not mere rhetoric? Perhaps, if by rhetoric is meant the terms on which men can agree to speak together. An alternative rhetoric and an alternative social creed prevailed before the Revolution both in America and Europe and continued to prevail in most of Europe. That creed also offered a way to consensus, but of a quite different sort. It affirmed divine sanction for a social hierarchy in which every man knew his place and was expected to keep it. The old creed was designed to suppress the aspirations of lower classes, to make them content with their lot....

The creed of equality did not give men equality, but invited them to claim it, invited them not to know their place and keep it, but to seek and demand a better place. Yet the conflicts resulting from such demands have generally, though not always, stopped short of large-scale violence and have generally eventuated in a greater degree of actual equality. After each side has felt out the other's strengths and weaknesses, some bargain, some equivalent to a Northwest Ordinance, is agreed upon, leaving demands not quite fulfilled, leaving the most radical still discontented with remaining inequalities, but keeping the nation still committed to the creed of equality and bound to move, if haltingly, in the direction it signals.[17]

So, for two centuries from the time of the American Revolution the creed of equality and the creed of public education have been bound together with extraordinary fidelity. Like the creed of equality, the creed of public education has often been charged with being merely rhetoric, and the search for alternatives has been prolonged and pervasive. But over and over again, the idea of public education, born in the Revolution, has been called upon to help promote social, economic, and political equality, while alternatives to public education have persistently had to face the charge that *they* promote inequality. And most of the time, as Morgan said of the alternatives to equality, advocates for alternatives to public education, whether charitable, philanthropic, entrepreneurial, or religious, often affirmed sanctions for a social hierarchy that tended to suppress the aspirations of the poorer classes.

Just as the Revolution did not give Americans equality but invited them to claim it, so did the Revolution generate the political values of public education without putting them into practice. These were generalized values that successive generations sought to carry out, in spite of shortcomings in practice and neglect of some old or new group that eventually claimed to be included in its benefits, groups that the originators of the idea did not or could not mean to include.

There have been two deep conflicts over the meaning of equality. Basically, does the phrase "all men are created equal" mean that in fact they *are* equal, or that they should be *treated* as though they are equal? By and large Americans have generally put their emphasis upon equal *rights* and equal *opportunity* rather than upon enforcing an equality of *condition* or income, which has been the stated goal of some extreme egalitarian communities and political parties.

The Fourteenth Amendment puts the idea in terms of the "the equal protection of the laws," but it was not until the civil rights movements of the 1950s and 1960s that positive government action was taken to wipe out long-standing restrictions on equality of opportunity in education, housing, voting, employment, and in a wide range of civil rights. The *Brown* decision of 1954 was a landmark in stressing equality of educational opportunity, and it was followed a decade later by the Civil Rights Act and the Voting Rights Act of 1965 and much else.

In a way, these moves reflected Rawls' second principle of justice, which argues that justice will require that any social or economic inequalities must be justified by arranging matters so that the greatest advantages will go to the least advantaged and that offices and positions are open to all under conditions of fair equality of opportunity. This means to me that totalitarian controls cannot be justified by government even if they do benefit the least advantaged:

> The distribution of wealth and income, and the hierarchies of authority, must be consistent with both the liberties of equal citizenship and equality of opportunity.[18]

But these are very difficult conceptions to realize in practice, and the more the government has been importuned to issue regulations on compensatory education or affirmative action for the benefit of the disadvantaged, the more the resistance has arisen to such regulations. Charges of government interference in business, labor, and educational institutions, charges of "reverse discrimination" occasioned by the *Bakke* case over admission to the medical school at the University of California at Davis have multiplied—and the continuing tension between the ideas of justice and equality on one side and the ideas of freedom and diversity and privacy on the other side have escalated in the course of the 1970s. So many of these tensions have arisen over education itself that the civic education programs have great resources for study and inquiry easily at hand—from desegregation and busing to open admissions and affirmative action.

The philosophical contrast between equality and freedom has been drawn most sharply in recent years by Rawls on one side and Robert Nozick, also professor of philosophy at Harvard, on the other side.[19] While Rawls argues that only those inequalities are justified that adhere to the benefit of the least advantaged through the action of the state, Nozick argues that justice requires that each individual has full entitlement to what he or she acquires justly and can dispose of it with no interference whatsoever from the state. Limited government and a minimal state are required for full freedom of individual rights; this is bound to result in certain inequalities because people indeed are unequal in talents, skills, and efforts, but *they*, not someone else, are entitled to what those talents, skills, and efforts produce. Equality imposed by the government is thus unjust, argues Nozick.

Yet, if all men are created equal and are entitled to the equal protection of the laws, a society that permits persecution, or segregation, or discrimination on the basis of race, religion, ethnicity, national origin, or sex is an unjust society. This persistent tension between equality and freedom should be faced in civic education programs as directly and as honestly in all its manifestations as possible. In recent years the tension has become especially strained with regard to the value of group diversity.

4. Diversity

I have already said a good deal about diversity in Chapter 1 under the heading of pluralism and in Chapter 3 regarding the history of citizenship education. Thus, I shall be brief here, but I should like to make it crystal clear that I believe respect for diversity and encouragement of diversity have been among the best elements of the American political system. Millions of immigrants were attracted to the U.S. because of the hope for life in a society that provided greater justice, greater freedom, and greater equality than they knew in their homelands—and of course they hoped for greater economic advantage as well. And millions found their hopes at least partially realized in a country of enormously diverse geography, ethnicity, language, religion, race, and culture. So, diversity is one of the major values to be studied, analyzed, and honored in any program of civic education for American schools.

But, like all the other values, diversity has its problems and costs as well as its advantages and benefits. The problem is often simply referred to as the tension between unity and diversity or order and liberty. I have referred to this tension or conflict with the two terms, civism and pluralism. The historical efforts to reckon with diversity have been variously defined: Nathan Glazer refers to the two traditions of inclusivity (welcome all comers) and exclusivity (keep the aliens out or in their place).[20] Robert Wiebe refers to the recurring emphasis upon the public and the private in the tradition of social segments in American life.[21] The various approaches to assimilation are often defined as Anglo-conformity (be like us or go away), the melting pot (we will all become something new), and cultural pluralism (we will each maintain our identities).[22] And John Higham identifies two persistent approaches that he calls integrationism (eliminate ethnic boundaries in the search for a greater community of the future based on an equality of individuals) and pluralism (maintain ethnic boundaries in the goal to hold fast to the small communities of the past based on the equality of groups).[23]

I have mentioned several views in Chapter 1 that see great significance in the reassertion of the values of pluralism. Others have cautioned against excessive pluralistic chauvinism.[24] For myself, I find merit in views that attempt to arrive at a balanced tension between the values of pluralism and political cohesion. For example, John Higham speaks of "pluralistic integration" and distinguishes between ethnic *boundaries* that keep people in or out of groups and ethnic *nuclei* that give identity and sustenance to different groups. In this sense, boundaries are permeable but nuclei are respected:

> In contrast to the integrationist model, it [the pluralistic integration model] will not eliminate ethnic boundaries. But neither will it maintain them intact. It will uphold the validity of a common culture, to which all individuals have access, while sustaining the efforts of minorities to preserve and enhance their own integrity....
>
> No ethnic group under these terms can have the support of the general community in strengthening its boundaries. All boundaries are understood to be permeable. Ethnic nuclei, on the other hand, are respected as enduring centers of social action....
>
> Many who are concerned about ethnic justice feel pessimistic about the ability of our society to develop the necessary appreciation of diversity. But it is possible,...that our greater problem in moving toward pluralistic integration may come in rediscovering what the participants in our kaleidoscopic culture have in common.[25]

The major point of my stress upon civism is exactly to rediscover what political values we have in common. Another view that I believe has merit in threading our way through the tugs between cohesion and pluralism is that distinction posed by Michael Kammen, Cornell historian and winner of the Pulitzer Prize for his *People of Paradox*. Kammen describes a plural society and distinguishes between "stable pluralism" and "unstable pluralism" as follows:

...."[P]lural society" connotes a polity containing distinct cleavages amongst diverse population groups. Often there will be a dispersion of power among groups bound together by cross-cutting loyalties, common values, and a competitive equilibrium or balance of power [stable pluralism]. Equally often there will be a conflict between racial, tribal, religious, and regional groups, to such a degree that the whole must be maintained by regulation and force. Because of the role of authority in any system of domination, there is commonly a psychological pressure upon subordinate cultural segments to deny legitimacy to the imposed order, and to reject law and authority as such [unstable pluralism].[26]

Thus, an unstable pluralism occurs when the cleavages in society threaten the very authority of the polity because of the conflict among racial, ethnic, religious, or regional groups, each of which forms its own political party and has its "own faction, each sect its own school, and each dogmatist his own ideology." On the other hand:

Stable pluralism requires a strong *underpinning* of legitimacy. A plural society is best insured by the rule of law—law made within the framework of an explicit constitution by elected representatives, executed by a partially autonomous administrative staff, and adjudicated by an independent judiciary. Insofar as all of these were created in 1787 and achieved in 1789, those dates do distinguish a genuine watershed in American history.

But stable pluralism in a democracy also requires a strong and lasting inventory of psychological legitimacy: understanding, acceptance, and pervasive confidence in the composite system necessary to make it run smoothly rather than by fits and starts.[27]

The building of a "strong and lasting inventory of psychological legitimacy" is one perceptive way to define the purpose of civic education for the schools, and leads us into the concepts of authority and participation on one side of our decalogue, and to privacy and due process on the other. I shall deal with these four concepts somewhat more briefly than the others, partly because there are excellent materials readily available for use in the schools on these concepts and partly because I have already dealt with aspects of these values in earlier chapters. For example, I follow quite closely the explication of the concepts of authority and privacy as published by Law in a Free Society; I have mentioned Stuart Langton's and Fred Newmann's work on participation; and I shall mention some extremely useful volumes on due process.

5. Authority

The role of authority can usefully be illustrated to students at all age levels, ranging from the need for rules on taking turns on the playground swing to the need for laws on murder and treason. At the heart of political authority is the difference between sheer power and authority. Power is usually considered to be the ability to control persons or conditions in such way as to direct their conduct or influence an outcome desired by the power wielder. The most common examples of sheer power to control events are military force and money.

On the other hand, authority is *legitimate* power, recognized as such and sanctioned by custom, institutions, law, constitution, or morality. Authority in a democratic polity is thus the exercise of influence and command by those in positions of power but done so within the confines of rules made by the consent of the governed and whose rule is considered over a period of time as legitimate. Robert M. MacIver, long-time professor of political philosophy and sociology at Columbia University, defined authority as follows:

> By authority we mean the established *right*, within any social order, to determine policies, to pronounce judgments on relevant issues, and to settle controversies, or, more broadly, to act as leader or guide to other men. When we speak of *an* authority we mean a person or body of persons possessed of this right. The accent is primarily on right, not power. Power alone has no legitimacy, no mandate, no office. Even the most ruthless tyrant gets nowhere unless he can clothe himself with authority.[28]

I would underline the fact that the *right* of an official to make decisions, to determine policies, and to maintain order derives not from the official's private capacity, but by virtue of a right conferred by the society. So the exercise of democratic political authority should be under the constraint of the values of fundamental justice and fairness as well as functioning to insure the greatest amount of freedom for the individual under rules of due process and with a fair distribution of privileges and resources in the society. Failing these constraints authority becomes authoritarianism. Without authority freedom becomes license or anarchy, pluralism becomes unstable, and individuals can be assured of little privacy or due process.

One final point. I would also underline MacIver's broad definition of authority as including the general right to act as leader or guide to others. Leonard Krieger, university professor of history at Chicago, points out that the idea of authority "as a consciously constituted or legitimate power to command or secure obedience" is a distinctly modern idea emerging during the sixteenth and seventeenth centuries as a background to the modern idea of citizenship in a nation state.

But he also points out that there was another meaning of authority that originated in Rome, not so much associated with power as with an uncoercive authority associated with persons or knowledge whose trustworthiness and responsibility are a guarantee that their deliberate judgments, convictions, and decisions are worth following as models or examples.[29] An *auctor* in Latin is a trustworthy writer, a responsible person, a teacher, a guarantor, a model. Meiklejohn appeals to the unique authority of the search for truth in a democratic society.[30]

It is in this latter sense of authority as trustworthiness that has been so eroded in recent years. Students have revolted against the authority of schools and colleges, against the authority of government officials, against the authority of parents, churches, business, and other institutions that in the past have claimed the right to guide the conduct and behavior of the young. This is what the Yankelovich survey referred to as "deauthorization," one of the reasons both the young and their elders have turned to privatism. This brings us to privacy.

6. Privacy

Let me say at the outset that I view privacy as one of the basic pluralistic values of a democratic political community along with freedom, diversity, and due process. I distinguish it from the privatism I described in Chapter 1, which I view as a perversion or corruption of privacy. As freedom is the right to live one's life in dignity and to seek one's self-development and self-fulfillment, so privacy is the right to be left along and to determine what information about oneself is communicated to others. In this I follow the privacy materials of Law in a Free Society:

> [Privacy] involves the right of individuals, groups, or institutions to determine for themselves when, how, and to what extent information about them is communicated to others.[31]

Infringement of this right was one of the most irritating of the eighteenth-century practices that led to the Third Amendment's guarantees against the quartering of troops in private households and the Fourth Amendment's guarantees that the people shall be secure in their persons, houses, papers, and effects against unreasonable searches and seizures. The revelations of the spying activities on American citizens by the CIA and FBI during the Vietnam War, the Watergate tapes, and the Ellsberg incident have led to new concerns about the protection of privacy. The development of electronic devices has added a 1984 quality to all kinds of business activities (such as computers that keep credit ratings on millions of consumers) as well as those of government agencies. The 1970s gave added bite to George Orwell's protest against the invasion of privacy and the unauthorized surveillance by Big Brother with attendant Doublethink, Records Department in the Ministry of Truth, Newspeak and Oldspeak, and the everpresent telescreen. The opening of school and university records revealing grades, test scores, and confidential ratings to the scrutiny of students and parents are examples of the new concern for privacy in education.

The most notable and—as it turned out—controversial legislative protection was the Family Educational Rights and Privacy Act of 1974 sponsored by Sen. James Buckley (R-N.Y.) and promoted most actively by the National Citizens' Committee on Education. Reacting to the revelations of Watergate and the unrest of the prior decade, Congress aimed at "opening up institutions," making them more accountable, and protecting the privacy of individuals. The Act denies funds to any school that prevents parents of children under 18 and students themselves over 18 from having access to all of their school records. Such records may not be released to others without written consent, except to school officials and to certain federal or state officials in connection with application for financial aid. The primary intent of the law was to prevent abuses whereby careless or incorrect materials that were damaging to a student's chances in further education or career were left in their files and to prevent releasing files to banks, credit agencies, police departments, and the like without the knowledge of the students or their parents. However, many college and university associations, led by the American Council on Education, protested vigorously that there were many ambiguities in the Act and that confidential recommendations would no longer be useful if the writers knew that the students could read them. As a result, a long process of rewriting the regulations in the Department of Health, Education, and Welfare was required.

7. Due Process

I continue from privacy to due process and thus interrupt the pendulum swing in my treatment of the conflicting values between cohesion and pluralism, because privacy and due process are so closely related. While privacy concentrates on a citizen's being left alone, the due process has to do with the rights of persons who have been accused of wrongs or injuries they have allegedly committed. The due process values center on the Fifth, Sixth, Seventh, and Eighth Amendments with their provisions for protection of individual rights in criminal cases and civil suits at law. Here the volumes issued by the Constitutional Rights Foundation are especially valuable for use in the schools on the subjects of criminal justice and civil justice.[32] There are many other useful sets of materials being produced by various projects and publishing companies.

Of special interest to educators has been the development in recent years of the concepts of due process as applied specifically to teachers, students, and parents. Again, there are excellent materials available. I think especially of the compilations and interpretations of the books by David Schimmel and Louis Fischer, both lawyers and professors of education at the University of Massachusetts.[33] Use of these materials focusing directly upon students and teachers could be interesting cases that start where the students and teachers are and lead on to the broader realms of adult citizenship.

I should think that students would be fascinated by the due process issues associated with the "children's rights" movement, which mushroomed in the late 1960s and early 1970s. A survey of 24 states by the *New York Times* in October 1976 revealed that cities in all of those states had active legal groups working for children's rights. It was correctly predicted that aggressive advocacy groups would make this a major concern of federal courts and of the U.S. Supreme Court in the following decade in the effort to gain due process rights for children that would be protected by the Constitution just as much as adult rights are protected:

> What they hope to do is establish that a child has a right to a safe, stable home, to a reasonable education, to due process of law and to freedom from abuse and neglect. They hope, in other words, to prove that adults and institutions have obligations to the young as well as powers over them.[34]

The landmark case in the U.S. Supreme Court was decided in 1967 when the Court ruled that children in juvenile courts must be given the same procedural rights that adults have with regard to notice of the charges and the right to a lawyer, to confront and cross examine witnesses, and to adequate warning of privileges against self-incrimination. This case had to do with a 15-year-old boy who had been sentenced to a state school for juvenile delinquents in Arizona without such protection (*In re Gault*, 387 U.S. 1 (1967)).

During the next decade the children's rights movement gathered momentum both in terms of research and in the courts. One of the most active research organizations was the Children's Defense Fund of the Washington Research Project, and among the scores of legal groups involved, the American Civil Liberties Union was prominent. State legislatures and the Congress were prodded to take action, notably by the Federal Juvenile Justice and Delinquency Act, sponsored by Sen. Birch Bayh (D-Ind.) and passed in 1974, and the Education of All Handicapped Children Act of 1975. In its October 1976 term the U.S. Supreme Court agreed to review at least five cases concerned with the constitutional rights of children. For example, the State of Pennsylvania was being charged with violating the due process provisions of the Fourteenth Amendment by committing four children to mental hospitals with the consent of their parents but against the will of the children. Thus, we see efforts being made to ascertain in what respects children's rights to due process may be defined as independent of those of their parents.

The drive to achieve more due process protection for children's private rights in the juvenile justice system was quickly directed at schools as well. The key case here is *Goss* v. *Lopez* (419 U.S. 565 (1975)), which involved nine high school students in Columbus, Ohio, who were suspended (during racial demonstrations and unrest in 1971) for up to 10 days without a hearing as permitted under Ohio law. The students charged that the law was unconstitutional under the Fourteenth Amendment because it deprived them of due process of their property (their right to an education) and of their liberty (by harming their record in school without a hearing). In January 1975 the Court declared in a five to four decision the law to be unconstitutional and ruled that students in high school are to be granted due process in suspensions. This must include oral or written notice of the charges of misconduct, an explanation of the charges and the evidence against them, and an opportunity to give their side of the story before suspension from school for 10 days or less.

The minority of four justices, all appointed by Richard Nixon, dissented, arguing that the decision was an unwarranted intrusion of the federal courts into what was the proper arena of authority for state legislatures and educational officials, i.e., school discipline. But the Court majority held firm when it ruled a month later in an Arkansas case that school board members and educational officials who discipline students unfairly and without due process by claiming ignorance of students' constitutional rights may be liable for damages. The majority argued that school officials must know the basic unquestioned constitutional rights of students. The same four minority of justices argued that this was too harsh a standard for laymen who served as school board members and who are generally immune from civil suits for their good-faith actions as public officials. When the character of the Court changed with the retirement of Justice Douglas, the new "Burger majority" began to draw back from children's rights, or so it seemed, when the Court decided in April 1977 that paddling of children in public schools was not a "cruel and unusual punishment" under the Eighth Amendment (*Ingraham* v. *Wright* 97 S. Ct. 1401 (1977)).

8. Participation

The idea of participation has undergone a great deal of criticism and modification since the founding of the Republic. Much of the original notion of "We the People" relating to popular consent and sovereignty of the people rested upon the idea that the citizens would participate actively in the making of the laws and indeed in the making of the fundamental contract known as the constitution. But the idea of citizen participation has had to change from the days of a Greek polis with its few thousand citizens or a New England town meeting with its few hundred citizens. Debates over the meaning of democracy as *direct* participation by the entire body of citizens as contrasted to a republic as meaning representative participation has continued from the Constitutional Convention and the Federalist Papers down to the present time.

I am arguing here that the *idea* of participation as a key value in a democratic political community should be studied and debated and

147

discussed by students along with the *practice* of participatory experience discussed in Chapter 4. There I analyzed the citizen participation movement in general and its counterpart in community action programs for students in schools. I refer the reader back to those sections to illustrate a major model or type of participation that has become increasingly important since the decade of the 1960s. After all, sit-ins, lie-ins, marches, freedom rides, and civil disobedience movements were a critical part of the idea of participation in the civil rights movement, along with draft card burnings and demonstrations on college campuses. "Participatory democracy" became a byword of the New Left movements of the 1960s and 1970s. The justification, costs, and benefits of all these forms of a more direct participation movement along with those described in Chapter 4 should be the subject of study.

But there is another model of participation that its advocates argue is more appropriate for the conditions of a modern technological society where the issues are so complicated that direct decisions by the masses of citizens should not be the rule. Rather, a representative model of participation should be revitalized to take better account of the expertise of professionals who, along with elected officials, are held accountable by the public. A good example of this model, along with criticism of direct participation reforms, is given by Stephen K. Bailey, now professor of education and social policy at Harvard, in the following extract:

> For reasons that are understandable in the sociology of reform, the air is filled with romantic half-truths about the possibilities and desirability of extending and increasing direct citizen participation beyond the activities and latencies just listed. Because the nation has recently been burned by abuses of power, some high-minded reformers and concerned educators have developed ("refurbished" is a better word) a democratic litany as superficially plausible as it is operationally specious and even dangerous. Two propositions seem to dominate: first, citizens should, wherever possible, participate directly in all political decision making; second, where they cannot participate directly, the decision processes of their representatives must be open to detailed and continuous public monitoring. Following in the footsteps of the reform movements at the turn of the century (especially the tarnished movements for the initiative, referendum, and recall), modern reformers seem to have little understanding of the complexity of the agenda of modern government, of the interest-group building blocks of public policy, and of the essential conditions of aggregating and exercising responsible political power. In consequence, they establish reform paradigms that are frequently irrelevant, naive, or mischievous....
>
> Because of the ultimate capacity of American citizens to make wise, fundamental value choices, attempts to induce them into making superficial technical choices are ill-advised. Representative legislators

and officials are supported by an educated bureaucracy, informed by myriad interest groups and experts, checked by an independent judiciary and a free press, and held accountable to the larger public through periodic elections, intermittent correspondence, and occasional face-to-face meetings. All this constitutes not only a reasonable apparatus for conducting modern public business in an economically and technologically complex free society like the United States, but also the *only* reasonable apparatus....

At some point in the process of public decision making, after various groups have made their demands known, after "participatory democracy" has taken place, temporal and spatial environments must be created that permit responsible authorities to sort out claims and counterclaims, analyze trade-offs, and develop face-saving formulas that optimize a series of inevitably conflicting values. In some circumstances, this cardinal aspect of democratic politics can best take place in the open. But in many cases, enforced openness through indiscriminate sunshine laws simply drives the process underground, or provides interest groups with a monitoring opportunity that they— not the general public or even the press—will exercise, and that inhibits the free give-and-take of honest compromise. Sunshine purifies, but an excess causes cancer....

Similarly, government can be immobilized if demands by any group for participation in the processes of decision making become a euphemism for minority control by veto or disruption. Some weight must always be given to intensity of feeling on the part of special interests (for example, labor; business; agriculture; banking; veterans; education; and religious, racial, and ethnic groups), but democracy is meaningless if responsible majorities cannot be formed and given the power to govern. This is why the health of American political parties—the great organizers of pluralities and majorities—is so important. This is why the antiparty sentiments of the American public are so dangerous. America's general ignorance about the significance and the workings of its party system is a defect so serious as to threaten the viability of the entire democratic enterprise.[35]

In this same statement Bailey goes on to put great emphasis on the development of political skills in civic education programs in the schools. Here he is close to the civic action programs proposed by Fred Newmann, but Newmann has trouble with Bailey's representative approach, which I believe he would call a "pluralist elitist model" of participation.[36] Newmann argues for more attention to what he calls a "participatory idealist model" in which he finds great value in the direct participation by citizens, especially at the local or "micro" level, with others of like-minded concern for the common good where the sense of community can be achieved in ways not possible on the massive "macro" level of national or international issues. Newmann thus argues for revitalizing of the "mediating institutions" (families, neighbor-hoods, churches, and voluntary organizations) that stand between the individual and the Goliaths of the corporate and governmental bureaucracies.

I confess that I am drawn to both of these views and hope that a view of participation can be worked out to take account of both, i.e., increasing the role of mediating structures, including more attention to schools as nuclei for such structures at the local level, and reinforcing the representative accountability of elected officials at the state and national levels. I confess that after living in California and witnessing Proposition 13 in 1978 and anticipating a rash of initiatives to be placed on the ballot in years to come, I have lost some faith in direct participation as compared with an open legislative deliberative process. "Direct participation" can be guided by special-interest and selfish purposes just as much as lobbying is by private pressures on legislators. Initiatives designed to amend constitutions by bypassing the deliberative process in legislatures or the judicial process of the courts can be as destructive of the public good as singular reliance on either one of the other governing powers can be. This brings me to the next concept in my decalogue of cohesive civic values.

9. Personal Obligation for the Public Good

This is perhaps the most difficult of the cohesive values to make clear and persuasive to Americans in the light of the traumatic events of the last two decades. As I have noted several times, our predecessors from the time of the Revolution spoke of the individual's obligation for the public good in terms of patriotism and loyalty to the nation as well as obedience to moral and religious commandments. These were powerful sanctions for civic education programs for generations, but both have been weakened in the past 50 years. The military defense of the nation as a reason for civic education probably reached its peak in World War II when a large proportion of the American people genuinely believed that defense against the Nazi and Fascist aggression and their inhuman persecution of minorities justified war. But the Korean War seemed less critical to the safety and security of the United States; and the Vietnam experience convinced vast numbers that it was an immoral war and thus not justified as a reasonable cause for patriotism.

In a quite different way the religious sanctions for civic education also declined, largely as a result of the very religious diversity that made necessary the secularization of public schools and the withdrawal of sectarian religious instruction. And the necessity of an ideological cold war against worldwide communism has been ameliorated to some extent in an era in which détente in military competition and efforts at strategic arms limitations have taken on high priority in foreign affairs of both Republican and Democratic administrations. Opening of cultural relations programs with the Soviet Union, the Peoples' Republic of China, and other communist nations scarcely makes anticommunism a viable justification for civic education. However, international crises in the 1980s could change all this.

Yet a sense of obligation and responsibility manifested by loyalty, patriotism, discipline, and duty is still needed as a social and political glue if the very structure of the democratic polity is to persist, let alone thrive. The schools, of course, cannot alone instill values of personal responsibility if and when all the other major social institutions are preaching and practicing advancement of self and private interests. But this is no reason for the schools not to try by reassessing what they *can* do and by seeking the aid of all community and public groups that are committed to the value claims of the democratic polity.

My argument is essentially that loyalty, patriotism, discipline, and duty should be defined in terms of the richest fulfillment of the total set of democratic values in the civic decalogue. The qualities of obligation or responsibility, now often thought of as old-fashioned or out-of-date, are to be judged by the extent to which individuals seek to put them into practice in their own lives and are ready to defend or promote for others the concepts of justice, freedom, equality, diversity, authority, privacy, participation, due process, and international human rights. This may seem exceedingly circular and vague in argument, but for philosophical and psychological justification for my argument, I come very close to Kohlberg's stage 5, to John Rawls' "public sense of justice," and to John Dewey's meaning of the public as distinguished from the private. Dewey's meaning of the public goes something like this: Human acts have consequences upon others; perception of these consequences leads to efforts to control action so as to secure *some* consequences and *not* others. Consequences of actions are of two kinds: those that only affect the persons directly engaged in a transaction are *private*; those that affect others beyond those immediately concerned are *public*. The effort to regulate these indirect consequences and care for the welfare of others is the realm of the public:

> The public consists of all those who are affected by the indirect consequences of transactions to such an extent that it is deemed necessary to have those consequences systematically cared for. Officials are those who look out for and take care of the interests thus affected.[37]

Significantly, Dewey argued that this supervision and regulation of the consequences of actions by individuals and by groups cannot be accomplished by the primary groups themselves. It is just such consequences that call the public into being. The public organized to conduct these affairs through officials is the state. When the association known as the public takes on the task of regulating the conjoint actions of individuals and groups, the public becomes a political state or political community.

The significance of a representative democracy is that every citizen-voter is an "officer of the public," a representative of the public as much as an elected official is. So every citizen has a dual capacity as a private person and as an officer of the public. The essential meaning of a representative democracy is so to organize its affairs that the public good dominates the private interest. Dewey points out that etymologically "private" is defined in opposition to "official"; a private person is one who is deprived of public position. His position recalls Aristotle's point that there are two kinds of "office of citizen": the official whose office is specifically defined and the citizen who continuously exercises his office as participant in the affairs of state. Dewey uses the term "officer of the public" to underline the fact that every citizen has a dual capacity and acts in both a public and a private capacity. When acting in a private capacity the citizen serves family, clique, or class:

> ...[E]very officer of the public, whether he represents it as a voter or as a stated official, has a dual capacity.... Rarely can a person sink himself in his political function; the best most men attain is the domination by the public weal of their other desires. What is meant by "representative" government is that the public is definitely organized with the intent to secure this dominance. The dual capacity of every officer of the public leads to conflict in individuals between their genuinely political aims and acts and those which they possess in their non-political roles. When the public adopts special measures to see to it that the conflict is minimized and that the representative function overrides the private one, political institutions are termed representative.[38]

The point here is that since "officers of the public" (i.e., all of us citizens) have this dual makeup, the civic education we devise should be focused upon those conditions and techniques that will enlist "insight, loyalty, and energy" on the side of our public and political role rather than upon our private role:[39]

> The essential need...is the improvement of the methods and conditions of debate, discussion, and persuasion. That is *the* problem of the public. We have asserted that this improvement depends essentially upon freeing and perfecting the processes of inquiry and of the dissemination of their conclusions.[40]

Kohlberg has added the emphasis on dealing with moral dilemmas to the processes of inquiry and discussion. In this respect he has followed up and elaborated Dewey's long-standing concern with democratic practice in school as one means of developing a sense of community and of responsibility among students as well as teachers. James Shaver seems to be speaking in the same vein when he reminds us that a "jurisprudential approach" provides a likely model for citizenship education in the schools. It not only helps students to grapple with political/ethical decisions but sets before them the necessity of wrestling with the fundamental constitutional rights and obligations of citizens, as judges are expected to do:

152

Because teachers and administrators often don't recognize the applicability of democratic constitutional principles to the school, opportunities are lost both to democratize the school and to teach the important concepts of citizenship....

...[T]he Supreme Court has unmistakably stressed students' responsibilities as well as rights....

In short, schools need not be permissive to be democratic. In fact, permissive schools would be nondemocratic because they would not give students essential experience in learning about and acting in regard to their responsibilities to other people and to the society.[41]

The role of civic education is thus at least twofold: it rests upon free inquiry as to rights and responsibilities, but it also seeks to promote commitment to put personal obligation for the public good of a free society above purely personal interests. The materials of Law in a Free Society devoted to the concept of responsibility put it this way:

Society seeks to achieve social order through the use of rules, and in this use of rules the community relies on the responsibility of its participants. The community relies on the individual's responsibility in two senses. First, it relies on the individual's capability for understanding the meaning of rules and for making choices guided by this understanding.... Second, the community also requires its members to exercise self-restraint in the pursuit of their personal goals; it relies on individuals who are responsible in the sense of caring for their fellow human beings, caring for the objectives sought to be achieved by law, and thus caring to comply with the rules which exist to realize those objectives....

Responsibility then is a key concept in a free society. If the individual's responsibility is removed and nothing takes its place, society no longer exists, and there is left merely a collection of unbridled individuals. If, on the other hand, responsibility for a person's actions is taken away from the individual and turned over to others, it is a tacit admission that the individual cannot or should not control his own destiny and is, therefore, not free.[42]

"Caring for fellow human beings" reminds us that the value of responsibility or obligation for the public good has its positive moral elements as well as its need to defend the public order when it is threatened. It reminds us that jingoistic patriotism, which in the past has been defined as the essence of loyalty or obligation to the nation, must now be replaced by a broader international outlook that honors the world's diversity of peoples but also seeks a new and larger cohesion based upon the concept of international human rights. This brings me to the final concept in my decalogue.

10. International Human Rights

We come, finally, to a concept and value for American civic education that I believe requires a basic change in our historical views of citizenship. In Chapter 2 I referred to two formative periods in the idea of citizenship. The first was the era of the Greek and Roman city-state republics; the second arose with the nation-states in the seventeenth and eighteenth centuries. Now I believe we are beginning to recognize that we are entering a third formative period when the idea of national citizenship must take account of the vast changes in the world situation that have suddenly burst upon our consciousness since the end of World War II. Increasingly popular terms to define the set of phenomena that began with the term "One World" in the 1940s are now "global inter-dependence" or simply "globalization." I cannot do more than mention the word here and list a few convenient sources of reference to illustrate various approaches to the growing interrelatedness of nations and peoples.[43]

An enormous amount of new educational material is being developed to make students aware of the many ways in which the earth has shrunk and the ways that events in one part of the world have an almost immediate impact upon conditions in other parts of the earth. The effect of raising oil prices or withholding oil production in the Middle East on the corporate and individual lives of people all over the world is only one of the latest and easiest examples to cite. Similar interdependence can of course be cited in the fields of technology, space, travel, commu-nication, multinational organizations, political blocs, cultural styles, pop music, mass media, and on and on. The immensity of the problems and the prospective overloading of the curriculum with teaching materials has led various groups to try to be somewhat selective in their approach. The Mid-America Program at Indiana University's Social Studies Development Center and Ohio State University's Mershon Center stress ways in which the children of local communities in a state like Indiana or Ohio can become aware of specific ways that they themselves and their community are linked with what happens halfway around the world. The Center for Global Perspectives concentrates on four concepts, interdependence, conflict, communication, and change, as basic tools by which children and youth from kindergarten to grade 12 can organize knowledge and think about their relation to the inter-dependent world.

The Institute for World Order deplores the easy popularity of the terms "interdependence" and concentrates on ways in which obstacles to "just world order values" can be overcome, and progress can be made toward achieving the transition toward a *preferred* world order and a planetary civilization.[44] World order education thus stresses ways that international violence can be reduced and how "tolerable conditions of worldwide economic welfare, social justice, and ecological stability can be achieved and maintained":

> The task now for social studies education is to foster both a passion
> for and a patience with the future, a deep commitment to world order
> values, and adequate preparation for the decades-long task of creating

a humanitarian transformation of the world system.[45]

I would like to call attention to the terms "just world order values" and "humanitarian transformation of the world system." Without implying my support for the total ideological framework involved in the world order approach, it seems to me that the value context for a basic international ingredient in civic education is now more urgent than ever before. The world situation has changed and the educational context has changed during the 20 years (1955-1975) in which I was deeply and directly involved in international education as director and associate dean for international studies at Teachers College and member of the Faculty of the School of International Affairs at Columbia. I was a member of the task force that drew up working papers as the basis for the International Education Act of 1966; I was deeply involved in technical assistance programs to aid lesser-developed, newly independent nations to improve their educational systems; and I wrote a good deal on the subject.[46] Thus, I feel special anguish about the recent setbacks, possibly fatal, to educational reform begun in the 1950s in Afghanistan and in the 1960s in Uganda.

My point about the change in approach is this: In the 1950s and 1960s a great motivation was to get American education to include more factual knowledge about other peoples of the world (largely through language and area studies impelled by the National Defense Education Act of 1958) and more factual knowledge about international relations, world affairs, and contemporary issues as a subdivision of political science. Comparative studies and foriegn student exchange programs were also highlighted. The International Education Act was supposed to internationalize the curriculum of American schools and colleges and give an academically solid and realistic education in world affairs for all Americans. But it did not get off the ground despite its passage by Congress at the insistence of Lyndon Johnson. One of the great ironies of the period was that international education became a casualty of Lyndon Johnson's international policies. While the ideas of global interdependence and a just world order were undoubtedly present in the 1960s, they were not the most visible concepts. "International understanding" and education for "development" or "modernization" were much more prominent themes.[47]

But, above all, there was relatively little relationship between the push for international studies and civic education in the schools. One of the distinctively new thrusts of the mid-1970s has been the effort to link these two educational movements. One of the key steps in this effort was taken at the Wingspread Workshop on Global Education in January 1976, called by Ward Morehouse, then director of the Center for International Programs and Comparative Studies of the New York State Education Department in Albany. The conference was sponsored by the Council of Chief State School Officers and attended by some two dozen persons. Besides Ward Morehouse as convenor, important contributions were made by Lee Anderson of Northwestern University, James Becker of Indiana University, Richard Remy of Ohio State University, and Judith Torney of the University of Illinois/Chicago Circle. We drew up a statement that was presented to the Chief State School Officers in May 1976. I believe Ward Morehouse and Judith Torney were responsible for the major parts of the paper. I contributed the first few paragraphs emphasizing the desirable linkage between citizenship education and global understanding. Substantial excerpts from that working paper are worth repeating here.

Toward the Achievement of Global Literacy in American Schools

Preliminary Report on the Wingspread Workshop on Problems of Definition and Assessment of Global Education (Racine, Wisconsin, January 25-26, 1976)

The New Civic Literacy: Citizenship Education and Global Understanding

For two hundred years the mainsprings of citizenship education in the United States have stemmed from the effort to develop among students the values and knowledge that would motivate them and enable them to play their parts as informed, responsible, and effective members of the American political system. At its best, civic education has helped to form the cohesive and unifying social base upon which to build a polity devoted to freedom, equality, justice, and popular consent. At its worst, civic education has tended to foster a jingoistic, aggressive chauvinism or an unreasoning, ethnocentric patriotism that has ill served America in the eyes of much of the world.

Today, there is a renewed concern among major professional groups, both governmental and voluntary, to promote a revitalized and realistic civic education devoted to the maintenance and improvement of constitutional self-government, embodied above all in the Bill of Rights. This movement, with it emphasis on law-related education, is paralleled by a revived movement to impel American education to take account of the realities of global interdependence which has been the focus of this workshop at Wingspread under the auspices of the Council of Chief State School Officers.

We welcome this renewed interest in citizenship education as one of the traditional goals of public education in our society. We believe that the task of enlarging understanding of America's role in the world and the relationship of global problems to those of our own society should be an integral and central part of citizenship education in the United States in the last quarter of the twentieth century.

Citizenship education and international education are both affected by their relationship in this new movement. In its concern for strengthening the American polity, citizenship education can no longer ignore the rest of the world. In its concern for recognizing the

156

necessities of an emerging world community, international education can no longer ignore the health and vitality of the American political community.

Education for interdependence means that basic civic literacy for American citizenship must include a reasoned and sympathetic awareness of the varying ways of life in other cultures, the changing world economic and political system, and the intimate way that global problems impinge upon and are linked with American communities, large and small. Education needs to sensitize more of our citizens to the manner in which actions taken in the communities of America affect life in communities around the world. Basic questions of foreign policy and America's role in the world constitute a major share of the judgments that American citizens must in turn make of their political leaders and their policies.

It is apparent to almost everyone that in recent years a startlingly large proportion of American citizens has lost confidence in the integrity, authority, and efficacy of public persons and governmental institutions. It is equally apparent that a large proportion of youth believe that our institutions do not practice the principles which the schools teach. It is significant that the two precipitating and reinforcing events surrounding these trends were the Vietnam War and Watergate, one international and one domestic. Insofar as education can help to reverse these trends of public outlook, it must conjoin its efforts for a revitalized citizenship education and a revitalized international education. The new civic literacy must embrace both.

The use of the term "civic literacy" recognizes that skills, attitudes and abilities required for participation in the political system (both domestic and international) are as basic as skills of reading and arithmetic. Of course, reading is more basic in the sense that one must be able to read well enough to comprehend a ballot or the political stories in a newspaper. But beyond that there are certain minimum levels of competency which are required by the nature of the political world and to the definition of which we address ourselves subsequently. These are not educational frills but necessities for today's society.

While I would hope for a greater linkage between citizenship education and international education, I do not believe that all of international studies should be subsumed under the rubric of civic education. There is simply too much. The 1980 catalogue of the Social Studies School Service of Culver City, California, lists hundreds of items having to do with global education. The paperbacks, simulations, filmstrips, multimedia kits, videocassettes, booklets, duplicating books, transparencies, and globes are listed under such headings as:

global perspectives in education	world issues
international relations	world ideologies
global economics	political ideologies and
food/population	political visions
human rights/terrorism	U.S. foreign policy

war and peace	China, Japan, India,
energy/environment	Indian subcontinent,
cultural geography	Soviet Union, Middle East,
cultural anthropology	Canada, Europe, Asia
regional studies: Africa,	geography
Latin America, Oceania,	future studies

While I believe that global studies should be given much greater attention throughout the total school curriculum, I believe that some principle of selection should be operating in order to define the scope of civic education. I would argue that the requirements of American citizenship in the world today mean that civic education should select from masses of information those examples of world studies that illuminate the other nine concepts in my decalogue of value claims. The Wingspread Workshop emphasized "political community," "human rights," "participation," and "cultural variability." It is but a short step from these to questions of justice, freedom, equality, diversity, authority, privacy, due process, and participation, as these values are honored or violated in various nations and in the relations among nations.

I would start with international human rights, examples of which come so relevantly from the holocaust, from Amin's Uganda, from Rhodesia's struggle to become Zimbabwe, from dissidents seeking freedom and due process in Iran, China, Cuba, or the Soviet Union, and from oppression by military dictators in the Middle East and Latin American countries. A basic set of study documents might include the United Nations Universal Declaration of Human Rights of 1948, the International Covenant on Economic, Social, and Cultural Rights of 1966 (finally ratified in January 1976); the International Covenant on Civil and Political Rights of 1966 (ratified in March 1976); and a Unesco statement headed by the formidable title "Recommendation Concerning Education for International Understanding, Cooperation and Peace, and Education Relating to Human Rights and Fundamental Freedoms."[48] The documents themselves are often tedious reading and contain difficult diplomatic language, but careful selection of concepts and examples from history and from the contemporary world could make illuminating comparisons with American achievements and lapses. The twofold aim is that of considering how to improve the American political system as well as of considering how the U.S. could play a more constructive and humanitarian role in the world.

This interrelationship of the political health and vitality of the U.S. itself with the state of the world at large is further illustrated by the concerns of the President's Commission on Foreign Languages and International Studies, headed by James A. Perkins, chairperson of the International Council on Educational Development.[49] The Commission recognized that pluralism in the U.S. should be viewed in relation to divergencies and differences on the international scene. The prominence of the multicultural emphasis in the deliberations of the Commission attest to the success of the pluralist movements in advancing their cause in recent years. I believe this represents a sound and desirable recognition of the interconnection of the international and the pluralist concerns. But I urged the Commission to recognize as well that both of those approaches should be related to the revival of a civic learning that for the first time in our history must take account of the international and pluralist concerns as well as the common cohesive civic values of the democratic political system.

My point is that these three influences (i.e., international, pluralist, and cohesive civic values) all directly address the national interest, but sometimes they work at cross purposes in the schools, each trying to make its separate claims upon the teacher of humanities and social studies. The schools are often caught in the middle as they attempt with one hand to develop new bilingual, multicultural, or ethnic heritage studies, and with the other hand to develop new civic or new global education programs. Or worse, to respond in only one way, or in no way.

Too often in the past these three aspects of the humanities and social studies curriculum have worked at cross purposes. I have pointed out how civic education has often stressed a jingoistic chauvinism or an ethnocentric patriotism; or "citizenship education" has often meant a conformist Americanization of immigrant and ethnic groups. On the other hand, multicultural studies often stress the diversities and differences of segmented ethnic groups to the neglect of concern for building a common viable political community. And international studies have often stressed the understanding of *other* peoples and cultures with little concern for what is happening to the American political community.

It is extremely important that education for civic cohesion and education for cultural pluralism be linked and interwoven with education for global interdependence. I urged the President's Commission to try somehow to mobilize these three constituencies together for joint action at the federal as well as state and local levels.

But just as the President's Commission was issuing its report in November 1979, the American diplomatic corps in Teheran was taken hostage. Several months later it was still too soon to discern the long-term effects of the revolution in Iran, the crisis over the American hostages, or the Soviet invasion and takeover in Afghanistan. The early knee-jerk reactions ranged, predictably, from the familiar shouts on the campuses of "Hell No, We Won't Go" (to the Persian Gulf) to the plaints in the sports arenas of "Hell Yes, We *Will* Go" (to the Moscow Olympics). The doves and hawks reemerged on the political horizons and the rhetoric warmed up as the presidential campaign proceeded.

159

Aside from the loud and raucous voices, however, the sober and careful judgment of scholarly and political observers in the spring and summer of 1980 was that the decade of the 1980s may very well be bringing us to a turn in the tide of world affairs—or, to change the metaphor, a fork in the road. Serious debate took place as to whether too much of a war atmosphere was being created in Washington or whether the President's budget had not gone far enough in rapid build-up of military strength. Were we approximately where we were at the time of Hitler's occupation of the Rhineland in 1935 or at the partition of Czechoslovakia in 1938; or, conversely, were we about to repeat the U.S. involvement in Vietnam of the 1960s? It was, of course, too early to be sure about such historic and fateful options. But it did seem clear that the processes of détente of the late 1970s had suffered serious blows, that the United States with its allies was engaged in a series of reassessments of America's role in the world vis-à-vis the Soviet Union, whether it was to be containment, confrontation, cold war, or hot war.

The responsible press tried to catch the early mood of scholars, commentators, and the public in general. Their reports ranged from George F. Kennan's belief that there was too much talk of war in Washington to the *New York Times* editorial that spoke of an appropriate "Stiffening of America" to regain a position of strength in the world. The early polls discovered a rather sudden and surprising rise of cold war mentality and even a militant mood among a large majority of U.S. citizens. In February 1980 a poll by the Associated Press and NBC reported two-thirds of Americans in favor of U.S. troops fighting the Soviets if they invaded Western Europe or the Persian Gulf. *Time* magazine found three-fourths in favor of reinstating draft registration, including two-thirds of those aged 18 to 24.

Such sudden and extensive shifts in public opinion might moderate if events cooled down, but they might not. In either case they raised fundamental questions about education and citizenship. Americans once again had to prepare for a thoroughgoing reexamination of education for citizenship. There are enormous challenges ahead but also certainly some opportunities. In an article with the headline "Excited by Crises, Students Ask for Mideast Lessons" (*New York Times*, 4 February 1980), Gene I. Maeroff wrote:

> Since the crisis in the Middle East...students throughout the country are showing uncharacteristic eagerness to learn more about the events unfolding before them on television. Children in the elementary schools are asking to have Iran pointed out to them on maps; youths in high schools are wondering whether the Russian intervention in Afghanistan means they may soon be going to war....
>
> No teacher interviewed could recall any news event since the Vietnam War that made so deep an impression on students.

So here was an opportunity to take advantage of students' interests fanned by world news, but as Maeroff went on to say:

...the spate of interest also discloses how little was taught about the Middle East until now.... As a result, youngsters are beseeching their teachers for more information.

And just when there seemed to be signs of a gathering sense of unity and cohesiveness around the government in the face of the assaults on the American diplomatic hostages in Teheran and the intrusion of Soviet troops toward Persian Gulf oil, the revelation concerning Abscam cast a pall of shock and depression about the extent of alleged bribery scandals among congressmen. Watergate deeply besmirched the Presidency; investigative reporters have recently exposed to public gaze pettiness and unedifying relationships within the Supreme Court; and now it seemed as if the steady stream of scandals affecting a few individual congressmen and their resignations under the cloud of wrongdoing since 1974 had become a flood affecting the integrity of the entire Congress.

Another low point in public attitudes toward government officials was approaching, but this time accompanied by worrisome suspicions about the role of the FBI and possible invasion of the rights of the persons involved. Many of the fundamental ideas and values of a democratic constitutional order were yet once again at stake: questions of justice, freedom, authority, privacy, due process, personal obligations for the public good, and basic human rights, all are to be considered as we view the role of government in relation to public and private persons. We must reexamine such fundamental ideas as they bear upon our view of ourselves as well as our view of the Iranian militants' violation of American rights in Teheran, or Soviet Russia's violation of Afghan rights, or the deprivation of dissident Andrei Sakharov's freedom in his own country.*

I like the way Anthony Lewis put the issue in his column in the *New York Times* (24 January 1980):

> For the West, for Americans especially, the brutal Soviet actions are as severe a test as we have had in a long time. The test is more than military strength. It is a psychological and moral challenge: a test of our maturity, our wisdom, our commitment. The details of our response will be debated in the months ahead. But some general principles ought to be clear.

Among those principles he mentions the following: "Steadiness is vital." "Hysteria has no place in our response." "Self-righteousness is to be avoided." "We must be true to ourselves, to our own vision of humanity."

It is his final point that especially bears on us as educators. Do we have a clear vision of humanity to which we can be true? Do we have a clear "vision of ourselves" that can and should be the basis of a

---

*See, for example, "A Letter from Exile," in the *New York Times Magazine*, 8 June 1980.

revitalized civic learning for the American citizen? This is the question that I have tried to answer in this book.

At the same time we must try to achieve this vision within the setting of a growing interconnectedness and overlapping of the national community and the wider world community. A decade ago two international scholars, Barbara Ward and René Dubos, put the idea cogently at a United Nations Conference on the Human Environment in the early 1970s:

> There are possibilities within the human environment for many different kinds of surroundings and ways of life...of developing the genius of each place, each social group, and each person—in other words of cultivating individuality.... The emotional attachment to our prized diversity need not interfere with our attempts to develop the global state of mind which will generate a rational loyalty to the planet as a whole. As we enter the global phase of human evolution it becomes obvious that each man has two countries, his own and the planet Earth.[50]

> ...From family to clan, from clan to nation, from nation to federation—such enlargements of allegiances have occurred without wiping out the earlier loves. Today, in human society, we can perhaps hope to survive in all our prized diversity provided we can achieve an ultimate loyalty to our single, beautiful, and vulnerable planet Earth.[51]

This states well the goal of combining the values of stable pluralism with the values of a cosmopolitan civism. I use "stable pluralism" in Michael Kammen's sense that the freedoms and diversities and privacies that we should honor, respect, and encourage must be based upon a strong underpinning of political and psychological legitimacy that in turn arises from the cohesive elements of civism. I use "cosmopolitan civism" in John Higham's sense of America's historically generous, open, tolerant approach to difference rather than its narrow, bigoted, provincial demands for conformity. Now, of course, "cosmopolitan" applies to the world itself. In viewing American history, Kammen speaks of a contrapuntal civilization in which we have arrived at a number of biformities—a collective individualism, conservative liberalism, pragmatic idealism, emotional rationalism, godly materialism:

> In short, the push-pull of both wanting to belong and seeking to be free has been the ambivalent condition of life in America, the nurture of a contrapuntal civilization.[52]

Higham makes something of the same point in his discussion of "pluralistic integration."

So I come to the need for an education that recognizes the persisting and continuing balance between a cosmopolitan civism and a stable pluralism. The need for such a balance is as great in the liberal education of colleges and universities, especially in teacher education, as it is in

162

elementary and secondary schools. A concerted revival of the civic learning is needed at all levels of the educational system. Whether the initial approach is through a pluralistic civism or a civic pluralism, the goal should be the same. I happen to think that the challenge of the 1980s points to the greater need for a vital pluralistic civism.

I would like to give the last word to a man whom I greatly admire for his contributions to the public as well as to the private sectors of American life. As president of Carnegie Corporation, as Secretary of Health, Education, and Welfare, as founder of Common Cause, and in countless other ways, John W. Gardner has consistently spoken up for the best in American education and politics. In an address in October 1979 John Gardner had this to say at the conclusion of a talk to alumni of the Stanford University Graduate School of Business:

> I am a strong defender of our pluralism, meaning by pluralism a philosophy and set of social arrangements that permit the existence of many competing ideas, many belief systems, many competing economic units. I habitually defend the private sector because it is the heartland of our pluralism. There, in both the profit and non-profit segments of the society, a multiplicity of thriving institutions, vital and diverse, provide the essential dynamism to our system.

> But a society in which pluralism is not undergirded by *some* shared values simply cannot survive. Pluralism that reflects no commitments whatever to the common good is pluralism gone berserk....

> At this moment, we are a nation in disarray. No point in mincing words. This is a moment when the innumerable interests, organizations and groups that make up our national life must keep their part of the bargain with the society that gives them freedom by working toward the common good. Right now. In this time of trouble. Their chance for long-term enjoyment of pluralism will be enhanced by a commitment to the common good as we go through this difficult passage. At least for now, a little less *pluribus*, a lot more *unum*.[53]

With such a text to conclude my decalogue, all I can say is Amen.

Chapter 5 Notes

1. Charles Frankel, "The Academy Enshrouded," *Change* (December 1977).

2. See, for example, summaries of research contained in the following studies: Byron G. Massialas, "Political Socialization and Citizen Competencies: A Review of Research Findings," and Judith V. Torney, "The Definition of Citizen Capacities and Related Psychological Research," in *Citizen Education Behavior Variables: Final Report* (Philadelphia: Research for Better Schools, 31 July 1978).

Steve McCurley and Judith Torney, "Summary of Selected Research," in *Citizen Education Today*, an early draft for the U.S.O.E. Citizen Education Staff, Fall 1977.

Byron G. Massialas, ed., *Political Youth, Traditional Schools* (Englewood Cliffs, N.J.: Prentice-Hall, 1972).

Jack Dennis, ed., *Socialization to Politics: A Reader* (New York: Wiley, 1973).

M. Kent Jennings and Richard G. Niemi, *The Political Character of Adolescence; The Influence of Families and Schools* (Princeton, N.J.: Princeton University Press, 1974).

Gabriel A. Almond and Sidney Verba, *The Civic Culture; Political Attitudes and Democracy in Five Nations* (Princeton, N.J.: Princeton University Press, 1963).

Judith V. Torney, A.N. Oppenheim, and Russell G. Farnen, *Civic Education in Ten Countries: An Empirical Study* (New York: Wiley, 1975).

Lee H. Ehman, "The American School in the Political Socialization Process," *Review of Educational Research*, Spring 1980, Vol. 50, pp. 99-119; and "Implications for Teaching Citizenship," *Social Education*, November-December 1979, pp. 594-596.

3. David Easton, *A Systems Analysis of Political Life* (New York: Wiley, 1965), chapters 11-13.

4. Nathan Glazer, *The Chronicle of Higher Education* (31 July 1978).

5. Ibid.

6. John Rawls, *A Theory of Justice* (Cambridge, Mass.: Harvard University Press, 1971), p. 458.

7. Ibid., p. 5.

8. Ibid., p. 302.

9. Ibid., p. 61.

10. Ibid., p. 302.

11. Ibid., p. 61.

12. See, e.g., Robert Nozick, *Anarchy, State, and Utopia* (New York: Basic Books, 1974); and William R. Torbert, "Doing Rawls Justice," *Harvard Educational Review* (November 1974).

13. For my views on freedom worked out in the crucible of the McCarthy era in the 1950s, see R. Freeman Butts, "Freedom and Responsibility in American Education," *Teachers College Record*, and "The Free Man in the Free Society," chapter 12 in *What Is the Nature of Man? Images of Man in Our American Culture* (Philadelphia: Christian Education Press, 1959), pp. 146-160.

14. Alexander Meiklejohn, *Political Freedom; The Constitutional Powers of the People* (New York: Harper, 1948, 1960), pp. 35-36. For an excellent high school text on freedom which could well serve as a model for the other civic values in the decalogue, see Isidore Starr, *The Idea of Liberty: First Amendment Freedoms* (Mineola, N.Y.: West Pub. Co., 1978).

15. Ibid., pp. 3-4.

16. Joseph Gales, ed., *Annals of Congress* (Washington, D.C.: Gales and Seaton, 1834), pp. 454-455. For full discussions, see Bernard Schwartz, *The Great Rights of Mankind; A History of the American Bill of Rights* (New York: Oxford University Press, 1977); and Henry J. Abraham, *Freedom and the Court: Civil Rights and Liberties in the United States*, 3rd ed., (New York: Oxford, 1977).

17. Edmund Morgan, "Conflict and Consensus in the American Revolution," in Stephen G. Kurtz and James H. Hutson, eds., *Essays on the American Revolution* (Chapel Hill: University of North Carolina Press, 1973), p. 308.

18. Rawls, *A Theory of Justice*, p. 61.

19. Robert Nozick, *Anarchy, State and Utopia* (New York: Basic Books, 1974). For a short but illuminating contrast between Rawls and Nozick see James S. Coleman, "Equality and Liberty in Education," *The Public Interest* (Spring 1976).

20. Nathan Glazer, *Affirmative Discrimination; Ethnic Inequality and Public Policy* (New York: Basic Books, 1974), chapter 1.

21. Robert H. Wiebe, *The Segmented Society; An Historical Preface to the Meaning of America* (New York: Oxford University Press, 1975).

22. Milton M. Gordon, *Assimilation in American Life; The Role of Race, Religion, and National Origins* (New York: Oxford University Press, 1964).

23. John Higham, "Integration vs. Pluralism: Another American Dilemma," *The Center Magazine* (July/August 1974): 67-73.

24. Harold R. Isaacs, "The New Pluralists," *Commentary* (March 1972): 75-79.

25. Higham, "Integration vs. Pluralism," pp. 72-73.

26. Michael Kammen, *People of Paradox; An Inquiry Concerning the Origins of American Civilization* (New York: Vintage Books, 1973), p. 60.

27. Ibid., p. 85.

28. Robert M. MacIver, *The Web of Government* (New York: Macmillan, 1947), p. 83. A very useful reconsideration of power as a positive and not merely negative concept is contained in David Nyberg, *Power Over Power* (Ithaca, N.Y.: Cornell University Press, forthcoming).

29. Leonard Krieger, "The Idea of Authority in the West," *American Historical Review* (April 1977): 249-270.

30. Meiklejohn, *Political Freedom*, p. 60.

31. Law in a Free Society, *Privacy*, Teachers Edition (Santa Monica, Cal: Law in a Free Society, 1977), p. 1.

32. Constitutional Rights Foundation, *Living Law: Civil Justice* (New York: Scholastic Book Services, 1978); and Constitutional Rights Foundation, *Living Law: Criminal Justice* (New York: Scholastic Book Services, 1978).

33. Louis Fischer and David Schimmel, *The Civil Rights of Teachers* (New York: Harper and Row, 1973); David Schimmel and Louis Fischer, *The Civil Rights of Students* (New York: Harper, 1975); and David Schimmel and Louis Fischer, *The Rights of Parents in the Education of their Children*

(Columbia, Md.: National Committee for Citizens in Education, 1977).

See also, Alan Levine et al., *The Rights of Students; the Basic ACLU Guide to a Student's Rights* (New York: Richard Baron, 1973). For a general survey of issues involved, see R. Freeman Butts, *Public Education in the United States* (New York: Holt, Rinehart & Winston, 1978), chapter 10.

34. Barbara Campbell, "Children's Rights Drive is Centered in Courtroom," *The New York Times* (31 Oct. 1976).

35. Stephen K. Bailey, *The Purposes of Education* (Bloomington, Ind.: Phi Delta Kappa, 1976), pp. 84-94. This extract from chapter 6, titled "The Enveloping Polity," was substantially reprinted in National Task Force on Citizenship Education, *Education for Responsible Citizenship* (New York: McGraw-Hill, 1977), pp. 32-40.

36. Fred Newmann, "Visions of Participation to Guide Community Learning" (Paper prepared for the Banff Conference on Community and the School Curriculum, sponsored by the Department of Secondary Education, University of Alberta, 9 Nov. 1978). For discussion of "mediating structures," see also, Peter Berger, *To Empower People: The Role of Mediating Structures and Public Policy* (Washington, D.C.: American Enterprise Institute for Public Policy Research, 1977).

37. John Dewey, *The Public and Its Problems* (Chicago: Swallow Press, 1954), pp. 15-16 (c. 1927, Holt).

38. Ibid., pp. 76-77.

39. Ibid., p. 82.

40. Ibid., p. 208.

41. James P. Shaver, "Democracy, Courts, and the Schools," *Theory into Practice* 17: 286-287.

42. Law in a Free Society, *On Responsibility; A Casebook* (Santa Monica, Cal: Law in a Free Society, 1972), pp. 1-2.

43. For emphasis upon global interdependence as it relates to education, see, for example, Lee Anderson, *Schooling and Citizenship in a Global Age* (Bloomington, Ind.: Mid-America Program for Global Perspectives in Education, 1978); the Interdependence Series published by the Aspen Institute for Humanistic Studies, especially Ward Morehouse, *A New Civic Literacy: American Education and Global Interdependence* (Princeton, N.J.: Aspen Institute, October 1975); R. Freeman Butts, *The Education of the West* (New York: McGraw-Hill, 1973), pp. 598-599; John H. Spurgin and Gary R. Smith, *Global Dimensions in the New Social Studies* (Denver: Center for Teaching International Relations, University of Denver, 1973).

For more current studies see the January 1977 and October 1978 issues of *Social Education* and the publications of the Center for Global Perspectives, New York City; the Mid-America Program for Global Perspectives in Education, Bloomington, Ind.; Consortium for Social Science Education, Boulder, Colo.; Center for Teaching International

Relations, University of Denver; Foreign Policy Association, New York City; Michigan Department of Education, Lansing; and New York State Education Department, Albany.

44. For a bibliography and a brief analysis of the world order approach, see the chapter by Saul H. Mendlovitz, Lawrence Metcalf, and Michael Washburn, "The Crisis of Global Transformation, Interdependence, and the Schools," in National Task Force on Citizenship Education, *Education for Responsible Citizenship* (New York: McGraw-Hill, 1977), pp. 189-212.

45. Ibid., p. 204.

46. R. Freeman Butts, *American Education in International Development* (New York: Harper and Row, 1963); "Teacher Education and Modernization" in George Z. F. Bereday, ed., *Essays on World Education* (New York: Oxford University Press, 1969); and "Civilization as Historical Process: Meeting Ground for Comparative and International Education," *Comparative Education* 3 (June 1967).

47. R. Freeman Butts, "America's Role in International Education," in Harold G. Shane, ed., *The United States and International Education*, Sixty-Eighth Yearbook of the National Society for the Study of Education (Chicago: University of Chicago Press, 1969).

48. Thomas Buergenthal and Judith V. Torney, *International Human Rights and International Education* (Washington, D.C.: U.S. National Commission for Unesco, 1976).

49. President's Commission on Foreign Languages and International Studies, *Strength Through Wisdom; A Critique of U.S. Capability* (Washington, D.C.: Government Printing Office, November 1979; See also *Background Papers and Studies.*

50. Barbara Ward and René Dubos, *Only One Earth; The Care and Maintenance of a Small Planet* (New York: Norton, 1972), p. xviii.

51. Ibid., p. 220.

52. Kammen, *People of Paradox*, p. 116.

53. "Remarks by John W. Gardner," unpublished manuscript delivered at the Stanford University Graduate School of Business, 6 October 1979, pp. 17-18.

Index